Writing Baseball

THE SOUTHERN ILLINOIS UNIVERSITY PRESS SERIES

Other Books in the Writing Baseball Series

The American Game

THE AMERICAN
★ GAME ★

BASEBALL AND ETHNICITY

EDITED BY

Lawrence Baldassaro

AND

Richard A. Johnson

WITH A FOREWORD BY

Allan H. (Bud) Selig

Southern Illinois University Press

Carbondale and Edwardsville

05 04 03 02   4 3 2 1

Chapter 4 originally appeared in *New Perspectives on the Irish Diaspora,* ed.
Charles Fanning (Carbondale: Southern Illinois University Press, 2000), 176–85.
© 2000 by the Board of Trustees, Southern Illinois University.
A slightly different version of chapter 5 originally appeared in *Past Time:
Baseball Across the Decades,* by Jules Tygiel, copyright 2000 by Jules Tygiel.
Used by permission of Oxford University Press, Inc.
A portion of chapter 6 previously appeared in "Ed Abbaticchio:
Italian Baseball Pioneer," *NINE: A Journal of Baseball History and
Social Policy Perspectives,* 8 (fall 1999): 18–30.

Library of Congress Cataloging-in-Publication Data

The American game : baseball and ethnicity / edited by Lawrence
Baldassaro and Richard A. Johnson ; with a foreword by Allan H.
(Bud) Selig.
  p. cm.
Includes bibliographical references and index.
  1. Baseball—Social aspects—United States. 2. Ethnicity—
United States. I. Baldassaro, Lawrence. II. Johnson, Dick, 1955–
GV867.64 .A44 2002
796.357—dc21   2001049600
ISBN 0-8093-2445-8 (alk. paper)
ISBN 0-8093-2446-6 (pbk. : alk. paper)

The paper used in this publication meets the minimum requirements of American National Standard for Information Sciences—Permanence of Paper for Printed Library
Materials, ANSI Z39.48-1992. ⊚

Writing Baseball Series Editor: Richard Peterson

To the memory of my parents,
Gerald and Olive Baldassaro,
who instilled in me a love of the game,
and to my son, Jim, who carries on the
challenging tradition of
rooting for the Red Sox.
—L. B.

To the memory of my father,
Dr. Robert Andrew Johnson (1914–2001):
physician, soldier, scholar,
father, and friend.
—R. J.

Contents

Illustrations

Foreword

ALLAN H. (BUD) SELIG

On 15 April 1997, at Shea Stadium in New York, Major League Baseball honored the great Jackie Robinson by celebrating the fiftieth anniversary of his historic entry into the big leagues. At that time, I said, "The day Jackie Robinson stepped on a major league field will forever be remembered as baseball's proudest moment."

Jackie's achievement, so ably assisted by Branch Rickey, was a seminal event not only for baseball but also for the entire country. For the first time, baseball, long hailed as our national pastime, truly became the game that represented all of America.

Throughout the early days of its history, baseball had attracted immigrants and members of diverse ethnic groups. For some, it was a way out of the ghetto; for others, it was a pleasant diversion from a difficult existence; and, for many, the game provided a measure of acceptance, a platform on which one could stand proudly and proclaim his status as an American.

The American Game: Baseball and Ethnicity describes baseball's role in the evolving ethnic changes that took place in America beginning with the Anglo-Americans, who contributed to the formation of the game a century and a half ago. In separate essays, the book examines the roles of various European ethnic groups as their members entered the game beginning in the latter part of the nineteenth century and continuing though the middle of the twentieth. They and their forebears came from Germany, Ireland, Italy, Poland, Czechoslovakia, and other Slavic nations. Some were Christians; some were Jews. As a whole, the ethnic representation in baseball was presented publicly as a metaphor for America's melting pot.

In truth, it was not quite the melting pot it was supposed to be. In his essay "Unreconciled Strivings: Baseball in Jim Crow America," Jules Tygiel examines how African Americans were excluded from baseball as they were from other aspects of American life. Baseball certainly regrets its role in the exclusion of African Americans for most of its early history, but it is proud that the breaking of baseball's color barrier took place before the integration of other American institutions.

Today, baseball truly is a melting pot and reflects the evolving American population as well as or better than any other sport or enterprise. In fact, with each year, more and more of our players come from foreign countries, notably the great talent that has come from the Caribbean and Latin America. At the start of the 2000 Major League Baseball season, 198 players, nearly 24 percent of all players on major league rosters, were born outside the fifty states. They represented sixteen different foreign countries and Puerto Rico.

The small Caribbean nation of the Dominican Republic had the most players with seventy-one, followed by Puerto Rico with thirty-three and Venezuela with thirty-one. Other nations represented were Aruba (three players), Australia (one), Canada (twelve), Colombia (two), Cuba (nine), Curaçao (one), Great Britain (one), Jamaica (one), Japan (six), Korea (three), Mexico (fourteen), Nicaragua (one), Panama (eight), and the Virgin Islands (one).

Because of this great influx of foreign talent and the growing interest in the sport around the world, Major League Baseball has embarked on an international strategy that will bring the game to peoples of various races and ethnic groups in all parts of the globe. In some respects, this strategy is the opposite of the phenomenon that took place during the game's first one hundred years, when different ethnic groups brought their influence to baseball. This international strategy will assure for decades to come that baseball will continue to be diverse and inclusive of all peoples and nationalities.

Acknowledgments

The editors wish to express their gratitude to the contributors whose essays made this collection possible and to Allan H. (Bud) Selig, who remains first and foremost a fan of the game.

A special note of thanks to Richard Peterson, general editor of the Writing Baseball series, for first suggesting this volume and to our editors, Karl Kageff, Carol Burns, and Robin DuBlanc, for their patient and knowledgeable guidance.

As always, Pat Kelly and Bill Burdick of the National Baseball Hall of Fame were both generous and expeditious in providing photos.

The American Game

★ 1 ★

Introduction

LAWRENCE BALDASSARO

Ever since athletes of German and Irish descent entered the major leagues in large numbers more than a century ago, the ethnic background of baseball players has fascinated fans and the media. Even before the turn of the century, major league teams were courting ethnic fans. In St. Louis, ads were placed in German-language newspapers. In the Polo Grounds, the section of the bleachers where Irish fans gathered was known as Burkeville, and in other parks, Irish fans sat in "Kerry Patches."

Beginning in the 1880s, ethnic tensions heightened as successive waves of new immigrants from southern and eastern Europe moved into big-city neighborhoods previously settled by earlier generations of new-comers. Cultures inevitably clashed; the "old" immigrants resented the new arrivals, not only for encroaching on their territory but for threatening to take away their jobs. Boxing promoters openly exploited these tensions by setting up bouts in which Irish, Italian, and Jewish fighters were pitted against each other.

For professional baseball, the new immigrants meant potential new customers. One way to tap into this market was to put "ethnic" heroes on the field. In the 1920s, commentators noted the influx of players of Italian and Slavic origins and wondered why there weren't more Jewish players in the big leagues. However, it wasn't until the mid-thirties that representatives of the new European immigrants—primarily Italians and

Slavs—appeared in the big leagues in numbers that approached their proportion of the total population. The era following World War II saw the most dramatic ethnographic shift with the belated entry of African American ballplayers.

The pattern of ethnic succession continues, as players of Hispanic and Asian origin provide a new infusion of excitement and renewal into America's game, from Fernando Valenzuela in the eighties to Hideo Nomo in the nineties to Ichiro Suzuki in 2001. Peter Gammons noted in a *Boston Globe* column in 1998 that, for many, "baseball is the sport of the two fastest-rising socioeconomic groups, Hispanics and Asian-Americans."[1] Anyone who has witnessed the Japanese media throngs covering Nomo and Suzuki and the national celebrations of Dominican fans cheering Sammy Sosa's heroics is inclined to agree.

The 1998 home run race between Sosa and Mark McGwire provided a vivid reminder of the racial and ethnic dimension of baseball history. In the process of shadowing McGwire, Sosa became a national hero, both to Dominicans living in his native land and those in the United States. He also became the standard bearer for all Hispanic ballplayers, a symbol of their growing impact on the game. Meanwhile, some commentators speculated that McGwire's broad base of fan support was due, in part, to his all-American image; he is, as one columnist called him, "a white guy of Irish ancestry."[2] (There was a time, of course, when someone of Irish descent was not a likely candidate for prototypical American.)

The demographics of big league baseball are shifting in yet another way. The game long ago spread far beyond U.S. borders, but major leaguers were almost exclusively American-born descendants of immigrants. Now, increasing numbers of foreign-born players are making it to the major leagues. On opening day of the 2001 season, 25.3 percent of the players on the major league forty-man rosters and 45 percent of minor league players were born outside the United States. Those players came from twenty-seven different countries around the globe. Accordingly, major league games were telecast to more than two hundred countries in 2001.

The international flavor of American baseball was strikingly evident in the pitching staff of the 1998 New York Yankees, winners of the World Series and considered by many one of the best teams ever. In addition to native-born Americans, the staff included Graeme Lloyd from Australia, Hideki Irabu from Japan, Orlando "El Duque" Hernandez from Cuba, and Ramiro Mendoza and Mariano Rivera from Panama. When, near the end of the 1998 season, late-night talk show host David Letterman announced his "Top Ten Signs the New York Yankees are Getting Arrogant," the number one item on the list was: "Sometimes they let an American guy pitch."

Of our major sports, only baseball has generated this fascination with ethnicity, presumably because baseball has long been associated with "American" values. Early in the twentieth century, baseball, already well established as the national pastime, was being hailed as a metaphor of the American melting pot, welcoming, in turn, a succession of ethnic groups. In *America's National Game*, published in 1911, A. G. Spalding insisted on the democratic nature of baseball, alluding to what would have passed at the time as the game's ethnic inclusiveness by writing: "The son of a President of the United States would as soon play with Patsy Flannigan as with Lawrence Lionel Livingstone, provided only that Patsy could put up the right article."[3]

Journalists pointed out the beneficial role of baseball as a means of acculturating the children of immigrants by instilling the American ideals of democracy and fair play. In the 18 July 1919 issue of the *Atlanta Constitution*, sportswriter Hugh Fullerton wrote: "Baseball, to my way of thinking, is the greatest single force working for Americanization. No other game appeals so much to the foreign-born youngsters and nothing, not even the schools, teaches the American spirit so quickly."

Similar thoughts were expressed in 1923 by Frederick G. Lieb, president of the Baseball Writers' Association, in an article titled "Baseball— The Nation's Melting Pot." Lieb concluded that "next to the little red school house, there has been no greater agency in bringing our different races together than our national game, baseball. Baseball is our real melting pot."[4] (Lieb was referring, of course, not to races but to ethnic groups. The real racial issue, the exclusion of African Americans from organized baseball, was simply not a topic of discussion at the time.)

In that same article, Lieb attempted, as many others would as well, to associate particular aptitudes with specific ethnic groups: "Slugging strength seems to be characteristic of the German element in professional baseball, while the Irish players usually are faster and think quicker."[5] Later commentators, reflecting widely accepted ethnic stereotypes, would characterize Italians as best suited to be catchers (because of their short, stocky builds), Slavs as muscular sluggers, and Jews as brainy ballplayers.

At times the expression of baseball's open arms policy was couched in language that now sounds like self-parody. In 1923, for example, *The*

Sporting News proudly proclaimed that "the Mick, the Sheeny, the Wop, the Dutch and the Chink, the Cuban, the Indian, the Jap or the so-called Anglo-Saxon—his 'nationality' is never a matter of moment if he can pitch, hit, or field."[6] Baseball's professed indifference to the ethnic background of its players (with the obvious exception of blacks) was a reminder of its role as a symbol of the American melting pot; all were welcome to participate in the great democratic ideal with its promise of equal access to the American Dream.

The melting pot theory has fallen out of favor with many. Its suggestion of a cauldron in which ethnic differences are fused into a homogeneous amalgam does not sit well in a postmodern culture. The metaphor of a mosaic, or a quilt, is now seen as a more appropriate expression of a multicultural society that, in theory at least, respects and retains ethnic differences. Several of the essays in this book suggest that baseball, in fact, embraces both of these metaphors. On the one hand, individual heroes have provided positive role models and helped foster a sense of pride and cohesion within their ethnic communities, with the subsequent potential for continued isolation from the larger community. At the same time, participation in baseball, either as player or fan, has provided a way for many to assimilate into American society.

Regardless of the metaphor of the moment, melting pot or mosaic, there is no question that baseball, more than any other sport and more than most American social institutions, has mirrored the gradual and often difficult process of assimilation experienced by a succession of ethnic and racial groups over the course of the twentieth century. For much of the first half of the century, baseball provided a window on the American Dream, creating in second-generation youth, especially those of European heritage, an awareness of those ideals that the arbiters of mainstream culture identified as "American" and serving as a bridge between the customs of their immigrant parents and the world they found outside the home.

With the exception of the first, each of the essays in this collection documents some form of discrimination, from verbal slurs to outright banishment in the case of African Americans. At the same time, for that small percentage of individuals blessed with great skill, the game offered a shortcut to financial reward and social status. Their success, in turn, instilled pride in their respective ethnic communities and offered hope that others might also prosper in America. And even for those whose talent never took them beyond sandlot baseball but who learned and followed the game, baseball, which remained undisputed as *the* American game for much of the twentieth century, provided a passport to at least a part of mainstream American culture, making them more recognizably "American" and less foreign. Even for African Americans, whose systematic exclusion from major league baseball overshadows the obstacles faced by all others who hoped to play professionally, baseball ultimately provided the first official avenue of integration.

Ever since Harold Seymour's groundbreaking study first appeared in 1960, students of the game have explored the ways in which baseball history mirrors the larger patterns of American life. The ethnic and racial dimension of major league baseball has been one of the more fertile grounds for study in recent years. *The American Game* brings together in one volume a variety of perspectives on this important aspect of baseball history. While this collection is obviously representative and not exhaustive in scope, its goal is to demonstrate how the gradual involvement by various ethnic and racial groups reflects the changing nature of baseball, and of American society as a whole, over the course of the twentieth century. These essays may also serve as a reminder that the history of baseball, like the history of this nation, consists of the contributions made by individuals from virtually every group that has made its way to these shores.

Notes

1. Peter Gammons, "Two Men Who Exceed Their Numbers," *Boston Globe Online,* 5 September 1998.

2. Leonard Pitts, "We Like Sosa, but We Love McGwire," *Milwaukee Journal,* 4 October, 1998, 4J.

3. Albert G. Spalding, *America's National Game* (1911; reprint, Lincoln: University of Nebraska Press, 1992), 6.

4. Frederick G. Lieb, "Baseball—The Nation's Melting Pot," *Baseball Magazine* 31 (August 1923): 393.

5. Lieb, 394.

6. *The Sporting News,* 6 December 1923, 4.

★2★

The Many Fathers of Baseball: Anglo-Americans and the Early Game

FREDERICK IVOR-CAMPBELL

Writer Henry Chadwick probably struck close to the mark in his intuitive insistence that baseball derived from the English game of rounders. Two arguments have been made that baseball was invented ex nihilo. The most familiar, the story that West Point cadet Abner Doubleday invented the game in Cooperstown in 1839, has been thoroughly discredited on several grounds, not least of which is that Abner Graves, who came up with the story, never said that Doubleday invented the game out of his own head, but only that he saw Doubleday outline a diamond on the field, and later on paper, "with a crude pencil memorandum of the rules for his new game, which he named '*Base Ball.*'"[1]

The second argument for ex nihilo creation comes from a purported statement by the first Knickerbocker Club president, Duncan Curry, that Alexander Cartwright "came up to the ball field with a new scheme for playing ball" and presented it to ballplaying friends who up to that time had simply "batted the ball to one another or sometimes played one o'cat." But writer William Rankin, who issued Curry's statement in 1910, had written it from his memory of a street corner conversation over three decades earlier at which he had taken no notes except "Mr. Alex. Cartwright is the father of base ball."[2] Our earliest description of the origins of the Knickerbocker Club, Charles A. Peverelly's brief club history in *The Book of American Pastimes*, says of Cartwright's contribution

6

only that "one day upon the field, [he] proposed a regular organization, promising to obtain several recruits."[3] Cartwright was not a member of the new club's rules committee.

We shall probably never know precisely who should receive credit for what, but the best evidence we have to date suggests that Cartwright did more than simply suggest organizing a club, but that he did not create baseball out of nothing. The fact that there were children's games called base ball, with rules similar to both rounders and the Knickerbocker game,[4] makes it extremely unlikely that anyone invented baseball in the way James Naismith invented basketball. That does not mean that what Cartwright and his Knickerbockers did was unsubstantial or inconsequential. Quite the opposite: without Cartwright, and without his club, we would not have the game we know today.

From Alexander Cartwright to the present, baseball has been graced by players of Anglo-American heritage, including many of the greatest. Daniel L. "Doc" Adams of the early Knickerbockers probably created the position of shortstop, and George Wright was the position's first memorable practitioner. Albert G. Spalding was the game's dominant pitcher in the early 1870s, and Adrian Anson dominated the field at first base and at the bat for enough years for his nicknames to evolve from "Baby" to "Capt." to "Pop." J. Lee Richmond pitched professional baseball's first perfect game in 1880, and John Montgomery Ward pitched the second five days later. Charles Radbourn earned the nickname "Old Hoss" by pitching Providence to the National League pennant in 1884 with what is still a record fifty-nine wins, then pitched them to victory in the game's first World Series with three wins in three days.

The list could be extended indefinitely, but great as many individual Anglo-American players were and are, it is not since baseball's earliest days that players of English descent have, as a group, dominated the game. It is an ironic coincidence that in September 1845, in the very month that the Knickerbockers organized to play their new game, the first wave of the blight that would destroy the potatoes drifted over the Irish countryside. With the great European migration to America of the latter nineteenth and early twentieth centuries, Anglo-American dominance of the game on the ball field rapidly diminished.

Off the field, too, innumerable non-Anglos have made their mark in baseball and have influenced the game in important ways, often helping soften or overcome typically Anglo biases. One need only look at Christian Von der Ahe, founder and for many years owner of the club that became the St. Louis Cardinals, and instrumental in the formation of the major league American Association in 1882. His league and club made Sunday baseball and the sale of liquor at the park respectable, and in time these innovations—long opposed by such Anglo-American power-houses as A. G. Spalding—became the norm. But for all the contributions of non-Anglos to the game and its governance, through the game's earliest years, and in many ways through much of the nineteenth century, Anglo-American influence was decisive to the game's development and direction.

In a very real sense, baseball is an English game, derived from English predecessors that were adapted and developed largely and most importantly by Americans of English heritage. All five persons most often identified as "fathers" of baseball—Alexander Cartwright, Daniel Adams, Henry Chadwick, Harry Wright, and A. G. Spalding—trace their ancestry to England. In a 1999 poll of the Nineteenth Century Committee of the Society for American Baseball Research, members were asked to name the most important off-field contributors to the early game; Chadwick, Spalding, Wright, and Cartwright received the most votes, followed in fifth place by John Montgomery Ward.[5] The contributions of these five, plus Adams, are worth looking at in some detail.[6]

Albert Goodwill Spalding. *Boston Herald* photo.

At the very least, we can say that without Alexander Cartwright's suggestion "one day upon the field" that he and his ballplaying friends form a club to play baseball, their game might never have spread beyond their own circle or advanced beyond its primitive state of development. The crucial contribution of the club's formation was the written codification of the rules of the game. Writing down the rules, first of all, forced the ballplayers to consider the distinctiveness of their game as contrasted with other games. Their prohibition of putting runners out by hitting them with a thrown ball, for example, eliminated a practice common in other forms of bat and ball games they knew about, and their formula for determining the length of baselines (forty-two paces from home to second and from first to third) assured a diamond significantly larger than that found in other known versions of baseball. By the decisions they made in codifying their rules, the Knickerbockers turned a children's game into sport for adults, setting it apart as a manly rival to that other game popular among many English immigrants, cricket. Written rules and the formation of a club to play by them made baseball a "real" game like cricket; it could no longer be perceived by outsiders merely as an idle, formless pastime.

Just as important, written rules made possible the ready communication of the Knickerbockers' game to others, allowing its spread far beyond what word of mouth could do. That baseball as we know it today grew from those first Knickerbocker rules is something not even the commission that declared Abner Doubleday the game's creator tried to deny.

If Alexander Cartwright had done nothing more than suggest that he and his friends form a club, the importance of his contribution to the game would be immeasurable. But it seems likely that he also contributed crucially to the nature of the game. Quite apart from the unreliable "Curry statement," there are in the literature two brief references to comments by Cartwright's grandchildren that their grandfather claimed a creative role in the game. Harold Peterson, in his biography of Cartwright, quotes granddaughter Mary Taylor, whom he interviewed: "Father [Alexander's son, Alexander III] remembered [his father's] talking about how he scrawled out the first rules in a notebook balanced on his knee."[7] And grandson Bruce Cartwright Jr. recounted in a 1938 letter to Alexander Cleland (the New York settlement house director who first proposed and helped organize baseball's Hall of Fame) that once, when he attended a baseball game with his grandfather, the elder Cartwright "drew a circle in the dust and then made a cross through it. While he was doing this, a crowd gathered; and he explained to them how he had devised the 'Baseball Square.'"[8] This allusion to the Knickerbocker baseball diamond, which was measured from home to second base and from first to third rather than from base to base as has been done since a rules revision in 1857, has a ring of truth to it and suggests that Cartwright's contribution to the origin of baseball includes a critical role in determining the architecture of the game.

However important his contribution to creating the Knickerbocker game, Cartwright had no significant influence on its further development. In 1849 he set out for California hoping to find gold, but instead moved on to Hawaii, where he lived the remainder of his life. He introduced Knickerbocker baseball to San Francisco and Honolulu before the game reached Philadelphia, Boston, or Chicago, and he retained his interest in the game until his death, but outside Hawaii the game developed without him.

Until recently, the most overlooked "father" of baseball was physician Daniel L. Adams.[9] He joined the Knickerbocker Club about a month after it was organized and quickly became one of its leaders. If we envision Alexander Cartwright as the father of baseball who planted the seed, then Doc Adams was the father who nurtured the infant. Elected vice president of the Knickerbockers in 1846 and president a year later, Adams served as a club officer for twelve of his sixteen Knickerbocker years. In his old age, Adams was interviewed by *The Sporting News*.[10] If his memory is to be believed—and there is little evidence to contradict it—then Adams held the Knickerbockers together through its early years. Until other clubs began to form in the 1850s—and even afterward—the Knickerbockers almost always played an intraclub game. For its first five years, the club struggled. "I frequently went to Hoboken," Adams recalled, "to find only two or three members present, and we were often obliged to take our exercise in the form of 'old cat,' 'one' or 'two' as the case might be. As captain, I had to employ all my rhetoric to induce attendance, and often thought it useless to continue the effort, but my love for the game, and the happy hours spent at the 'Elysian Fields' led me to persevere." For several years Adams made the baseballs himself, "not only for our club but also for other clubs when they were organized," and he personally supervised the turning of the bats. "Base ball playing for the first six or seven years of its existence," Adams recalled, "was the pursuit of pleasures under difficulties."

In 1854, as baseball gained in popularity and other clubs were beginning to organize, the Knickerbockers and two other clubs revised the playing rules a little for clarity. But just two years later, so many new clubs had formed in the New York area that a further expansion of the rules was needed to explain the game more extensively and clearly to players who were unfamiliar with the Knickerbocker brand of ball. The Knickerbocker Club took the lead in calling a convention for early 1857. Fourteen clubs were represented at the first session in January, and Doc Adams was elected president of the convention. At its second session, in February, the delegates (representing sixteen clubs this time) were presented with a thoroughly revised set of playing rules, more than double the length of the 1854 rules. Adams recalled chairing the rules committee, but reports in the press listed William H. Van Cott of the Gotham Club as the committee chair and L. F. Wadsworth as the Knickerbocker representative to the committee.[11] Whatever the truth, it is clear that the proposed rules revisions reflected a strong Knickerbocker influence and may indeed have been prepared by Adams, as he claimed.[12] Adams was correct that the proposed revised rules were "in the main adopted."[13] One rule important to Adams and his club was rejected, though, which would have required fielders to catch fair balls on the fly for a putout, rather than permit an out on a first-bounce catch. This proposed revision, which corresponded to the rule in cricket, was advocated, as *Porter's Spirit* put it, "with a view of making the game more manly and scientific,"[14] and although it was rejected by the first convention and several annual conventions thereafter, the Knickerbockers themselves played the "fly game" in all their intraclub encounters.

Ironically, although the Knickerbockers issued the call for the 1857 convention and the next one in 1858, the effect of the meetings was to make their club irrelevant to the further development of baseball. The gathering together of ball clubs (they established a formal association at the 1858 convention) and the new rules turned the game's focus irrevocably from intramural play to interclub competition, and the game drifted gradually away from the Knickerbocker ideal of healthy exercise among friends toward combative rivalry. And, increasingly, it became a spectator sport.

In May 1858, Harry Wright, a twenty-three-year-old English-born cricketer who gave his residence as Hoboken, New Jersey (where his father was employed as a cricket professional), was elected to membership in the Knickerbocker Base Ball Club.[15] Two months later, he was picked to play right field for New York against Brooklyn in baseball's first all-star game at the Fashion Course racetrack near Flushing, Long Island. Even though spectators were charged fifty cents admission to defray the cost of preparing the grounds, four thousand persons attended the game.[16] No thought was given to reimbursing the players. Ten years later, Wright was in Cincinnati, preparing the game's first all-salaried team for its inaugural season.

Harry Wright remained a Knickerbocker for five years before moving his membership to the more competitive Gotham Club in 1863. In August 1865, he was hired by the Union Cricket Club of Cincinnati as professional bowler, a summer position he had previously held in Hoboken in addition to his amateur play as a baseballer. He continued his double life in Cincinnati, pitching for the Cincinnati Base Ball Club, which shared the cricket club's grounds. After the 1867 season—perhaps stung by their 53-10 defeat at the hands of the touring National Club of Washington (even though the Nationals found Wright's pitching "the most troublesome they ever faced," according to reporter Henry Chadwick, who was traveling with the club[17])—Cincinnati decided to bolster its first nine with a few professionals, and hired Wright to pitch in 1868 for the same $1,200 he had earned from the cricket club.[18] Wright's change of professions from cricket to baseball, as Warren Goldstein points out, "while it could not have seemed especially consequential at the time either for the clubs, for Harry Wright, or for the history of baseball and cricket, in fact constituted one of the most significant events in the history of all three."[19] Baseball was on the ascendancy, cricket in decline, and Harry Wright would quickly carry the Cincinnati club, and baseball itself, to a level of excellence and popularity unimaginable in November 1867 when he was first hired to pitch.

After a successful 1868 season in which Cincinnati's few losses came at the hands of strong eastern teams, the club decided to make itself fully professional. It may not have been Harry Wright's idea to hire professionals for every position on the 1869 team—that was a decision made at a meeting of the club in September 1868—and we cannot even be certain that Wright was the one who decided whom to hire, though he is usually given the credit for this. Harry Ellard, writing in 1907, gives his father George—one of the club's founders and the creator of its signature knickerbocker trousers and red stockings—credit for selecting and hiring the team. But no one questions that it was Wright who molded the players into the nine whose tours to both coasts and undefeated season launched professional baseball as a permanent feature of the American scene.[20] It is for the influence on baseball history of this first foray into full and open baseball professionalism that Harry Wright is regarded as the "father of professional baseball."

As manager, Wright was responsible for arranging the club's games, and Goldstein argues that Wright's "largely unheralded . . . business management was an outstanding contribution to Cincinnati's success," and that Wright's "efforts to subject an extremely irregular and unpredictable set of encounters (baseball games) to the systematic supervision of business management carved out new territory in the material history of the game." Equally significant in baseball history was the new manager-player relationship Wright established. A decade older than most of his players, Wright (who with the hiring of pitcher Asa Brainard switched from the box to center field for 1869) was able to put himself across as something of a father figure. Goldstein views as central to Wright's managerial innovation "the way he altered relations among the nine, firmly establishing his authority over the players in every aspect of the game. Wright negotiated contracts with them, and he ordered them about on the ballfield and off. His control over the players' lives off the field was never as complete as he would have liked, but he did establish the *principle* of that authority."[21] As baseball management became more and more complex, the dual roles of business manager and field manager came to require two persons, but the idea of the manager acting in loco parentis has remained an ideal (sometimes even approaching actuality) in baseball since Wright's day.

Wright's lasting influence was solidified by a quarter-century of successfully managing both clubs and players—but not in Cincinnati. After his undefeated 1869 season, a few losses in 1870 disheartened the Cincinnati Club officers, who gave up on professionalism and disbanded the team. Wright and several of his players moved on to Boston, a newly formed club in the newly formed National Association of Base Ball Players, where he led his team to four association pennants in five years. In 1874, Wright organized and led his team and the Athletics of Philadelphia on a tour—in the middle of the baseball season—to England in an unsuccessful attempt to implant baseball there. (He sent his young pitcher, Al Spalding, ahead to make the arrangements.)

When the National League was formed in 1876, usurping and destroying the pioneer National Association, Wright's willingness to bring Boston into the new league—even though four of his best players had been hired away from him unlawfully by the Chicago club, whose president was the league's chief founder—was an important factor in making the National League immediately respectable. Wright's influence as an effective manager continued until his retirement in 1893. In a tribute to Wright following his death in 1895, Henry Chadwick praised his accomplishments, then moved on to an assessment of his character, noting that "by his sterling integrity of character alone he presented a model every professional ball player can copy from with great gain to his

Henry Chadwick

individual reputation and to public esteem and popularity. Let us trust that in the coming time we may look upon his like again."[22]

Spectators and writers are adjuncts of baseball we have long taken for granted. The English-born Henry Chadwick was one of the earliest and most influential exemplars of both, but before he reported baseball, he covered cricket matches. It was in the autumn of 1856, at about the time the Knickerbockers were first considering calling a convention of ball clubs, that Chadwick discovered baseball. He never tired of telling the story of how, while returning home to Brooklyn from a cricket match in Hoboken, he came upon a baseball game at Hoboken's Elysian Fields. "The game was being sharply played on both sides," he recalled, "and I watched it with deeper interest than any previous ball match between clubs that I had seen." He had seen baseball before, but this game transformed him: "It was not long before I was struck with the idea that base ball was just the game for a national sport for Americans, and, reflecting on the subject, it occurred to me, on my return home, that from this game of ball a powerful lever might be made by which our people could be lifted into a position of more devotion to physical exercise and healthful out-door recreation than they had hitherto, as a people, been noted for."[23] Chadwick had found his calling, and his efforts over the remainder of his long lifetime to promote, improve, preserve, and document the game made him the most universally acknowledged "father" of baseball. In his later years he was routinely referred to as "Father Chadwick."

Chadwick's multifaceted contribution to baseball was so great that it is difficult to assess and nearly as difficult to overstate—though Chadwick himself, no shrinking violet, sometimes managed the feat, at times incurring the ire (or at least the annoyance) of other baseball writers. As a journalist, he made it his goal to see that the daily papers reported baseball matches. (Before he undertook this task, most baseball reportage appeared in weekly sporting papers.) As a member for many years of baseball's rules committees, he influenced the nature of the game. He devised the first scoring system and box score that explained games in full statistical detail, and while his scorebook proved unnecessarily complex (he numbered players by batting order rather than by their positions in the field), it established a model for others to improve upon.[24] As a writer and analyst, he taught countless readers the finer points of baseball as he understood them, and in the guides he prepared from 1860 (he originated the annual baseball guide) until the year of his death in 1908, he informed and educated millions of readers about the game.

When Chadwick came to baseball in the mid-1850s, it was still a game oriented to exercise and sportsmanship among friends, yet it had also developed into a game where skilled play was beginning to be valued over mere exercise. "First nines" were formed for matches between clubs and, as Chadwick discovered in his revelatory experience at Elysian Fields, the game—as played at a skilled level—was fun to watch.

Too little notice has been given to the fact that Henry Chadwick, uniquely among the fathers of baseball, came to the game as a spectator, not a player. Whatever he said about the game as healthful exercise, he was attracted by watching it, not playing it. On the rare occasions he played baseball, it was as a "muffin," one of the unskilled class, as he might have put it. Muffin games, when they were watched at all, were watched for their comical aspects, not for excitement or aesthetic pleasure. He preferred skill over prowess and encouraged skilled running, fielding, and place hitting, while railing against sluggers who swung for the fences, depriving fielders of the opportunity to interact in a display of agility and swiftness. His efforts to shape the game were aimed at increasing the pleasure of the aesthetically minded spectator.[25]

Chadwick liked the game he was first captivated by in 1856, and while he grudgingly became an admirer of professional play that became ever more skilled through his lifetime, he never reconciled himself to the less attractive features that accompanied it: drunkenness, gambling, and the occasional corruption of participants that it brought, and "kicking" by players against umpires. He saw himself as the conscience of baseball, and while his rants often had little direct effect—and at times even antagonized those who agreed with him—his loud and lifelong concern for upright behavior kept that issue in the forefront of the baseball world's consciousness and likely did much to keep the game one of the more respectable professional sports.

Chadwick first laid eyes on Albert Goodwill Spalding, with whom he would later develop a lifelong professional relationship as editor of Spalding's annual baseball guide and other Spalding sports publications, in the summer of 1867 when, as a reporter traveling with the touring National Club of Washington, D.C., he watched the heretofore unknown sixteen-year-old pitch the Forest Citys of Rockford, Illinois, to victory over the highly favored Nationals. In his extensive report of the game for his sporting weekly, the *Ball Players' Chronicle,* Chadwick did not single out Spalding for special mention, but the young pitcher did not go unnoticed; by 1871, at the age of twenty, he was starring for Harry Wright's Boston club in the National Association's inaugural season. In each of his six full seasons of professional league ball, Spalding won more games than any other pitcher, and was especially dominating in 1872–75, when he pitched Boston to successive National Association championships.

During the 1875 season, he negotiated with William A. Hulbert of the Chicago club—against association rules, which forbade the signing of players under contract to another club—to play for and manage Chicago in 1876. Hulbert and Spalding avoided trouble with the association by abandoning it after the season to form a new league, the National League. With its centralized scheduling of games and more businesslike organization and management, the National League attracted even the misused Harry Wright and his Boston club into its ranks.

While Spalding may not have had quite the inspiriting role in creating the National League that he sometimes claimed,[26] he shared with Hulbert the main effort of organizing the league, preparing its rules and constitution, and setting it in operation. Spalding, as team manager, was also responsible for preparing his players (himself included) for the league's inaugural season. But as if this weren't enough to keep him occupied, in the first months of 1876 the ambitious twenty-five-year-old launched his entrepreneurial career, opening, with his younger brother Walter, "a Base Ball emporium" on Randolph Street, Chicago. A. G. Spalding & Bro. (which became "& Bros." a couple of years later) began strongly, securing the franchise for the National League ball. By 1877, the young firm was publishing the official rules and league constitution, and the next year launched *Spalding's Official Base Ball Guide,* an annual publication that would be a baseball fixture well into the twentieth century (and of course an ideal venue for Spalding & Bros. to advertise their wares).

In his inaugural managerial season, Spalding piloted and pitched

Chicago to the club's first pennant. Arm trouble and the press of business took him off the playing field the next year, and after Chicago finished in fifth place, his managerial career was over as well. He remained with the club as secretary, however, and when Hulbert died in 1882, the club's stockholders elected him president. He retained the presidency until 1891, and even after relinquishing it to James A. Hart, remained a power behind the scenes. He remained active and influential in National League affairs while becoming wealthy in sporting goods and sports publishing.

In the latter part of the nineteenth century and well into the twentieth, the three big names in American sporting goods were Spalding, Reach, and Wright & Ditson. Albert James Reach was born in London but reared in Brooklyn. A highly regarded player for his hometown Eckford club, Reach was lured away in 1865 by the Athletics of Philadelphia, for whom he played through 1877. Like Spalding, Reach opened a sporting goods store and quickly expanded into manufacturing as the A. J. Reach Co. In 1882, with the organization of the American Association, Reach, like Spalding in the National League, became the official supplier of Association baseballs and the publisher of an annual Association guide. A year later, when the National League replaced its Worcester franchise with one in Philadelphia, Reach and his business associate Ben Shibe invested in half ownership of the new club, nicknamed the Phillies.[27] Reach was named president of the club, a position he retained until 1902.

George Wright, Harry's younger brother and, like Reach and Spalding, a noted ballplayer, opened his store in Boston in 1871. The business became Wright & Ditson in the autumn of 1879 with the addition of Henry A. Ditson to the firm. Wright, who that season had played shortstop and managed Providence to its first National League pennant, decided to return to Boston, his former club, the next year to be closer to his business, a decision that spurred the National League to create the immediately infamous "reserve rule" permitting clubs to retain players against their will. Wright managed somehow to evade Providence's reserve of his services, but his playing career was virtually over, as he played only nine games for Boston over the next two seasons. In 1884, he influenced the establishment of a Boston club for the renegade Union Association in return for the association's baseball, score book, and annual guide franchises,[28] but when the association folded after its inaugural season, so did Wright & Ditson's place among the big three as a supplier of major league baseballs.

Reach and Wright & Ditson retained their corporate names well beyond the long lifetimes of their founders (Reach died in 1928 at age eighty-seven, Wright in 1937 at ninety), but by the early 1890s, both firms had become parts of Spalding's empire. Wright, who remained with the company, expanded Wright & Ditson's line into sports like golf and tennis, which displaced baseball as the firm's signature sports; A. J. Reach, which at the time Spalding acquired it was producing the official ball for a number of minor leagues, became the manufacturer of all the balls that bore the Reach or Spalding labels.

Peter Levine, in his incisive introduction to his biography of Spalding, sees him as a product of his times, as a "representative figure" rather than an "individual genius."[29] It took no genius to see that what the loosely organized National Association of 1871–75 lacked was structure, and the business philosophy of the times called for top-down control. The idea that professional baseball was a business was not a new idea in 1876, but until Hulbert and Spalding organized the National League, it had been an idea incompletely implemented.

Perhaps the main reasons Spalding's influence on baseball was as great as it was were the clarity of his vision and his persistence in its pursuit. "Like every other form of business enterprise," he wrote, "Base Ball depends for results on two interdependent divisions, the one to have absolute control and direction of the system, and the other to engage—always under the executive branch—the actual work of production."[30]

With its independent clubs and volatile workforce, the National League never ran as efficiently as Spalding would have liked, but innovations like the reserve rule did stabilize club rosters and limit salary increases. And by reducing the input of players in club and league governance to next to nothing, the National League achieved a measure of authoritarian stability comparable in some ways to big business.

Those involved "in the actual work of production"—the players—did not find management's increasing control of their vocation and lives an unalloyed blessing. The fact that they were earning money in an occupation they loved, and earning more money for fewer hours' work than most would have been able to do in other occupations, didn't entirely compensate for the disrespect heaped on them by policies that restricted their freedom to move from one employer to another, while they themselves could be shunted to other clubs or dismissed entirely at their employer's will. One eminent player, John Montgomery Ward, argued in a

famous 1887 article for *Lippincott's* magazine that baseball's reserve rule
made the ballplayer a chattel, in his career a slave to his owners.[31] Ward
appears to have assessed the purpose of the reserve rule accurately: "In
the enactment of the reserve-rule the clubs were probably influenced by
three considerations: they wished to make the business of base-ball more
permanent, they meant to reduce salaries, and they sought to secure a
monopoly of the game."[32]

As new leagues emerged that threatened the National League's he-
gemony, a "National Agreement" was drawn up in which the leagues
agreed to respect one another's player reservations. Most leagues found it
worth their while to join in the agreement. Ward did not view the reserve
rule as a good idea with bad consequences but as evil in its very concept:
"Ideal wrong will always work itself out in practical wrong, and this has
been no exception. The rule itself was an inherent wrong, for by it one
set of men seized absolute control over the labor of another, and in its
development it has gone on from one usurpation to another until it has
grown so intolerable as to threaten the present organization of the
game."[33] Although the reserve rule's threat to "the present organization
of the game" proved less deadly than Ward supposed, his view of the
baseball establishment's "absolute control" over the ballplayers' labor
was, if also somewhat overstated, a sentiment Spalding would have applauded.

In some ways, Ward and Spalding were very much alike. In addition
to their Anglo-American heritage, both grew up middle class in small-
town America and developed into pitching phenoms at an early age. Ward
led the National League in earned run average (1878) and pitching wins
(1879), and in 1879 pitched Providence to a pennant—all before the age
of twenty. While still a player, Ward, as Spalding had done, became a
successful manager. And, like Spalding, Ward was extraordinarily ambitious. But Ward's ambition led him into law, not business—he earned his
law degree from Columbia in 1885 in the midst of his playing career—
and he led the player revolt that came closer than any other crisis to
toppling the National League from the pinnacle of the baseball world.

In the summer of 1885, the two major leagues added to the National
Agreement a $2,000 salary cap, though they held off announcing it until
October, just days after John Ward and eight New York Giants teammates
organized themselves into the Brotherhood of Professional Base Ball
Players. The brothers elected Ward president—"unsurprisingly," Bryan

DiSalvatore observes, "as he almost certainly conceived of the organization, called the formation meeting in the first place, and composed the group's guiding documents."[34]

It is simplistic to describe the conflict that culminated in the "Brotherhood War" of 1890 as a duel between Ward and Spalding, but they were the most prominent and influential figures on the opposing sides. Ward was in Australia as a member of Spalding's around-the-world baseball tour in the 1888–89 off-season when he learned of organized baseball's latest innovation, the "Brush Classification Plan," which the National League had adopted just days after the touring ballplayers set sail from San Francisco. This plan, named for its originator, John T. Brush, then owner of the National League's Indianapolis club, ranked players in five categories, with a maximum salary of $2,500 for players in the top category. Trapped as he was halfway around the world, Ward was powerless to respond to this move, but when he at last arrived home, he began laying plans for the formation of a brotherhood league. Although the plan was not made public until November, Ward revealed it to Brotherhood leaders in July.[35]

In sharp contrast to business practices of the times—which concentrated "ever-larger amounts of capital in fewer and fewer hands," stirring labor unrest and "rapidly increasing enmity between workers and owners"[36]—the Players' National League included players in league governance and encouraged them to invest in their clubs. It seemed like an idea whose time had come: most of the National League's best players bolted to the new league, and attendance at National League games, which had risen to a record 1.35 million in 1889, fell to 776,000 in 1890. Players' League clubs attracted over 980,000 spectators to their games, outdrawing their National League counterparts in six of the seven cities that fielded teams in both leagues, including Spalding's Chicago. Only in Brooklyn, where the National League club retained most of its players from 1889, did the Players' League finish second in attendance.[37] Ironically, Brooklyn was where Ward himself chose to play and to manage the Players' team.

Henry Chadwick, in the 1890 edition of *Spalding's Official Base Ball Guide,* described the revolt as the work of spoiled and ungrateful New York players led by a deceitful Ward (whom he did not mention by name), who had lured the defecting players down a road they had not wished to travel. He then went on to argue at length how the reserve rule had worked only to the benefit of players, with two pages of figures showing how each defecting player's pay had increased in the years since the reserve rule was instituted. Ward, Chadwick observed, ranked second only to noted catcher Buck Ewing in total accumulation.[38] Chadwick, as Spalding's employee, was of course promoting Spalding's view, but it was his own opinion also.

While the Players' League was a relative success in 1890, attendance was less than the investors in the new clubs had hoped for, and they were willing—even eager—to discuss peace with the National League. But if the Players' League was shaky, the National League was on the brink of collapse. Its linchpin New York club had had to be shored up financially by the league and other owners during the season, and its Cincinnati club had been sold to a Brotherhood backer. But in the negotiations that followed between the leagues, the Players' League owners capitulated, and the league that Ward had proclaimed in its first and only annual guide as "a living monument for all time to come"[39] was dead. Ward—who, curiously, seems to have distanced himself from much of the post-season discussion—was excluded from the negotiations, which were engineered by Spalding as head of the National League's conference committee. "Different versions of the intrigues between Players' League and major league club owners exist," writes Peter Levine, "but they all agree on two points—that the end result was the demise of the Brotherhood and that the chief undertaker was A. G. Spalding."[40]

Ward returned to the National League as a player and manager, and as a lawyer represented effectively a number of disgruntled players in their personal wars with the baseball establishment, but his influence over the governance and direction of the game was over. His lasting contribution to the game off the playing field is his passionate writing in defense of workers' dignity and in opposition to baseball's love affair with the oppressive business philosophy that ruled his day.

Are there threads in their English heritage that bind these six men together? Has their "Englishness" given a distinctiveness to their contributions to baseball? They represent the extremes of English presence in America, from descendants of the New England Puritans, with their wary hostility toward the old country, to first-generation newcomers. Not surprisingly, perhaps, Spalding was delighted to defeat the English at cricket during the baseball tour of 1874—abandoning "good form" for an aggressive baseball-type offense—and grasping at the frailest evidence to "prove" an exclusively American origin for baseball. Chadwick, not burdened with a historic opposition to the home country, was able to recognize the British progenitors of the American game.

Much is made (and was made at the time) of the Spalding-Chadwick dispute over baseball's origins, but there was much more that bound the two than divided them—and, indeed, bound all six subjects, as best we can tell. Chadwick and Spalding (and Cartwright, Adams, Harry Wright, and Ward) shared a characteristically British-American morality —Christian but not overtly religious, strict without sectarian rigidity— and a sense (without smugness) of moral superiority over the less enlightened classes. The original Knickerbocker rules required the umpire to note in a book "all violations of the By-Laws and Rules during the time of exercise," and the expanded code prepared by Doc Adams and his fellows forbade all participants in a game from betting on it. Obedience to the umpire and quiet submission to his decisions were mandated.

The writings of Chadwick, the teaching of Harry Wright, and the views of baseball governance promoted by Spalding all envisioned a baseball world characterized by integrity, decorum, temperance, and submission to authority—a game attractive to the "better class of people," a game ladies would not be embarrassed to witness. Even Ward, who as the players' advocate was closer to the culturally diverse working class, forbade the sale of liquor at Players' League games and prohibited games on Sunday,[41] thereby siding philosophically with the National League of Spalding, Wright, and Chadwick against the "beer and whiskey league" American Association.

As the baseball fraternity grew increasingly diverse ethnically and culturally, Chadwick saw his ideal compromised at nearly every turn. He never abandoned the professional game, though toward the end of his life he found more pleasure watching high school ball. The last piece he wrote before his death paid tribute to a school headmaster who, playing first base with his students, disputed an "out" call by the umpire on a pickoff play because he knew he had missed the tag.[42]

Notes

1. Henry Chadwick, ed., *Spalding's Official Base Ball Guide* (1908), 42. These are the words of Albert G. Spalding describing Graves's recollection.

Graves himself may have believed Doubleday was creating a new game, but the name "base ball" was not new in 1839, and there is nothing in what Graves is reported to have said that indicates that Doubleday was doing anything more than describing and writing out the rules for a game he had learned from someone else. The classic refutation of the Doubleday creation story is Robert Henderson, *Ball, Bat and Bishop: The Origin of Ball Games* (New York: Rockport Press, 1947; Detroit: Gale, 1974). Recent research has suggested that the Abner Doubleday who became a Union general may not have been the one Graves remembered but another Abner Doubleday who lived in the Cooperstown area. See Peter Morris, "The *Other* Abner Doubleday," *Nineteenth Century Notes* (spring 1999): 6. In either case, there is no credible reason to suppose that someone brought Doubleday's game from Cooperstown to Manhattan, where everyone agrees that the game first codified in 1845 by the Knickerbocker Base Ball Club is the game from which today's baseball descends directly.

2. Curry's statement was published in Alfred H. Spink, *The National Game* (New York: National Game, 1910), 54, 56. Rankin discusses his Cartwright no tation in "Game's Pedigree," *The Sporting News*, 2 April 1908, 2. Another Rankin column, "Baseball's Birth," *The Sporting News*, 8 April 1905, 2, contains a brief version of Curry's purported comments on baseball's origin.

3. Charles A. Peverelly, *The Book of American Pastimes* (New York: self-published, 1846), 340.

4. Robert Henderson was the first to point out that Robin Carver, *Boy's and Girl's Book of Sports* (Providence, R.I.: Cory & Daniels, 1835) contains rules for "Base, or Goal Ball" that are nearly identical to rules for rounders published in William Clarke, *The Boy's Own Book* (London: Vizetelly, Branson, 1829).

5. "Baseball's Nineteenth Century Best," *Nineteenth Century Notes* (spring 1999): 2.

6. Daniel Lucius Adams was an eighth-generation Yankee whose first American Adams ancestor, Henry, settled near Boston before 1645. Daniel L. Adams family genealogy, preserved by Adelaide (Mrs. Daniel Putnam) Adams, New York, N.Y.

Alexander Joy Cartwright Jr. was descended from a long line of seafarers; his first American progenitor arrived in New Hampshire from Devonshire, England, shortly after 1660. Harold Peterson, *The Man Who Invented Baseball* (New York: Scribner's, 1973), 91–94.

Henry Chadwick was born in Exeter, Devonshire, England, in 1824 and immigrated to the United States in 1837, settling in Brooklyn. Among the numerous sources for this information is Chadwick's obituary in the *Brooklyn Daily Eagle*, 20 April 1908, 3.

Albert Goodwill Spalding was a ninth-generation American whose first American ancestors, John and Anna (Heald) Spaulding (as the name was then spelled) were born in England and died in Chelmsford, Mass., according to his genealogy on the Latter Day Saints Web site. Information in *Spalding's Official Base Ball Guide* (1908): 18–19, however, claims that Spalding descended from an Edward Spalding, who arrived in Virginia from England in 1619 and moved later to Massachusetts.

John Montgomery Ward was descended on his paternal grandparents' side from Lt. John Ward, an English immigrant who settled in Branford, Conn., in 1648, and English settlers who came to America in 1623. Bryan DiSalvatore, *A Clever Base-Ballist: The Life and Times of John Montgomery Ward* (New York: Pantheon, 1999), 25–31.

William Henry "Harry" Wright was born in January 1835 in Sheffield, Yorkshire, England, to an English father and Irish mother. He came to the United States with his parents either a year or so after his birth or shortly before the birth of his brother George, who was born in January 1847. Sources differ.

7. Peterson, 189.

8. James A. Vlasich, *A Legend for the Legendary: The Origin of the Baseball Hall of Fame* (Bowling Green, Ohio: Bowling Green State University Popular Press, 1990), 149.

9. *New York Times,* 13 April 1980, sec. 5, p. 2, reprinted large portions of a memoir of Adams written by his son R. C. Adams years earlier, but it was not until the publication of John Thorn's "The Father of Baseball?" in *Elysian Fields Quarterly* 11, no.1 (1992): 85–91 (reprinted in recent editions of *Total Baseball* as "The True Father of Baseball") that scholars began to examine more seriously Adams's contribution to the game.

10. 29 February 1896. The interview is reprinted in Dean A. Sullivan, ed., *Early Innings: A Documentary History of Baseball, 1825–1908* (Lincoln: University of Nebraska Press, 1995), 13–18.

11. *Porter's Spirit of the Times,* 31 January 1857, 357; 28 February 1857, 420.

12. In one of its three accounts of the convention, *Porter's Spirit* (7 March 1857, 7) reports: "Although many old Base Ball players were connected with the new clubs, it was generally conceded, and expected, that the Knickerbockers would, from their well-known experience, as to the requirements of the game, take the lead in proposing the necessary reforms. They, accordingly, submitted [to the convention] a new code of laws, in which they clearly defined every point in the game."

13. Interview, in Sullivan, 16.

14. *Porter's Spirit of the Times,* 7 March 1857, 7.

15. Knickerbocker Base Ball Club book (1 April 1854–22 February 1859), 147, Spalding Collection, New York Public Library.

16. Preston D. Orem, *Baseball (1845–1881) from the Newspaper Accounts* (Altadena, Calif.: self-published, 1961), 18–22. Orem reproduces the primitive

box score prepared for the game. Wright batted ninth and was the only player on either side not to score a run. His team edged Brooklyn 22-18. Wright did not play in either of the other two games in the match.

17. *Ball Players' Chronicle,* 25 July 1867, 1. Chadwick wrote further: "certainly [Cincinnati] will encounter no such difficult pitching as that of Harry Wright's, who only wants well-trained support in the field to be the most troublesome pitcher in the country. His thorough good humor and his excellent judgment make him quite, a model to copy from. The Cincinnati clubs may congratulate themselves on having such a player to train them."

18. Harry Ellard, *Base Ball in Cincinnati: A History* (Cincinnati: self-published, 1907; Cincinnati: Ohio Book Store, 1987), 40, 43.

19. Warren Goldstein, *Playing for Keeps: A History of Early Baseball* (Ithaca, N.Y.: Cornell University Press, 1989), 104. Goldstein provides the most insightful analysis I have seen of Harry Wright's contribution to baseball history. Also useful is Harold Seymour, "Baseball's First Professional Manager," *Ohio Historical Quarterly* 64 (October 1955): 406–23.

20. Ellard, 138, 141.

21. Goldstein, 112–13. Wright's authority over his players *on* the field wasn't always as great as he liked, either. In one 1875 letter to Henry Chadwick, he complained about his difficulty in positioning his outfielders: "Leonard . . . and McVey dislike exceedingly when playing in the field, to be told to change their positions when certain players come to the bat, that move to the right or to the left. I never have any trouble with Andy when I tell him, but McVey will get ugly and show his temper now and then. He says that he has played in the field long enough and knows the strikers well enough to know when to change his position without being told." Wright to Chadwick, 2 January 1875, Harry Wright Correspondence, vol. 2, Spalding Collection, New York Public Library.

22. Henry Chadwick, ed., *Spalding's Official Base Ball Guide* (1896): 164.

23. Henry Chadwick, *The Game of Base Ball* (New York: Munro, 1868; Columbia, S.C.: Camden House, 1983), 10.

24. Jules Tygiel, in *Past Time: Baseball as History* (New York: Oxford University Press, 2000), ch. 2: "The Mortar of Which Baseball Is Held Together," explores in depth and with insight the significance of Chadwick's seminal contribution to baseball statistics.

25. In 1870, for example, Chadwick criticized the lively ball and the heavy hitting that resulted. "What is wanted," he argued, "is first a change in the public estimate of batting skill, and then, when crowds are found laughing at and ridiculing muffin home run hits and appreciating the really skillful style of first base hits only, the players will soon be found repudiating the muffin batting." *New York Clipper,* 9 July 1870. Two decades later, he was still criticizing heavy hitters like Mike Tiernan and Roger Connor, who "both have the power to excel in the art of batting, if they would get out of the old rut of fungo hitting, and apply

themselves to the study of the art, the aim and intent of which is to forward runners around the bases by scientific hitting." Henry Chadwick, ed., *Spalding's Official Base Ball Guide* (1892): 95–96.

26. Peter Levine, *A. G. Spalding and the Rise of Baseball* (New York: Oxford University Press, 1985), 25. Intriguingly, Henry Chadwick, who initially excoriated the National League organizers for their highhanded ways before becoming a loyal league supporter himself, later also claimed to be one of its cofounders.

27. Donald Dewey and Nicholas Acocella, *Encyclopedia of Major League Baseball Teams* (New York: HarperCollins, 1993), 413.

28. Jerry Jaye Wright, "What's in a Name? George Wright's Influence, Favors, and Deals During the Organization of the Boston Unions of 1884," manuscript, n.d.

29. Levine, xii, xiii.

30. Albert G. Spalding, *America's National Game* (1911; reprint, Lincoln: University of Nebraska Press, 1992), 270.

31. John Montgomery Ward, "Is the Base-Ball Player a Chattel?" *Lippincott's* (August 1887): 310–19.

32. Ward, 311.

33. Ward, 313.

34. DiSalvatore, 177. DiSalvatore provides the most thorough discussion in print of Ward's Brotherhood activities. Also useful is Cynthia Bass, "The Making of a Baseball Radical," *National Pastime* (fall 1983 [misdated 1982]): 63–65.

35. DiSalvatore, 267. DiSalvatore provides a detailed account of the Brotherhood War, but also see Levine, 59–65, for a focus on Spalding's role.

36. DiSalvatore, 281.

37. Robert L. Tiemann, "Nineteenth Century Major League Attendance," manuscript, 1999. Officially released attendance figures for 1890 are suspect, as each league was intent on demonstrating its superior drawing power, but if the announced figures were inflated, they were probably inflated for both leagues, so relative attendance may be close to the mark.

38. Henry Chadwick, ed., *Spalding's Official Base Ball Guide* (1890): 14–23.

39. *The Players' National League Official Guide for 1890*: 6.

40. Levine, 63. DiSalvatore, writing fifteen years after Levine, makes a good effort to sort out the varying accounts and in chapters 23 and 24 presents a satisfying summation of events leading to the demise of the Players' League.

41. DiSalvatore, 276–77.

42. Henry Chadwick, "Uncle Harry's Letter," *Brooklyn Daily Eagle,* 13 April 1908, 3.

⋆ 3 ⋆

German Americans in Major League Baseball: Sport and Acculturation

LARRY R. GERLACH

Ruth. Gehrig. Wagner. Klem. Stengel. Kuhn. Ripken. The names and achievements of the luminaries residing in baseball's Teutonic Valhalla are familiar to fans and nonfans alike. Less well known is the overall involvement of German Americans in the national pastime. In contrast to the attention given sport in ethnographic studies of African Americans, Irish, Italians, Jews, and Latins, historical and sociological studies of German Americans have ignored sport as a social institution, an agent of assimilation, or source of ethnic pride and achievement.[1] And because German immigrants rather easily assimilated into mainstream American society, baseball writers and historians have paid much less attention to their ethnicity compared with other groups.[2] Despite their perceived, and ultimately actual, status as unexceptional ethnics, German Americans have enjoyed prominence in all aspects of baseball history.

Since the eighteenth century, Germans have constituted the largest non-English-speaking ethnic group in America. Germanic immigration grew steadily after the arrival of the "Pennsylvania Dutch" in 1682, surged after the ill-fated Revolution of 1848, and increased dramatically after the American Civil War.[3] From 1846 to 1904, Germans were by far the largest immigrant group, totaling nearly two million émigrés from 1881 to 1892. The majority of German emigrants settled in the Midwest, many on farms and in small towns, but most in the burgeoning cities of

27

Chicago, Cincinnati, Milwaukee, and St. Louis. The largest ethnic group in Chicago from 1860 to 1920, Germans comprised 25 percent of the city's population in 1870 and that same year totaled 23 percent of Cincinnati and 51 percent of St. Louis, the fourth largest city in America.[4]

German immigrants arrived heavily laden with cultural baggage, settled in ethnic neighborhoods like Cincinnati's "Over the Rhine," and perpetuated their *kultur* through language, food, and customs as well as ethnic schools, newspapers, social organizations, theaters, and sports clubs, including turnvereins. Founded in Prussia in 1811 to promote liberal intellectual development and physical training for German youth, turner societies featured not games but calisthenics gymnastics. The first American turner society was established in Cincinnati in 1848, and by 1860 they numbered more than 150 nationwide. German sporting traditions did not include team sports, but the turnverein's encouragement of physical recreation led naturally to participating in American sports, which were, after all, more fun than calisthenics and a means of joining in the larger public culture.[5]

Bat and ball games, not unknown in Germany, were the rage in the northeastern urban areas in mid-century, and Germans quickly gravitated toward baseball rather than cricket.[6] Indeed, they were present at the recorded origins of the game—three of the known members of the 1845 Knickerbockers and the two other contemporary New York City clubs were German.[7] German American participation increased as the popularity of the game spread across the nation after the Civil War. Turners, such as those in St. Louis, sponsored baseball teams, as did German social clubs like the Schneiders, Laners, and Landwehrs in New Orleans.[8]

The claim that Germans embraced baseball because "its geometric order, its requirement of technical skills as well as brute strength and quick reflexes, its disciplined pattern appealed to something in the German psyche" is specious given the ethnic inclusiveness of what truly was America's national sporting pastime.[9] Unlike other immigrant groups who saw pugilism as a means of socioeconomic mobility, Germans disdained prize fighting: the baseball diamond, not the boxing ring, was their sporting venue of choice. Besides the primary attraction of pleasure, participation in the uniquely American sport was an easy means of assimilation and gaining recognition for one's ethnic group. And with its transformation from amateur recreation to commercial entertainment after the Civil War, baseball also afforded economic opportunity for the talented few.

Many first-generation German parents, like Willie Kamm's, did not know "baseball from shmaseball," but encouraged their sons to pursue the professional game.[10] According to data on parental ethnicity compiled by Lee Allen, historian for the National Baseball Hall of Fame, nearly half of the National Association (1871–75) players were British, with Germans comprising 30 percent and the Irish 20 percent. But from the advent of the National League to the end of the century, a majority of major leaguers were of German or Irish ancestry. From 1876 to 1884, 21 percent of the players entering the league were of German ancestry, 34 percent were British, and 41 percent were Irish; from 1885 through 1890, 24 percent of the new players were German, 36 percent were Irish, and 31 percent were British; and from 1891 to 1899, Germans increased to 30 percent while the Irish declined to 22 percent and the British rose to approximately 40 percent.[11] German and Irish players so dominated some rosters that teams on St. Patrick's Day staged intrasquad games between the two ethnic groups.[12] While British, German, and Irish ballplayers experienced interethnic tensions, they showed more unity than their compatriots in industries with more diverse workforces because of their special athletic talents and anticipation of increased income.[13] But since Germans were mostly either independent farmers and shopkeepers or members of labor's aristocracy, they saw baseball more as a means of expanding their lower-middle-class opportunities than as a vehicle for socioeconomic mobility as did the Irish.[14]

First-generation Germans have been present throughout the history of major league baseball. Joseph Miller, an infielder who appeared in one game with Washington in 1872 and twenty-eight games with two teams in 1875, was the lone German-born player in the National Association, the initial professional circuit. George Meister played only one year, with Toledo of the American Association in 1884, but it was an eventful season as it marked the debut of teammate Moses Fleetwood Walker, the first African American major leaguer. In all, thirty-four major league players were born in Germany and another, Jake Gettman, Volga Deutsch, was born in Frank, Russia.[15] Twenty-two of the German-born players debuted before World War I, eleven in the nineteenth century.

Most native Germans were not players of distinction. Of the twenty-four who appeared before the end of World War II, only six played more than two years. Native German position players were marginal hitters; despite anemic batting averages, catcher Fritz Buelow (1899–1907) and third baseman Willie Kuehne (1883–92) enjoyed substantial careers because of their defensive skills. The best of the German natives was Charlie Getzien, nicknamed "Pretzels," an ethnic reference to his twisting curve ball. He posted a modest 145-139 record in nine seasons (1884–92) but was the National League's best pitcher in 1886–87 when he went 30-1 and 29-13 for Detroit. (The ten German-born players who debuted after World War II, including Glenn Hubbard and Craig Lefferts, were sons of U.S. armed forces personnel and not German ethnics.)

American-born players of German ancestry gave fans much more to cheer about. Outfielders George Bechtel and John "Count" Sensenderfer, third baseman Levi Meyerle, who in 1871 won the first batting title with the highest average in baseball history (.492), and pitcher George Zettlein, reputedly the hardest thrower of the day, were stars of the 1870s, professional baseball's formative decade. Lou Bierbauer, "Move-Up Joe" Gerhardt, Herman "Germany" Long, Heinie Peitz, Fred Pfeffer, Heinie Reitz, Jake Stenzel, and George "Stump" Weidman were notable German Americans who played from the advent of the National League in 1876 to the end of the century. But save for Gerhardt and Pfeffer, two of the finest second basemen of the day, German Americans did not approach the premier status of the British and Irish players. Ex-players frequently became managers, but before World War I, there were relatively few managers of German descent, and only Al Buckenberger (1889–1904) and Gustavius "Gus" Schmelz (1884–97) enjoyed notable tenures.

By far the greatest impact of German Americans on nineteenth-century baseball came from the ranks of owners and administrators. While baseball became more ethnically heterogeneous on the playing field after the Civil War, British Americans dominated management until the appearance of the American Association in 1882. Germans brought the brewer's art to America in the 1840s, and in 1881 a quintet of beer barons—Chris Von der Ahe of St. Louis, John H. Park of Louisville, Harry Von der Horst of Baltimore, and John Hauck and Justus Thorner of Cincinnati—laid plans for a second major league. With the addition of franchises in Philadelphia and Pittsburgh, also backed by beer and liquor money, the American Association embraced cities with large German populations.

It was the Germanic mentality of owners and fans alike that gave the new league its distinctive qualities. Whereas the National League in 1880 had expelled Thorner's Cincinnati Red Stockings for violating its Sabbatarian and temperance restrictions, the new circuit scheduled games on

Sunday, sold beer and alcohol to spectators, and reduced admission prices by half to accommodate working-class fans.[16] Second-generation Germans were enthusiastic baseball fans, and the so-called "beer and whiskey league" catered to them. The German-language press did not normally cover sports, but newspapers in Cincinnati and St. Louis carried advertisements for the local team. The *Sporting Life*, the nation's first modern sports periodical, founded in Philadelphia in 1883 by German American sportswriter F. C. Richter, devoted considerable space to American Association baseball. Cincinnati and St. Louis, and later Chicago, promoted players of German ancestry as gate attractions as the Browns did with local-born pitcher Charley "Silver" King (b. Koenig) and the famous "pretzel battery" of pitcher Ted Breitenstein and catcher Heinie Peitz. The American Association, whose success led the National League to adopt alcohol sales and, where possible, Sunday baseball, was the marketing model for major league baseball.

The personification of the American Association was Christian Frederick Wilhelm Von der Ahe, the most important owner of the nineteenth century and the most innovative owner in major league history.[17] Von der Ahe, who emigrated from Westphalia as a teenager, found fame and fortune by coupling beer and baseball—and thus founding an American tradition. He knew little about baseball, but in 1881 bought the St. Louis Brown Stockings and helped found the American Association as a means of increasing patronage of his Golden Lion Saloon, located just two blocks from Sportsman's Park. The self-proclaimed "Der Poss Bresident" was a hands-on owner. Believing of money "dot is to schpend," he hired excellent players, including captain Charles Comiskey, who led the Browns to four straight pennants from 1885 to 1888 and a world championship in 1886. Von der Ahe's Germanic sense of gemütlichkeit made the game an occasion for diverse entertainment. "German tea" was available from roaming vendors, stands located throughout the park, or from concessionaires in the *biergarten* adjacent to right field. He delighted fans with fireworks, oompah bands, merry-go-rounds, water-slide rides, horse races, and a variety of amusements including Wild West shows. Sportsman's Park was the first to boast a stadium club, women's restrooms, and a special seating section for ladies. An innovative promoter, Von der Ahe dressed waiters in his saloon with Browns caps and shirts and sold beer mugs, pennants, posters, and sporting goods bearing the Browns logo. He hired boys to display handbills advertising games and placed full-page ads in the local German-language newspaper, *Anzeiger des Westerns*. He even arranged for a game-day express cable car, the "Cannon Ball Train," to whisk fans to the ballpark.

The press attributed Von der Ahe's success to his German ethic, but also poked fun at his heavy accent, fractured syntax, and malapropisms.[18] In time, his ostentatious behavior, boozing, and carousing as well as his personal peccadilloes and financial problems led to the sale of the Browns in 1899. The designation "half-genius, half-buffoon" is probably correct.[19] But it was Von der Ahe who infected St. Louis with the baseball fever it still possesses and who, by turning Sportsman's Park into a self-described "Coney Island of the West," significantly expanded baseball's commercial horizons and anticipated by more than half a century the entrepreneurial strategies designed to make the ballpark a place of more entertainments than just the baseball game.

German Americans came to the fore in major league baseball in the first two decades of the twentieth century. The Midwest had surpassed the Northeast as the primary producers of major leaguers, and many ball-players of German descent came from Chicago, Cincinnati, Pittsburgh, and St. Louis.[20] While the percentage of German American entrants into the majors remained consistent during the first two decades of the century—28 percent from 1900 to 1909, 32 percent from 1910 to 1915, and 31 percent from 1916 to 1919—the prominence of those players increased dramatically.[21] German Americans who reached stardom included Addie Joss, fireballing Hall of Fame pitcher who never had a losing season and posted the second-best career ERA (1.89) in history; Heinie Groh, who invented the "bottle bat"; Hans Lobert, the "fastest man in baseball," who easily beat Jim Thorpe in a hundred-yard dash and outraced a horse around the bases; Ed Reulbach, master curveballer who completed 201 of 300 starts and compiled a .632 career winning percentage with a 2.28 ERA; Herman "Germany" Schaefer, baseball's first "funny man," also known as "the Mad Dutchman," who on 4 September 1908 "stole" first base from second, thereby prompting a rule prohibiting running the bases in reverse order; Wally Schang, switch-hitting catcher for three different World Series champions; Frank "Wildfire" Schulte, who in 1911 won the National League's first Most Valuable Player Award; "Dutch" Stengel, later known as "Casey"; Harry Steinfeldt, slick-fielding third baseman in the famous Tinker-to-Evers-to-Chance infield; and Rube Waddell, Hall of Famer who recorded a 2.13 ERA over thirteen seasons. Not all German ballplayers gained fame for exemplary performances. Fred Merkle cost his team an important game by neglecting to touch second base in 1908; Lee (b. Hoernschemeyer) Magee fixed games while with Cincinnati in 1918; and in 1919, the Giants released Heinie Zimmerman, who had won the Triple Crown in 1912, for throwing games.

These and other German players received considerable press coverage, but nothing like that accorded the leader of the Teutonic brigade, Honus Wagner, baseball's first German American superstar.[22] One of six children born to immigrant parents, Johannes Peter Wagner was raised in a working-class community near Pittsburgh. He initially attended public school but then enrolled in a German-language Lutheran school and participated in the local turnverein. Known by the anglicized John Peter or German diminutives (Hans, Hannes, Hanus, or Hones), Wagner worked in the coal mines and steel mills as his father and brothers did before embarking on a career in professional baseball in 1895. His father did not understand baseball but supported his son's ambition; two years later, he reached the majors with Louisville of the National League. With the Pittsburgh Pirates from 1900 to 1917, Wagner dominated the game with his bat and glove. Hitting over .300 for seventeen consecutive seasons, he earned eight league batting titles and recorded a career .327 average. John McGraw, Edward Barrow, and Branch Rickey were among those naming the Pirates shortstop "the greatest baseball player of all time," and when the Hall of Fame elected its first group of inductees in 1936, Wagner tied with Babe Ruth for the second most votes, seven behind Ty Cobb.[23]

Wagner did not speak English with a German accent, but his evident ethnicity drew notice. While he was at Louisville, his manager, Fred Clarke, dubbed him "Dutch"; teammates called him Hans and Honus; and appreciative bleacher fans once sang him a German song. After he arrived in Pittsburgh, a sportswriter, taken by the way Wagner ran the bases, called him "the Flying Dutchman" after the famous opera by German composer Richard Wagner. Universally admired, Wagner was never the target of negative ethnic actions or commentary.[24] His celebrity status derived from his personal character as well as on-field achievements. Wagner's modesty and decorum contrasted with the brawling, boozing, and betting ethos of turn-of-the-century baseball. He smoked and chewed tobacco but further enhanced his role-model image in 1910 by demanding that the Piedmont Tobacco Company stop distribution of a cigarette card bearing his picture because it might entice young boys to

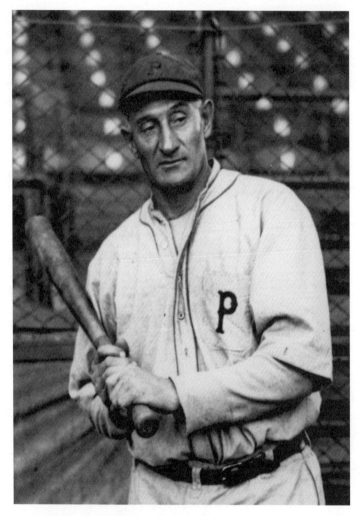

Honus Wagner. National Baseball Hall of Fame Library, Cooperstown, N.Y.

smoke.[25] A source of cultural pride for German Americans, Wagner, as one who had achieved the American Dream, was also an inspiration to all immigrant and working-class Americans.

Umpires solidified the German presence in baseball. With the advent of the two-umpire system and front-office support for an arbiter's decision, umpires became highly visible symbols of authority and discipline. The first prominent German umpire was Bill Klem (b. Klimm), son of immigrants, who reached the National League in 1905. Generally regarded as the greatest umpire in baseball history, Klem, who pioneered using the inside chest protector and calling balls and strikes from over the catcher's shoulder, holds the record for seasons (37), World Series (18), and World Series games (108) umpired. After his retirement in 1941, he served as the first modern chief of umpires and was elected to the Hall of Fame in 1953. Egotistical, sharp-tongued, and shorter than most umpires at five feet, seven inches, "the Old Arbitrator" umpired with imperious rectitude and unquestioned authority. It was Klem who said, "I never missed one in my life" and ended arguments by drawing a line in the dirt with his foot and ejecting anyone who crossed it.

Hulking Charles "Cy" Rigler joined the National League in 1906 and until 1935 was the temperamental counterpart to Klem, using humor and diplomacy to run the game. Rigler, who ranks second to Klem in the number of World Series and World Series games worked, originated hand signals to indicate balls and strikes in 1905 while a minor league umpire. George Hildebrand (1913–34), inventor of the spitball and the first arbiter of German descent in the American League, umpired a record 3,510 consecutive games. Although their autocratic demeanor could easily have promoted stereotypical commentary about Teutonic despots, the press rarely mentioned the ethnicity of German American umpires.

German Americans gained increased notoriety as owners. Temperamental and tyrannical Andrew Freedman, second-generation German Jew, nearly ruined the New York Giants from 1895 to 1902, but Barney Dreyfuss, who emigrated from Freiburg at age seventeen, used "benevolent despotism" to build the Pittsburgh Pirates into a powerful club from 1901 to 1932. August "Garry" Herrmann, owner of the Cincinnati Reds from 1902 to 1927, provided fans with a festive atmosphere at the ballpark and a World Championship in the infamous Black Sox Series of 1919. The greatest owner of German descent in the early twentieth century was Jacob Ruppert Jr., inheritor of the leading brewery in New York state and president of the New York Yankees from 1915 to 1939.[26] Determined to assemble a winning club, Ruppert hired Miller Huggins as manager in 1918 and began buying outstanding players, most notably Babe Ruth in 1919. The next year Ruppert hired Ed Barrow as the club's general manager and began plans to build baseball's grand palace, Yankee Stadium, which opened in 1923. Ruppert, who preferred to be called "Colonel" after his rank in the New York National Guard, "ran his ballclub with all the discipline and singleness of purpose of a Prussian oberlieutenant."[27] The architect of the most fabled professional sports franchise in America was the first owner to make numbers a regular part of uniforms (1929).

German Americans also were a conspicuous presence in baseball's governance structure. Former umpire John Heydler was the National League's secretary-treasurer from 1903 to 1918, interim president in 1909, and president from 1918 to 1934. While secretary, he created in 1912 the earned-run average (ERA) as a statistical measurement of pitching effectiveness. A weak executive as president, Heydler nonetheless actively supported the creation of the office of commissioner and was the first baseball executive to urge the creation of Cooperstown's Hall of Fame.

The second most influential baseball executive during the first two decades of the century was Garry Herrmann, owner of the Cincinnati Reds, who is best known for his leadership role on the National Commission. From the merger of the American and National Leagues in 1903 until the appointment of a commissioner in 1921, the three-member National Commission, composed of the president of each league and an independent chairman, governed major league baseball. The chairman frequently cast the tie-breaking vote, and although Herrmann owned a National League club and was a personal friend of American League president, Ban Johnson, the owners annually elected him to the commission because of his fairness and integrity. Known as "the Great Conciliator," his most enduring contribution on the commission was arranging a permanent annual playoff between league champions, for which he is called the "Father of the World Series."[28]

The son of German immigrants and a member of the North Cincinnati turnverein, Herrmann gloried in his ethnicity. The press thought him "as German as sauerkraut" and frequently referred to his "guttural Teutonic accent" and love of beer and German food. The "beer garden atmosphere" that Herrmann brought to Cincinnati baseball carried over into National Commission meetings, where invariably "beer, knackwurst, cheese, [and] sauerkraut topped the menu." He is the only German American involved with major league baseball whose ethnicity was regularly mentioned in the press.[29]

German Americans were noted for labor radicalism (seven of the eight convicted in the 1878 Haymarket bombing were Germans), so it is not surprising that they were leaders in the several ill-fated attempts at unionizing ballplayers. Former baseball writer William "Billy" Voltz founded the Brotherhood of Professional Base Ball Players (1885–91), but no other German Americans were prominent in its administration. Lou Bierbauer, Willie Kuehne, and Fred Pfeffer were the only notable *deutsch* defectors to the BPBBP's Player's League in 1890. Charles "Chief" Zimmer, the first catcher to position himself directly behind home plate on every pitch, was the founding president of the Protective Association of Professional Baseball Players (1900–3). In 1901, Zimmer devised a loophole that allowed National Leaguers to jump with impunity to the new American League. David Fultz, attorney and former player, was elected president of the Fraternity of Professional Baseball Players (1912–15), created to improve working conditions for players and prevent contract abuses; Chicago Cub Ed Reulbach was the fraternity's first secretary.

The rise of German Americans to prominence in baseball before World War I occurred within a broader context of cultural adjustment and ethnic tensions. The largest immigrant group in the United States, comprising some 25 percent of the Caucasian population in 1910, they assimilated faster and easier than other non-British groups. Nonetheless, Anglo-Saxon Protestants generally were suspicious or resentful of their Teutonic neighbors because of their harsh-sounding language, supposedly intemperate lifestyle, opposition to "blue laws" forbidding baseball and other recreations on Sunday, political and economic radicalism and, for the largest Germanic subgroup, Catholicism. But notable contributions by German Americans in science, technology, education, and music (as well as their political power in many communities) mitigated anti-German sentiment. As a result, they were subjected to verbal slurs and stereotypical comments, suspicion and political opposition, but little overt hostility or discrimination.[30]

German American ballplayers pursued assimilation and countered ethnic negativism in a variety of ways. Americanization meant anglicization —hence, Honus Wagner was commonly called Honus Wagner, not Hanus Vaagner. And since English equivalents of German given names (for example, Henry instead of Heinrich) were the rule, surnames were the most obvious signifiers of ethnicity. German American players altered surnames far less frequently than those of Czech, Greek, Italian, Jewish, and Polish descent, perhaps in part because of their numerical prominence.

Yet anglicization was not uncommon. Parents or grandparents were responsible for most name changes, but forty-two German American players modified their surnames in the late nineteenth century and the beginning of the twentieth. Some alterations shortened or simplified unwieldy names without disguising ethnicity—Schulte from Schultenhenrich, Starnagle from Steurenagel, and Schreck from Schreckengost. But other changes masked ethnicity. English versions of the German were common—Koenig became King, Moeller Miller, Schnell Snell, Schmidt Smith. Still others were Anglo-Saxon creations—Hoernschemeyer became Magee, Baerwald Bell, Funkhouser Lee, Schuerholz Sherry, Winbigler Abbot, Weichbrodt Roach, and Louis Staub the original Bull Durham. All but eight name changes occurred before World War I: fifteen were players who debuted between 1872 and 1899, while nineteen appeared from 1902 to 1915. Anglicization did not always hide ethnicity, as George "Dutch" Smith (1884–98) could attest.

Official nicknames, the names by which ballplayers are publicly known, is a common indicator of ethnicity.[31] Herman "Dutch" Dehlman (1872–77) was the first of the ninety-four players before 2000 who bore nicknames that reflected their German heritage. Some were Germanic variations of given names, such as Fritz for Frederick (seven), Hans or Honus for John (five) and Gus for August or Augustus (four). Twenty players were called "Heinie," twelve as a variant of Henry and eight signifying German ancestry. The most common German American nickname, "Dutch," the corruption of "Deutsch," was bestowed upon forty-four players.[32] (So common was "Dutch" as an informal nickname that Heinie Meine listed his ethnicity as Dutch instead of German.)[33] Four players received the nationalistic tag "Germany," including Herman Long (1889–1904), who was also dubbed the original "Flying Dutchman." Monikers for "Pretzels" Getzien and John "Count" Sensenderfer and Irvin "Kaiser" Wilhelm referenced ethnic food and presumed Teutonic titles. Still others carried ethnic terms of endearment; the German fans of Chicago and Milwaukee embraced Fred Pfeffer and Joe Hauser as "ours," calling them "Unser Fritz" and "Unser Choe." Some were false ethnic signifiers. Otto "Oom Paul" Krueger (1899–1905) obtained his nickname not from German music, but because he pronounced his surname the same as Paul Kruger, leader of the Boer War, 1899–1902, instead of the Germanic "Kreeger."[34] Heinie Meine was known as "the Count of Luxemburg," not for association with the European country, but because he lived in the unincorporated community of Luxemborg (later LeMay) south of St. Louis.

The frequency of German-related nicknames fits the overall pattern of baseball nicknames and society's changing sensitivity about ethnic origins. Germanic nicknames slowly increased in the nineteenth century (eighteen), peaked from 1900 to 1919 (thirty-six), diminished between the world wars (twenty-five), and disappeared thereafter. Perhaps because of the recent flood of post–Civil War immigration, none of the eleven native Germans who played in the nineteenth century had an ethnic nickname, and only five American-born players, four debuting in the 1890s, were called Heinie or Dutch. Perhaps because of subsequent acculturation, most of the German players accorded nicknames during the first two decades of the twentieth century were dubbed Heinie (ten) or Dutch (sixteen) as innocuous signifiers of heritage.[35]

Language maintenance is a key component of culture, and virtually all second-generation players, from Fritz Pfeffer in the 1880s to Lou Gehrig in the 1920s, learned German at home and sometimes also in school.[36] Like Honus Wagner, they spoke fluent German as well as English without an accent. So, too, did some third- and fourth-generation players like Charlie Gehringer and Babe Ruth. Because their use of German was private and their English unaccented, language was not an obvious indicator of ethnicity. The press readily noted those who, like Chris Von der Ahe and Garry Herrmann, spoke with an accent and invariably tied their imperfect English to stereotypical comments about Germans generally.

Major league baseball promoted itself as "a democratic, catholic, real American game" because of ethnic inclusiveness (save for African Americans), but the ethnic insensitivities and prejudices that pervaded American society at large crept into the game in the form of verbal taunts and the perpetuation of stereotypes.[37] Besides being hardworking, earnest, frugal, disciplined, and fond of beer and wurst, Germans initially were presumed to be strong, stocky, and slow, generally unsuited for a quick and agile game like baseball. The achievements of numerous players quickly destroyed the unathletic stereotype, and by the turn of the twentieth century, German Americans had become so prominent in baseball and society at large that they, like the Irish, had become unremarkable ethnics.

Still, occasional newspaper commentary expressed the ethnic attitudes of reporters and readers alike. William A. Phelon, sportswriter for the Cincinnati *Times-Star*, penned a poem stereotyping Germans as well as the hotheaded, spendthrift Irish and the "Sphinx-like" Indians:

> The slow, methodic German seldom kicks,
>   Counts it "a business," works for those who pay
> His salary—works earnestly, and it's a cinch—
>   Plants heaps of shekels for a rainy day.[38]

Such comments, like the remark that Fred Schulte had the "typical German thrift of his ancestors," were benign. Typical was a *Pittsburgh Dispatch* article on 12 May 1908 that referred to Honus Wagner as "the doughty German," "the big Teuton" and "the Flying Dutchman" without further ethnic attribution. Teams with a high percentage of Germans also received notice. William F. Kirk wrote in the *New York American* on 11 August 1908 about "Das German Cubs, [Jimmy] Sheckard, [Harry] Steinfeldt, [Jimmy] Slagle, and all the rest of 'em [Solly Hofman, Johnny Kling, Jack Pfiester, Ed Reulbach, Fred Schulte, and Heinie Zimmerman]" and on 26 September 1908 noted "the Gingery Germans from Zinzinnati" took a twin bill from the Giants as "Messrs. [Dick] Hoblitzel, [John] Ganzel, [Hans] Lobert, [George] Schlei, [Bob] Bescher et al. [Jack Doscher, Jake Volz, and Jake Weimer], worthy Teutons all, were raking in the chips. Ach, du lieber!"[39] While ethically conscious sportswriters frequently mentioned the ancestry of German players, they rarely, and never negatively, commented about their culture.

German Jews, for whom religion rather than nationality defined their ethnicity, were subjected to widespread suspicion and hostility that occasionally affected non-Jewish Germans. Some, like Johnny Kling and Jacob Atz (b. Zimmerman), suffered verbal abuse from anti-Semites.[40] Others, like Levi Meyerle, Benny Kauff, and Ed Reulbach, were incorrectly identified as Jewish in the press. When Charley "Buck" Herzog reached the New York Giants in 1908, writers assumed from facial features that he was Jewish. One scribe wrote: "The long-nosed rooters are crazy whenever young Herzog does anything noteworthy. Cries of 'Herzog! Herzog! Goot poy, Herzog!' go up regularly, and there would be no let-up even if a million ham sandwiches suddenly fell among these believers in percentages and bargains." Finally, after receiving Happy New Year wishes on Rosh Hashanah, Herzog told a reporter he wanted it known that he was "a Dutchman." "They've got me wrong. I'm as Dutch as sauerkraut," he explained, noting that he had broken his nose as a child and that it had not been set properly.[41]

The outbreak of war in Europe in August 1914 unleashed latent Germanophobia. Long-standing anti-German sentiment was compounded by the efforts of many Germans to oppose U.S. intervention on behalf of the Allies. The assault on "hyphenism" directed at German Americans following the sinking of the *Lusitania* in May 1915 erupted into full-blown anti-German hysteria after the United States declared war on Germany in April 1917. By the fall of 1917, "a fierce hatred for everything German pervaded the country." Individuals suffered verbal harassment and physical beatings, while the nationwide effort to purge everything that smacked of the "Hun" took the form of attacking German American organizations, prohibiting teaching the German language, destroying property, removing German literature from libraries, closing German newspapers, firing German professors, banning Beethoven symphonies, renaming towns, and changing the name of sauerkraut to "liberty cabbage," and hamburgers to "liberty sandwiches."[42]

Major league baseball escaped the virulent anti-German hysteria that swept the nation during World War I. Indeed, 31 percent of the 342 newcomers to the majors between 1916 and 1920 were of German descent.[43] The prominence of German American players, umpires, and executives, notably Heydler and Herrmann, and of sportswriters such as Fred Lieb, H. G. Salsinger, and F. C. Richter blocked societal xenophobia. Indeed, when major league baseball and its press responded to America's entry into the war with highly publicized displays of patriotism and support for the war effort, German American baseballers played their part. In one of the most symbolic gestures, members of John McGraw's "Prussians," as the New York Giants were called because of "the preponderance of Germans on the team and their fighting qualities," marched across the field of the Polo Grounds before the fourth game of the 1917 World Series with flags of the Allied nations that were fighting "the House of Hohenzollern."[44] Herrmann, as chair of the National Commission, wrote articles encouraging support for the war, while the press published ethnically sanitized articles. *Baseball Magazine,* the premier monthly magazine devoted to the sport, ran a series of laudatory articles on Honus Wagner without reference to his ethnicity and an article on Herman Schaefer without using his customary nickname, "Germany," or any other ethnic signifiers.[45] Wagner, baseball's elder statesman, became a principal spokesman for the war effort in Pittsburgh after his retirement in 1917 by making speeches on behalf of the Allied cause, encouraging men to enlist, selling Liberty bonds at movie theaters, coordinating recycling programs for the Red Cross, and even playing in a benefit baseball game.[46]

Although one would never know about the nation's anti-German crusade from reading baseball publications, German ballplayers, despite being protected and privileged cultural celebrities, were not immune from the Germanophobia. Some, like Irvin "Kaiser" Wilhelm (1903–15), ignored ethnic nicknames, but others changed theirs. Even two veteran "Heinies," Groh of Cincinnati and Zimmerman of the Giants, asked teammates and sportswriters to call them "Henry." Charles Stengel, known in the minors and the first two years after reaching the majors in 1914 as "Dutch," was now called "Casey" after his hometown, Kansas City. Most players who entered the majors during the war years did not anglicize their surnames, but some, like John Fluher, who debuted in 1915 as William Morris, did so. The story of Alfred Holmes "Fritz" Von Kolnitz illustrates ethnic ambivalence. Sensitive to his obviously Prussian-sounding name, he used the name "R. H. Holmes" when entering professional baseball in 1913, but a year later used his legal name upon joining the Cincinnati Reds. Von Kolnitz subsequently enlisted in the army in 1917 and reached the rank of major, thereby becoming the highest-ranking big leaguer to serve in World War I. (Wilhelm also fought in the war, as did German-born Robert Troy, who played for Detroit in 1912 and was killed in action.)

World War I had a devastating cultural impact on German Americans, but the end of hostilities in November 1918 ushered in a Golden Age of prosperity for American society—and Germans in baseball. As in the past, there were few outstanding pitchers of German ancestry, as "slugging strength" continued to be the primary characteristic of Teutonic ballplayers.[47] The 1920s began with Joe Oeschger sharing the record for most innings pitched in a game (twenty-six), and Billy Wambsganss making the only triple play in World Series history, but it was the heavy hitting that dominated the offensive production of the 1920s and 1930s, especially in the American League, that catapulted German Americans to stardom. During those two decades, players of German descent won eleven American League batting titles, eight consecutively from 1920 to 1927, and three batting championships in the National League. They were named Most Valuable Player five times in the American League and three times in the National. Babe Ruth broke the single-season home run record three times, while Chuck Klein earned the Triple Crown in 1933.[48] Even George Uhle, the American League's top hurler in 1926, recorded the highest career batting average for a pitcher (.288). For all their individual achievements, the prominence of German Americans in baseball was magnified by their presence on the New York Yankees, the era's most dominant team, and by Babe Ruth and Lou Gehrig, the game's dominant players.[49]

George Herman Ruth Jr. was the oldest of eight children born to second-generation German Americans of Pennsylvania Dutch origin.[50] His surname was an anglicized version of either Rut (root) or, more prophetically, Ruthe (wand or rod).[51] Debuting with the Boston Red Sox in 1914, Ruth became the best left-handed pitcher in baseball, going 23-12 with a league-best 1.75 ERA in 1916, and the next year posting a 24-13 and 2.01 ERA while completing thirty-seven of thirty-eight games started. Despite his pitching success, which included a record thirty-one consecutive scoreless innings in the World Series, in 1918, Ruth played increasingly in the outfield to take advantage of his hitting. Sold to the New York Yankees in 1920, he became the greatest hitter in baseball history, recording phenomenal .847 and .846 slugging percentages in 1920–21, setting seasonal and career home-run marks that lasted until 1961 and 1973, respectively, and posting an eighth-best career .342 batting average. During his fifteen peak years as an outfielder, he led the league in homers twelve times and slugging percentage thirteen times.[52] His prodigious homers both captured the imagination of baseball fans and changed offensive strategy from the "inside" game of bunts and stolen bases to power hitting.

Ruth was the most publicized and recognized sports figure of the day, a true national hero like Charles Lindbergh and Alvin York. His rags-to-riches story, from waterfront waif to the national pastime's greatest star, coincided with America's Horatio Alger mythology while his flamboyant, garrulous, hedonistic, profane, arrested adolescent behavior fit the emerging social ethos of the Roaring Twenties.[53] Although the Ruthian image countered traditional German cultural norms, he had been raised in a strong German environment. Germans were the largest ethnic group in Baltimore, and Ruth learned German customs and language from his parents. But as an adult, he eschewed ethnic identification and kept his linguistic skills private. Sportswriter Fred Lieb, a second-generation German, was surprised to hear Ruth speaking German to Lou Gehrig's immigrant mother and including "some indelicate German words and

George Herman "Babe" Ruth. From the private collection of Richard A. Johnson.

phrases into his conversation."[54] Thus, unlike other highly publicized players such as Andy Cohen, Tony Lazzeri, Joe DiMaggio, and Hank Greenberg, Ruth's ethnicity was never an issue; indeed, it was rarely a topic of print conversation. Even his nicknames—Babe, the Bambino, the Sultan of Swat—were non-Germanic. Ruth's own ethnic sensibilities likely were blunted partly because both parents died before he was twenty-three, but primarily because his incorrigible behavior led to committal at age seven in the St. Mary's Industrial School for Boys, where he grew up under the influence of Brother Mathias and the Xaverian Brothers.

Whereas Babe Ruth was a thoroughly Americanized persona, Lou Gehrig always retained a fundamental "Germanness."[55] Born Heinrich Ludwig Gehrig in 1903, he grew up in Yorkville, a predominantly German section of Manhattan, and attended the local turnverein with his father. During World War I, young Lou endured anti-German taunts—"Heinie," "dumb Dutchman," "Krauthead"—from other kids. His mother wanted him to pursue a college degree instead of baseball, but his father, while not understanding the game, supported Lou's desire to cash in on sport. He became a regular with the New York Yankees in

1925, forming with Ruth the greatest batting tandem in baseball history. For the 1927 Yankees, generally considered the best team in history, Gehrig hit 47 homers, drove in a record 175 runs, and posted a .373 batting average while earning league Most Valuable Player honors. A powerful slugger who won the Triple Crown in 1934 and a second MVP in 1936, he had a record 23 grand slams and a career .340 batting average, ninth highest in history. Called "the Iron Horse" for his strength and endurance, he played in 2,130 consecutive games, a record that stood until broken by another player of German descent, Cal Ripken Jr., in 1995. Because of his modesty and strong work ethic, Gehrig was promoted as a role model for youth. When General Mills decided in 1934 to use athletes to advertise cereal, Gehrig was the first real-life sports figure chosen to adorn a Wheaties box.[56]

The press frequently attached ethnic references to Gehrig. Most were stereotypical appreciations of his strength and work ethic, but some reflected the influence of his domineering parents in his private and public lives. Unlike Ruth, Gehrig embraced his German heritage. Through adulthood, he conversed with his parents in German, a practice that annoyed his wife, Eleanor, who knew no German. Fred Lieb, a close friend of the Gehrig family, later remarked: "What struck me as some what odd for Americans in the later 1920s was that Mom and Lou would converse almost entirely in Mom's native tongue, German."[57] Despite his evident Germanness, he was never given an ethnic nickname, although his wife and close friends called him "Dutchman" in private.

Gehrig's career was cut short in 1939 by a rare muscle disease, amyotrophic lateral sclerosis, later called Lou Gehrig's disease. The disease, his courageous farewell speech at Yankee Stadium on 4 July 1939, and the release in 1942, a year after his death, of *The Pride of the Yankees,* a biographical movie that emphasized his German heritage, transformed a great ballplayer into a legendary folk hero.

Ironically, as German Americans ascended to unparalleled prominence in baseball, their personal and public ethnic identity began to diminish. In the early 1920s, talk of baseball as an ethnic melting pot focused on the numerous German and Irish players, and by the 1930s, their proportion among American Leaguers remained sizable at 25 and 42 percent, respectively.[58] But the anti-German xenophobia of World War I had a devastating effect on German culture and greatly accelerated acculturation.[59] Prior to World War I, virtually all German American players married within their ethnic group, but by 1933, eighteen of the

Charlie Gehringer. Courtesy of the Sports Museum of New England.

forty-nine American Leaguers identified as German were "full-blooded,"
while thirty-one were of mixed parentage; three years later, twenty-seven
were "Germans" and twenty-five "part-German."[60] Because ethnic intermarriage invariably destroys cultural identification, Yankees Earle Combs
(Scots-German), Myril Hoag (German-Irish), Waite Hoyt (German-English), and Miller Huggins (German-English) did not think of themselves
as ethnics. Germans dispersed residentially faster than other immigrant
groups, so many players, like Harry Heilmann and Mark Koenig, grew
up in non-German neighborhoods and had no ethnic identification. Players of German descent now infrequently spoke German.[61] One who did
was Detroit's Charlie Gehringer, whose insistence on the Germanic pro-
nunciation of his name (Geh-ringer, not Gehr-in-ger) elicited no negative

comment in the press and did not prevent his appearance on a Wheaties box in 1938, the year after being named league MVP. Language was an affectation for Charlie Grimm, who earned the nickname "Jolly Cholly" partly for telling "delightful stories [jokes] in a heavy German accent."[62] Ethnic commentary, some of it negative, even exclusionist, persisted in sport pages until World War II, but it focused on Italians, Jews, and Slavs—Germans were thought of not as ethnics, but as acculturated Americans.

Through intermarriage and the loss of language, German Americans had become essentially un-German. That only seven players anglicized their names after World War I and that "Dutch" was the most common nickname for German Americans (twenty-six) from 1920 to 1940 indicate that their ethnicity was of no significance. Replaced as ethnic gate attractions by Jews and Italians, players of German ancestry were now simply baseball celebrities. Thus, much was written, then and after, about Babe Ruth's fabled "called-shot" home run off Charlie Root in the 1932 World Series, fueled by Yankee anger at Chicago's treatment of Mark Koenig, without any mention that all three principals were of German ancestry. Similarly, managers Charlie Dressen and Charlie Grimm and umpires Charles "Cy" Pfirman, George Magerkurth, and Larry Goetz performed without comment about their German heritage. In recalling their baseball careers, pre–World War II players of German descent rarely mentioned ethnicity and, even more telling, their interviewers never raised the issue.[63]

World War II did not produce a repeat of the anti-German hysteria that swept the nation a quarter-century before. Americans of German extraction rejected en masse the various pro-Nazi organizations founded by recent pro-Hitlerian immigrants collectively known as the Bund, chief among them the *Amerikadeutscher Volksbund* led by German-born *Bundesleiter* Fritz Kuhn, the "American Führer."[64] Anti-German sentiment was replaced by anti-Japanese xenophobia after the bombing of Pearl Harbor in December 1941. Issei and Nisei were herded into concentration camps while German Americans, including Bundists, were ignored; baseball newspapers and magazines published anti-Japanese, not anti-German, articles.[65] German Americans comprised 30 percent of the U.S. armed forces, among them such high-profile ballplayers as Charlie Gehringer, Tommy Henrich, Pete Reiser, and Red Ruffing.

World War II and the fight against Nazi racism marked the end of the public, if not the private, kind of ethnic commentary and stereotyping that had filled the pages of sports publications for the previous seventy-five years. Thus, a magazine article on St. Louis Cardinals second baseman Albert "Red" Schoendienst of Germantown, Illinois, entitled "Bei Mir Bist du Schoen-dienst" contained no mention of his ethnicity.[66] Anglicization ceased, as did the ethnic nicknames so common before the war. Reflecting declining concerns with European ethnicity, only five players received German nicknames after World War II, all "Dutch" and all in the 1950s; there have been none since 1957. Persons of German extraction continued to make major contributions to baseball, but without ethnic attribution. Surnames are no longer cultural indicators of ethnicity, as acculturation and intermarriage have eroded ethnicity for most Americans of European ancestry. For Commissioners Ford Frick, William Eckert, Bowie Kuhn, and Peter Ueberroth; for owners such as August Adolphus Busch Jr. of the St. Louis Cardinals and George Steinbrenner, the modern-day "Boss President" of the New York Yankees; for managers like Whitey Herzog and Buck Showalter; for umpires like Bruce Froemming and Harry Wendelstedt; and for countless players from Warren Spahn and Andy Messersmith to Mike Schmidt and Cal Ripken Jr., their German heritage was of no matter or mention. While un-German in terms of public perception and personal identification, Americans of German descent, like John Smoltz, second cousin of Charlie Gehringer, continue to make important contributions to baseball history.

Notes

1. For example, Robert Henry Billigmeier, *Americans from Germany: A Study in Cultural Diversity* (Belmont, Calif.: Wadsworth, 1974); La Vern J. Rippley, *The German-Americans* (Boston: Twayne Publishers, 1976); Frank Trommler and Joseph McVeigh, eds., *America and the Germans: An Assessment of A Three-Hundred-Year History*, 2 vols. (Philadelphia: University of Pennsylvania Press, 1985); Alice Kessler-Harris and Virginia Yans-McLaughlin, "European Immigrant Groups," in *American Ethnic Groups*, ed. Thomas Sowell (Urban Institute, 1978), 107–37; Dieter Cunz, *The Maryland Germans* (Princeton, N.J.: Princeton University Press, 1948); Rudolph A. Hofmeister, *The Germans of Chicago* (Champaign, Ill.: Stipes Publishing, 1976); Guido A. Dobbert, *The Disintegration of an Immigrant Community: The Cincinnati Germans, 1870–1920* (New York: Arno Press, 1980); Audrey L. Olson, *Saint Louis Germans, 1850–1920: The Nature of an Immigrant Community and Its Relation to the Assimilation Process*

(New York: Arno Press, 1980). The lone exception is Richard O'Connor, *The German-Americans: An Informal History* (Boston: Little, Brown, 1968), which briefly notes the celebrity status of Honus Wagner and Babe Ruth.

2. See G. Edward White, *Creating the National Pastime: Baseball Transforms Itself, 1903–1953* (Princeton, N.J.: Princeton University Press, 1996), 245–74; Steven A. Riess, *Touching Base: Professional Baseball and American Culture in the Progressive Era,* rev. ed. (Urbana: University of Illinois Press, 1999), 156–211.

3. Prior to becoming a nation-state in 1871, "Germany" was a loose linguistic confederation of some thirty-five states, kingdoms, and free cities. See Aaron Spencer Fogleman, *Hopeful Journeys: German Immigration, Settlement, and Political Culture in Colonial America, 1717–1775* (Philadelphia: University of Pennsylvania Press, 1996); Mack Walker, *Germany and the Emigration, 1816–1885* (Cambridge: Harvard University Press, 1964); Charlotte L. Brancaforte, *The German Forty-Eighters in the United States* (New York: Peter Lang Publishing, 1989); Carl F. Wittke, *Refugees of Revolution: The German Forty-Eighters in America* (Philadelphia: University of Pennsylvania Press, 1952); A. E. Zucker, *The Forty-Eighters: Political Refugees of the German Revolution of 1848* (New York: Russell & Russell, 1950).

4. From 1820 to 1966, German immigrants to the United States surpassed those of any other country by some two million persons. *Statistical History of the United States from Colonial Times to the Present* (Stamford, Conn.: Fairfield, 1965), Series C 88–114, 56–57. For community populations, see Hofmeister, 10, 33; Trommler and McVeigh, 1:191; Dobbert, 30; Olson, 46–47.

5. On turners, see Ralf Wagner, "Turner Societies and the Socialist Tradition," in *German Workers' Culture in the United States, 1850 to 1920,* ed. Hartmut Keil (Washington, D.C.: Smithsonian Institution Press, 1988), 221–39; August J. Prahl, "The Turner," in Zucker, 79–110; Henry C. A. Metzner, *A Brief History of the American Turnerbund,* rev. ed. (Pittsburgh: National Executive Committee of the American Turnerbund, 1980).

6. A game called "Ball-Stock" was played in the early nineteenth century in the region ultimately known as Germany. Robert W. Henderson, *Ball, Bat, and Bishop: The Origin of Ball Games* (New York: Rockport Press, 1947), 141. For the ethnic makeup of baseball and cricket clubs, see George B. Kirsch, *The Creation of American Team Sports: Baseball and Cricket, 1838–72* (Urbana: University of Illinois Press, 1989), 111–78.

7. Robert F. Burk, *Never Just a Game: Players, Owners, and American Baseball to 1920* (Chapel Hill: University of North Carolina Press, 1994), 5.

8. J. Thomas Hetrick, *Chris Von der Ahe and the St. Louis Browns* (Lanham, Md.: Scarecrow Press, 1999), 5; Dale A. Somers, *The Rise of Sports in New Orleans, 1850–1900* (Baton Rouge: Louisiana State University Press, 1972), 118, 201.

9. O'Connor, 309.

10. Kamm interview, in Lawrence S. Ritter, *The Glory of Their Times: The Story of the Early Days of Baseball Told by the Men Who Played It* (New York: Macmillan, 1966), 265.

11. Burk, 44, 67, 90, 131.

12. Lee Allen, *The Hot Stove League* (New York: A. S. Barnes, 1955), 26.

13. Burk, 93.

14. In 1880, 72 percent of St. Louis Germans were skilled laborers, white-collar workers, or merchants. Margaret LoPiccolo Sullivan, "Ethnic Elites and Their Organizations: The St. Louis Experience, 1900–1925," in *Immigrant America: European Ethnicity in the United States,* ed. Timothy Walch (New York: Garland Publishing, 1994), 216. See also Keil, 111; Keil, "German Immigrant Workers in Nineteenth-Century America: Working-Class Culture and Everyday Life in an Urban Industrial Society," in Trommler and McVeigh, 1:189–206; Riess, 185–86.

15. The number of German natives ranks third behind players from Latin America and Great Britain. Bill Deane, "Foreign-Born Players," in John Thorn and Pete Palmer, *Total Baseball* (New York: Warner Books, 1988), 414–15.

16. David Nemec, *The Beer and Whiskey League: The Illustrated History of the American Association, Baseball's Renegade Major League* (New York: Lyons & Burford, 1994).

17. See Hetrick; Richard Egenriether, "Chris Von der Ahe: Baseball's Pioneering Huckster," *NINE: A Journal of Baseball History and Social Policy Perspectives* 7 (spring 1999): 14–39.

18. He was quoted as exhorting the Browns players in 1883: "Und I understand dot some of you fellers took some classes of beer ven I vasn't looking last night. Now if I fint any of you fellers boosing, I vill fine effery one vich booses ten dollars. Ond as my od secretary Dave Reet used to say, 'if the show fit, vear it.'" And again in 1885: "See here now, I don't vont some foolishness from you fellows. I vant you to stop dis slushing and play ball. Of you vin de 'schampion-ship,' I gif you a suit of clothes and a benefit game extra, and of you don't you vill have to eat snowballs all vinter." Hetrick, 22, 36.

19. David Quentin Voigt, *American Baseball: From Gentleman's Sport to the Commissioner System* (Norman: University of Oklahoma Press, 1966), 138.

20. Riess, 184; Frederick G. Lieb, "Baseball—The Nation's Melting Pot," *Baseball Magazine* 24 (August 1923): 393–95, 410.

21. Burk, 171, 204, 223. For comparison, the British comprised 40 percent and the Irish 23 percent of the newcomers in the first decade of the century and 39 percent and 18 percent, respectively, for the second decade.

22. Excellent biographies are Dennis DeValeria and Jeanne Burke DeValeria, *Honus Wagner: A Biography* (New York: Henry Holt, 1996); William Hageman, *Honus: The Life and Times of a Baseball Hero* (Champaign, Ill.: Sagamore Publishing,

1996); Arthur D. Hittner, *Honus Wagner: The Life of Baseball's "Flying Dutchman"* (Jefferson, N.C.: McFarland, 1996).

23. John J. McGraw, *My Thirty Years in Baseball* (1923; reprint, Lincoln: University of Nebraska Press, Bison Books, 1995), 201; Fred Lieb, *Baseball As I Have Known It* (New York: Coward, McCann, & Geoghean, 1977); James A. Vlasich, *A Legend for the Legendary: The Origin of the Baseball Hall of Fame* (Bowling Green, Ohio: Bowling Green State University Popular Press, 1990), 45.

24. Legend has it that during the 1903 World Series, Detroit's Ty Cobb yelled from first base, "Hey, Kraut Head, I'm comin' down on the next pitch." Wagner supposedly replied, "Come ahead," and then put him out with a forceful tag in the mouth; Cobb needed stitches to sew up his lip. Hittner, 184–85, and DeValeria and DeValeria, 222, dismiss the "Krauthead incident" as apocryphal.

25. Hittner, 244–45.

26. Ruppert and engineer Tillinghast L'Hommedieu Huston purchased the team in 1914; the latter, in military service during World War I and essentially a silent partner, sold out to Ruppert in 1923.

27. Jimmy Powers, *New York Daily News,* 3 November 1940.

28. See the relevant sections of Burk; White; Eugene C. Murdock, *Ban Johnson: Czar of Baseball* (Westport, Conn.: Greenwood Press, 1983); Harold Seymour, *Baseball: The Golden Age* (New York: Oxford University Press, 1971).

29. *The Sporting News,* 30 April 1931 and 22 December 1962; Garry Herrmann File, *The Sporting News* Archives, St. Louis. Hall of Fame historian Lee Allen said, "Garry was a walking delicatessen. A connoisseur of sausage, he carried his own wherever he went. When he presided at a hotel suite or in a bar, his party sat around one or more tables that were piled high with roast chickens, boiled hams, cheeses of every description, Thuringian blood pudding, liver sausage, baked beans, radishes, coleslaw, potato salad, green onions, and every type of fermented drink that was known to Bacchus." David Pietrusza, Matthew Silverman, and Michael Gershman, *Baseball: The Biographical Encyclopedia* (Kingston, N.Y.: Total/Sports Illustrated, 2000), 496.

30. E. Allen McCormick, ed., *Germans in America: Aspects of German-American Relations in the Nineteenth Century* (New York: Columbia University Press, 1983); Kathleen Neils Conzens, "German-Americans and the Invention of Ethnicity," in Trommler and McVeigh, 1:131–47; Christine M. Totten, "Elusive Affinities: Acceptance and Rejection of the German-Americans," in Trommler and McVeigh, 2:185–203.

31. Data on nicknames are taken from player entries in John Thorn et al., eds., *Total Baseball,* 6th ed. (New York: Total Sports, 1999); player files in the National Baseball Library, Cooperstown, N.Y., and *The Sporting News* Archives; James K. Skipper Jr., *Baseball Nicknames: A Dictionary of Origins and Meanings*

(Jefferson, N.C.: McFarland, 1992). Nicknames bestowed by teammates, family, and friends that remained largely private are not included in this analysis. For example, Ty Cobb called Floyd Herman "Dutch," but Herman was known "officially" as "Babe." Walter M. Langford, *Legends of Baseball: An Oral History of the Game's Golden Age* (South Bend, Ind.: Diamond Communications, 1987), 149.

32. Not all those nicknamed "Dutch" were German. The "Dutch" accorded Bob Holland and Johnny Vander Meer was an accurate reflection of their nationality. Hubert Leonard (1913–25), of Belgian descent, was called "Dutch" because "he looked like a Dutchman." F. C. Lane, "'Dutch' Leonard's Three Ambitions," *Baseball Magazine* 18 (November 1916): 47–49. Austrian-born Kurt Krieger was dubbed "Dutch" because of his Germanic heritage.

33. Biographical questionnaire, Meine File, *The Sporting News* Archives.

34. *St. Louis Post-Dispatch,* 11 January 1959.

35. Skipper, xxi–xxii.

36. Trommler and McVeigh, 1:223–82.

37. *The Sporting News,* 6 December 1923.

38. Quoted in Allen, 24.

39. Quoted in G. H. Fleming, *The Unforgettable Season* (New York: Holt, Rinehart, and Winston, 1981), 65–66, 163, 256.

40. Reiss, 190. Atz, of Irish-German parentage, changed his name after his club in North Carolina found itself in financial difficulty and paid players with the remaining funds in alphabetical order. The money ran out before reaching Zimmerman, so he signed his next contract "Atz." *The Sporting News,* 31 May 1945.

41. Joe Vila, *The Sporting News,* 17 September 1908; Gym Bagley, *New York Evening Mail,* 28 September 1908, quoted in Fleming, 224, 265.

42. See Frederick C. Luebke, *Bonds of Loyalty: German-Americans and World War I* (De Kalb: Northern Illinois University Press, 1974).

43. Burk, 223.

44. *The Sporting News,* 18 October 1917. The players were Buck Herzog, Walter Holke, Heinie Zimmerman, Bennie Kauff, and Ferdie Schupp.

45. For example, Herrmann's "Baseball's Immediate Future: How Baseball May Best Serve the Interest of the Nation During the Present World War," *Baseball Magazine* 19 (July 1917). Typical of the Wagner articles are Barney Dreyfuss, "Hans Wagner's Comeback," *Baseball Magazine* 19 (August 1917): 432, 458; and Hans Wagner, "Twenty-One Years in the Major Leagues," *Baseball Magazine* 20 (March 1918): 395–97. See also "Schaefer, the Grand Comedian of the Diamond," *Baseball Magazine* 23 (July 1919): 164, 184.

46. DeValeria and DeValeria, 277–79.

47. Lieb, "Nation's Melting Pot," 394.

48. The batting champions are George Sisler, 1920 (.407) and 1922 (.420);

Harry Heilmann, 1921 (.394), 1923 (.403), 1925 (.393), and 1927 (.398); Babe Ruth, 1924 (.378); Heinie Manush, 1926 (.378); Lou Gehrig, 1934 (.363); Charlie Gehringer, 1937 (.371); and Johnny Mize, 1939 (.349) in the American League, and Paul Waner, 1927 (.380), 1934 (.362), and 1936 (.373) in the National. The American League MVPs are Sisler, 1922; Ruth, 1923; Gehrig, 1927 and 1936; and Gehringer, 1937; the National League MVPs are Waner, 1927; Frankie Frisch, 1931; and Chuck Klein, 1932.

49. German American Yankees in the 1920s included Wally Pipp, Muddy Ruel, Wally Schang, and eight members of the 1927 club, arguably the best team in history—Gehrig, Ruth, Mark Koenig, Bob Meusel, George Pipgras, Dutch Ruether, and half-Germans Waite Hoyt and Earl Combs. Stars of the 1930s included Babe Dahlgren, Tommy Henrich, Charlie Keller, Myril Hoag, Red Ruffing, Hal Schumacher, and Billy Werber.

50. The best biographies of Ruth are Robert W. Creamer, *Babe: The Legend Comes to Life* (New York: Simon and Schuster, 1974); and Marshall Smelser, *The Life That Ruth Built: A Biography* (New York: Quadrangle, 1975).

51. In 1923, Fred Lieb ("Nation's Melting Pot," 394) said Ruth's ancestral surname was Eckhardt, and toward the end of his career, several sportswriters wrote that it was Erhardt or Gerhardt. Creamer, 24–25, convincingly disputes the claims.

52. Ruth led the American League in slugging percentage thirteen times, homers twelve times, walks eleven times, on base percentage ten times, runs eight times, and RBIs six times. In baseball history, he ranks first in slugging percentage (.690), batting runs (1,322), and runs created (2,847); second in home runs (714), RBIs (2,213), walks (2,056), on-base percentage (.474); and tied for second in runs scored (2,174). For his season and career statistics, see Thorn et al., 1,225, 1,791.

53. For a suggestive portrait of Ruth as societal symbol, see Richard C. Crepeau, *Baseball: America's Diamond Mind, 1919–1941* (Orlando: University Presses of Florida, 1980), 73–101.

54. Lieb, *Baseball As I Have Known It,* 153–54.

55. The standard life of Gehrig is Ray Robinson, *The Iron Horse: Lou Gehrig in His Time* (New York: W. W. Norton, 1990).

56. The first sports figure on a Wheaties box was the fictional All-American boy, Jack Armstrong.

57. Lieb, *Baseball As I Have Known It,* 174, 179.

58. Of the two hundred American Leaguers in 1933, 25 percent (forty-nine) were Germans and 42 percent (eighty-four) were Irish; three years later, there were fifty-two Germans and eighty-four Irish. *The Sporting News,* 8 June 1933 and 11 June 1936. No comparable data are available for the National League. For the early 1920s, see Lieb, "Nation's Melting Pot."

59. Many German Americans shed tangible evidence of their heritage by

anglicizing names, reducing cultural activities, and ceasing to speak German. Despite immigration, the 1920 Census showed a "dramatic decline" of 33 percent in the number of Americans admitting to German birth or ancestry. La Vern J. Rippley, "Ameliorated Americanization: The Effect of World War I on German-Americans in the 1920s," in Trommler and McVeigh, 2:215–31.

60. *The Sporting News*, 8 June 1933 and 11 June 1936.

61. See Marion L. Huffines, "Language-Maintenance Efforts among German Immigrants and Their Descendants in the United States," in Trommler and McVeigh, 1:241–50; and Bernhard Kettemann, "'Words Don't Come Easy'—German as an Immigrant Language in the USA," in *The European Emigrant Experience in the U.S.A.*, ed. Walter Holbling and Reinhold Wagnleitner (Tubingen, Germany: Gunter Narr Verlag, 1992), 269–83.

62. Langford, 55.

63. The exceptions are Willie Kamm and Joe Hauser. See the remembrances of Heinie Groh, Kamm, Hans Lobert, Billy Wambsganss, and Paul Waner in Ritter; Hauser and George Uhle in Eugene Murdock, *Baseball Players and Their Times: Oral Histories of the Game, 1920–1940* (Westport, Conn.: Meckler, 1991); Waite Hoyt and Jake Miller in Eugene Murdock, *Baseball Between the Wars: Memories of the Game by the Men Who Played It* (Westport, Conn.: Meckler, 1992); Charlie Grimm, Mel Harder, Babe Herman, and George Uhle in Langford.

64. Sander A. Diamond, *The Nazi Movement in the United States, 1924–1941* (Ithaca, N.Y.: Cornell University Press, 1974).

65. For example, *Baseball Digest* 2 (November 1942): 54; (April 1943): 57–58; and (August 1943): 9–31.

66. *Baseball Digest* 4 (October 1945): 13.

★4★

"Slide, Kelly, Slide":
The Irish in American Baseball

RICHARD F. PETERSON

Baseball historians have long recognized the ascendancy of Irish players in the early history of baseball. By the end of the nineteenth century, Irish stars dominated baseball and its greatest teams. The legendary Baltimore Orioles, managed by Ned Hanlon, won consecutive National League pennants in 1894, 1895, and 1896 with Hall of Famers Big Dan Brouthers, Hugh Jennings, and John McGraw in the infield and Joe Kelley and Wee Willie Keeler in the outfield. A decade earlier, so many New York Irish fans came out to see the stellar pitching of Tim Keefe and Smiling Mickey Welch, both winners of more than three hundred games in their professional careers, and the slugging of "the Mighty Clouter" Roger Connor, the Babe Ruth of his day, that the bleachers at the Polo Grounds were called "Burkeville." At other ballparks, the Irish sat in "Kerry Patches" to watch the colorful Mike "King" Kelly, generally regarded as the most popular baseball player of the nineteenth century. A. G. Spalding's sale of Kelly in 1887 from the Chicago National White Stockings to the Boston Beaneaters for the unheard-of price of ten thousand dollars was the biggest and most controversial deal of the era. Kelly's baserunning was so spectacular and his behavior on and off the field so flamboyant that he inspired the popular song "Slide, Kelly, Slide" and often performed on the vaudeville stage to packed houses during the off-season.

This predominance of Irish players in baseball's evolution into America's national pastime is most frequently interpreted within the traditional and popular view of the game as both an opportunity for individual success and a melting pot for ethnic groups. Conventional historical wisdom has it that once organized baseball shook free of both its amateur beginnings in the 1840s and the Knickerbocker hold on the game as a polite pastime for Protestant gentlemen, it opened its fields, especially after baseball became professional in 1869, to an increasing tide of immigrant players. The first immigrant wave of Germans and Irish supplanted the English and Scottish and transformed the game in the last few decades of the nineteenth century from a rural diversion and class signifier into an expression of America's democratic character and its competitive spirit. By the twentieth century, baseball had further evolved to the point that the ethnic origins of players had become an essential part of baseball's character and even a matter of pride. Of course, even as German and Irish players became assimilated into the national game and some of them emerged as ethnic heroes, other ethnic and racial groups, such as the Italians, Jews, and African Americans, would face the same prejudices and obstacles but would also have the same opportunity, when their time came, to prove themselves on the playing field. A 1931 editorial in *The Sporting News,* baseball's bible, declared, as if in anticipation of Joe DiMaggio, Hank Greenberg, and Jackie Robinson, that the "Sons of Erin" had "better beware. . . . They will be challenged to prove their racial superiority one of these days."

The problem with this theory of the melting pot and the ethnic hero, besides its paradoxical nature, is that it relies heavily on a romantic vision of baseball as a moral and heroic proving ground, an immigrant field of dreams. This vision, while one of the formative principles for baseball histories, perhaps finds its perfect expression in Lucy Kennedy's *The Sunlit Field,* generally recognized as the first adult baseball novel written by a woman. Published in 1950, two years before the appearance of Bernard Malamud's *The Natural,* Kennedy's historical romance, set in 1857, follows its runaway sixteen-year-old Irish heroine, Po (for Pocahontas) O'Reilly, from Fall River, Massachusetts, where the capitalist Eaters and their thread mills threaten her spirit, to Brooklyn, where she discovers that her dying father's dream of America as "a fabulous place—like a great open sunlit field" comes to life on a baseball field, where "the men flashed about, stretching their bodies in long beautiful arcs, or leaped into the air to catch the ball with easeful sureness in bared cupped hands. Yes, these were the tall men!"

In *The Sunlit Field*, baseball also becomes an epic battlefield for ethnic clashes and class rivalries, when Kennedy turns one of the most celebrated events in early baseball history—the 1858 three-game Fashion Race Course Series between what A. G. Spalding in *America's National Game* described as "picked nines representing the foremost clubs of New York and Brooklyn"—into a bloodletting, to-the-death contest between the hirelings of the Knickerbockers and Po Reilly's tall men. The real series, the nineteenth-century precursor to the modern-day World Series, was played over a span of three months and was remarkable not only for its fierce rivalry but for the demand by its organizers for a fifty-cent admission fee and for the heavy amount of gambling on player performance and the outcome of the games. In her novel, Kennedy does not change the historical outcome of the series—New York won the deciding third game after the teams split the first two—but she does condense the series into a three-day event and transform the games into a ruthless attempt by the upper-class Knickerbocker Club to buy baseball supremacy by hiring "shooting stars" or "revolvers" to beat the upstart, working-class Brooklyn nine by any means, including bribery, cheating, and dirty play.

The dream of baseball as a field for individual opportunity and social assimilation survives Brooklyn's loss in *The Sunlit Field*. By the end of the novel, the game of baseball as a professional sport emerges as the immigrant's best hope for participating successfully in the democratic and competitive spirit of America. But Lucy Kennedy's novel remains to the end far more historical romance than historical writing. While *The Sunlit Field* envisions baseball as heroic ground for immigrants, baseball histories, even when celebrating the glory of the game, have tended to see baseball's assimilation of ethnic and racial groups through the distorted lens of ethnic and racial stereotypes—and this has been especially so for the Irish. Lawrence McCaffrey in *The New York Irish*, observing that "Irish players came to represent American adaptability and their skills in this arena gave them a more acceptable persona," also notes, "but athleticism also reinforced nativist opinion that the Irish were strong of back and weak of mind."

One of the most blatant, if not outrageous, examples of the historical stereotyping of Irish ballplayers occurs in one of baseball's most popular historical texts, *The Bill James Historical Baseball Abstract*. In writing about the Irish domination of baseball in the 1890s, James at first appears to reject nativism and stereotypes by declaring that "many people, in the same stupid way that people today believe that blacks are born athletes, thought that the Irish were born baseball players." But in the very next sentence, after observing that "of course people also associated the roughness and unruliness of the players with their ethnic background," he notes that "the Irish have, indeed, always been known for that." In other words, while it is stupid to think of the Irish as born baseball players, to think of them as born rowdies may be another matter.

Adding ethnic insult to injury, James, beginning with his section on baseball in the 1880s, a decade when the players were "mostly eastern, mostly Irish, and a little rough," sets up a special category for baseball's "Drinking Men." The category, with its listing of Charlie Sweeney, King Kelly, Curt Welch, and Duke Farrell among its eight most notorious drunks, is obviously tilted toward the Irish. In the next section on the 1890s, James, in writing about the decade most dominated by Irish players, continues his category for Drinking Men. By listing Tom McCarthy, Marty Bergen, and Willie McGill among his five baseball lushes of the 1890s, the category once again raises the glass to the Irish. When James gets to the 1900s, the decade when baseball "gradually began to shed its Irish flavor," his category for the game's Drinking Men disappears, apparently no longer required. And, notes James, with baseball becoming more temperate and respectable, baseball attendance dramatically improved: "Whereas baseball in the nineteenth century was in danger of becoming a game of the Irish, by the Irish, for the Irish, it now began to appeal to a broader cross-section of the public."

The Bill James Historical Baseball Abstract obviously relies on blatant stereotyping in its association of baseball's early rowdyism with the predominance of Irish players in the 1880s and 1890s, but there is ample historical evidence to support James's attitude toward the Irish, an attitude shared by baseball historian Benjamin Rader, who in his own commentary on late-nineteenth-century ballplayers in Baseball: A History of America's Game notes, "(at least for the Irish) drinking, brawling, and display were a conspicuous part of their male homosocial world." Curt Welch, listed among James's Drinking Men, once purportedly dedicated his season to beer. His heavy drinking forced him out of baseball at the age of thirty-one, and he died three years later of alcoholism. Also on James's list, Charlie Sweeney, according to the biographical entry in the Society for American Baseball Research's (SABR's) Nineteenth Century

Stars, "was vilified in the press for his public drunkenness and for assaulting another player." Several years after his career was over, Sweeney was convicted of manslaughter and sentenced to ten years in prison for killing a man in a barroom argument. But Sweeney's conduct and fate pale beside that of Marty Bergen, a brilliant but emotionally disturbed player who, in the middle of an erratic career and nine days after the turn of the century, used an ax to kill his son and daughter and then cut his own throat with a razor.

Even baseball's earliest historians had no trouble finding and displaying examples of Irish misconduct on and off the playing field. In *America's National Game,* published in 1911 and generally regarded as the first official chronicle of baseball, A. G. Spalding uses, as one of the turning points in baseball's development into the national pastime, a meeting between William Hulbert, president of the National League, and Jim Devlin, one of four Louisville players banned from baseball for conspiring with gamblers to throw games. According to Spalding, Devlin, after being reduced to abject poverty by his expulsion, came to Hulbert's office and fell to his knees to plead for mercy on behalf of his starving family. Moved to tears, Hulbert put a fifty-dollar bill into Devlin's palm but told him: "That's what I think of you, personally; but damn you, Devlin, you are dishonest; you have sold a game, and I don't trust you. Now go; and let me never see your face again; for your act will not be condoned as long as I live."

The banning of Devlin, despite the claims of Spalding, hardly kept baseball free of gambling and scandal but, thanks to Spalding's chronicle, Devlin became baseball's most conspicuous example of the crooked ballplayer, at least until the fixing of the 1919 World Series. Devlin, a thirty-game winner for Louisville in 1876 and 1877 and one of baseball's emerging stars at the time of his expulsion, was further proof that the Irish were prolific in the late nineteenth century not only for their playing skills, competitive nature, and success on the ball field but for their alcoholism, hoodlumism, and self-destructiveness. They have provided historians with the best examples of the "poor moral conduct and . . . ill-mannered behavior both on and off the field" that Steven A. Riess in *City Games: The Evolution of American Urban Society and the Rise of Sports,* his study of sports in the Progressive Era, sees as the cause of ballplayers' low prestige in the early history of professional baseball.

The epitome of the nineteenth-century Irish ballplayer for baseball historians is the colorful and controversial figure of Mike "King" Kelly.

Listed by Bill James as the most handsome and dashing ballplayer of the 1880s, Kelly is described in SABR's *Baseball's First Stars* as "the brainiest, most creative, and most original player of his time." The most spectacular base runner of his day, Kelly once stole a remarkable 84 bases in just 116 games. He was also an excellent hitter, leading the National League in batting twice and in runs scored three times. During his major league career, he led Cap Anson's Chicago club to three straight National League pennants from 1880 to 1882 and to two more in 1885 and 1886. He was elected to the Hall of Fame in 1945.

Yet, when baseball historians portray Kelly, their accounts draw far more attention to his heavy drinking, his flaunting of baseball rules, and his troublesome and often unmanageable behavior than to his accomplishments. In *Baseball: An Illustrated History*, the book derived from Ken Burns's popular television documentary on the history of baseball, the narrative relates story after story of Kelly's drunkenness and trickery. Readers, after looking at a cartoon of Kelly in the clubhouse sleeping off a nightly bender, learn about the time Kelly, when asked if he drank while playing, replied, "It depends upon the length of the game," and about the time he held up a game while he and "several wealthy gentlemen in box seats toasted one another." The narrative also quotes the solemn words of Henry Chadwick, baseball's pioneer journalist and an early reformer of the game, condemning Kelly's outrageous conduct: "To suppose that a man can play properly who guzzles beer daily, or indulges in spiritous liquors, or who sets up nightly gambling or does worse by still more enervating habits at brothels is nonsense."

The stories of Kelly when he was sober enough to play ball are usually about his trickery and cheating. On the base paths, he routinely skipped second base on his way to third if the umpire was watching the ball being retrieved in the outfield. When he was the catcher for his team, he would cover home plate with his mask to prevent the base runner from scoring. But the most outrageous apocryphal story of Kelly's on-the-field cunning has to do with his leaping, game-ending catch in the twilight gloom to save a Chicago victory. When he came off the field and was asked for the ball by his manager Cap Anson, Kelly supposedly replied, "The ball? . . . It went a mile over me head." Of course, there is also the story of the time Kelly, sitting out the game because of a hangover, saw a foul pop fly heading toward the bench, cried out, "Kelly catching for Boston," and jumped up and caught the ball for an out.

Kelly, however, was a piker compared to the infamous Baltimore

Orioles and their galaxy of Irish stars and miscreants. The Irish-dominated Orioles were led on the field by the pugnacious John McGraw, who was called Muggsy by his enemies for his foul mouth and dirty play. In the Ken Burns history, McGraw is described in the words of the sportswriters of his day as "the toughest of the tough . . . an abomination of the diamond." Bill James in his *Baseball Abstract* named McGraw the best third baseman of the 1890s but also listed him as the decade's least admirable superstar. McGraw's own biographer, Charles Alexander, called him the worst umpire baiter in the history of baseball.

McGraw's Baltimore Orioles may have been one of the best teams in the early history of baseball, but they are also generally regarded as one of baseball's most infamous nines. Although they were the era's most

John McGraw. Courtesy of the Sports Museum of New England.

skilled team at playing inside or scientific baseball, they have been remembered for abusing umpires and intimidating, and even maiming, opposition players. In his highly regarded history of baseball, *Baseball: The Golden Years,* Harold Seymour cites a complaint by *The Sporting News* that the Orioles were "playing the dirtiest ball ever seen in the country" and summarizes its description of such dirty tactics as tripping and spiking base runners or grabbing their shirts as they went by. The Orioles would also bunt between the mound and first base to run into and spike opposing pitchers. They bowled over infielders as they rounded the bases, and they crowded around and jostled any catcher waiting for a throw home. As for umpires, one of their favorite targets, John Heydler, who was an umpire during the 1890s and later became president of the National League, offers the following indictment of the Orioles:

> We hear much of the glories and durabilities of the old Orioles, but the truth about this team seldom has been told. They were mean, vicious, ready at any time to maim a rival player or an umpire, if it helped their cause. The things they said to an umpire were unbelievably vile, and they broke the spirits of some fine men. I've seen umpires bathe their feet by the hour after McGraw and others spiked them through their shoes. The club never was a constructive force in the game. The worst of it was they got by with much of their brow beating and hooliganism. Other clubs patterned after them, and I feel the lot of the umpires never was worse than in the years when the Orioles were flying high.

The most obvious, albeit superficial, way to counter the historicizing of the Irish ballplayer in the nineteenth century as something of a cross between an irresponsible drunk and a vicious hooligan is to offer examples—and there are many—of Irish ballplayers who, despite the ethnic stereotype of the "Sons of Erin," were not alcoholics, rowdies, or blackguards. For every Irish ballplayer in SABR's two-volume biography of nineteenth-century stars who fits the stereotype of the Irish born to drink, brawl, and break the law, there is a player like the idolized The Only Nolan, the respected Billy McLean, or the redoubtable Connie Mack, each greatly admired for his skill, his integrity, or his career achievements. For every Irish ballplayer who qualifies for James's list of Drinking Men, there is an enshrined Hall of Famer like Orator Jim O'Rourke. A Yale Law School graduate, O'Rourke, when told that to sign a contract

Connie Mack with fellow Hall of Famers Mickey Cochrane (left) and Lefty Grove (right). Courtesy of the Sports Museum of New England.

with Boston and its Protestant financial backers, he would have to drop the "O" from his name, responded: "I would rather die than give up my father's name. A million dollars would not tempt me." For every Jim Devlin, banned from baseball for life for throwing games, there is a Kid Gleason, who retained his reputation for fairness and honesty as a manager even after eight of his Chicago White Sox players threw the 1919 World Series. Among the overflow crowd of five thousand in attendance at Gleason's funeral were Baseball Commissioner Kenesaw Mountain Landis, who had banned Shoeless Joe Jackson and his fellow Black Sox from the game, and fellow managers and Irishmen John McGraw and Connie Mack.

Among the nineteenth-century greats listed position by position in Alfred H. Spink's *The National Game*, first published in 1910, are several Irish players praised for their "sterling character," "excellent disposition," and "splendid habits." James Deacon McGuire, who caught and managed for over thirty years and later coached at Albion College, was known to have "never been fined, never put out of a game by an umpire." Long John Reilly, one of the early power hitters in his years with Cincinnati, won public acclaim for his modest conduct and was widely regarded as a model for self-discipline and team play in an era characterized by its rowdiness. Tommy Burns, the third baseman for Cap Anson's pennant-winning Chicago teams of the 1880s, never drank or smoked and was respected for his fairness and honesty as a player and a manager. Silent Mike Tiernan, who starred as a slugger and a base stealer with New York in the 1890s, earned his nickname for his dignity and his calm. In a 1902 article in the *Gael,* he was described as being "as honest as the sun, a sober gentlemanly professional player, . . . a credit to his team, . . . possessed [of] a record of never having been fined for disputing an umpire's decision."

Other Irish ballplayers in Spink's *The National Game* are singled out for their "braininess" and were instrumental in revolutionizing the professional game. Irish-born Tommy Bond, who won forty or more games in three consecutive seasons from 1879 to 1881, was one of the first to "throw the ball rather than pitch it" and is credited with perfecting the curveball after learning how to throw it from Hall of Famer Candy Cummings. Another Hall of Famer, Charles A. Comiskey, destined to become one of the most dominant and controversial baseball magnates of the twentieth century, revolutionized the position of first base in the late nineteenth century by playing far off the base when fielding his position. James Fogarty, a left fielder described by Spink as one of the "greatest who ever lived," was one of the first outfielders to earn a reputation for his defensive play because of his great speed, powerful throwing arm, and ability to make sensational catches. Tim Murnane, popular with his teammates because of his cheery disposition and credited with the first stolen base in National League history, eventually, after a brief stint umpiring, became one of the leading baseball writers of his day. He became renowned as a champion of the game's traditions and its old-time ballplayers and is credited with writing the first baseball column.

There were many stellar Irish ballplayers important to the early history of American baseball whose conduct did not conform to an ethnic stereotype, but the real historical issue of the Irish in baseball resides not in the character of the Irish but in the character of the professional game in the late nineteenth century. Steven Riess has pointed out that "the professionalization of the sport did not begin in earnest until after the Civil War in response to the strong demand by upper-middle class amateur clubs for winning teams." These ringers or revolvers were not only given money, they were often given jobs or placed on company payrolls as well. As baseball in the 1870s became a means to earn money, it attracted young men who were poor and uneducated and otherwise trapped economically and socially within their underprivileged class.

That baseball's origins were in the Northeast and that professional play was concentrated in seaboard cities—Philadelphia, New York, Brooklyn, Baltimore, and Boston—also had a major impact on the character of baseball in the nineteenth century. Riess notes that 83 percent of the players in baseball's first professional league came from cities, and 40 percent of those players were from cities along the eastern seaboard. With baseball's professional game emerging as one of the few ways of escaping urban slums, it is hardly surprising, considering the waves of Famine and post-Famine Irish immigrants settling into shantytowns in America's cities, that the "Sons of Erin" seemed to have a natural affinity for baseball and its rowdy play.

As for the rowdyism in baseball, the obvious cause, rather than the ethnic character of the ballplayers, would seem to be the loosely organized, financially unstable, and fiercely competitive nature of the early professional game. With the biggest payouts and profits going to the most successful players and teams, with the most skilled players rotating to the highest bidder, and with less successful teams going bankrupt and failing to meet their payrolls, baseball quickly became a cutthroat business on and off the field. The Pittsburgh club earned its team name not because of its swashbuckling play but because it stole players under contract to another team.

When baseball formed the National League in 1876 and took its first major step toward becoming a business monopoly, the owners, who now saw themselves as magnates, instituted within a few years a reserve clause to gain absolute control over player movement and salaries. With players now in virtual bondage to the owners, the game became even more combative—Spalding applauded it as "war"—because victory or defeat determined a player's survival in the game and his livelihood. If extra money could be made by associating with gamblers, some players were willing to take the risk.

The early professional game may have been something like a war, but not because of the ethnic stereotype of the Irish as drunken brawlers. That the stereotype of the Irish seemed to fit the early character of baseball is undeniable, but it is also undeniable that the game's economics demanded a combativeness from its players and victories on its playing fields. Once baseball became a moneymaking opportunity, created ironically by the same class that had turned Irish immigrants into servants and day laborers, the Irish were among the first—and became the foremost—to seize upon the game as a means to rise out of the urban ghetto. It is true that some Irish players in the first decades of professional baseball could not handle their new financial success and celebrity status and ended their careers and sometimes their lives in disgrace and tragedy. But it is also true that many performed so well and conducted themselves with such integrity that they became a major reason for the advancement of baseball into a major sport, a big business, and a national pastime worthy of the support and passion of the American public.

While baseball historians are fond of their stories of the wild Irish and the rowdy days of the early professional game, the Irish, in reality, played the game as they found it. Once they became a major part of early baseball, however, they played with such fierce determination and success that, although they were early targets for nativism, many of them also were eventually elected into baseball's hallowed Hall of Fame. The Irish belong in Cooperstown, not for their notoriety but for their achievements on the field and their contributions in the transformation of a leisurely pastime for gentlemen into America's national game.

Works Cited

Ivor-Campbell, Frederick, Robert L. Tiemann, and Mark Rucker, eds. *Baseball's First Stars*. Cleveland: Society for American Baseball Research, 1996.

James, Bill. *The Bill James Historical Abstract*. New York: Villard, 1986.

Kennedy, Lucy. *The Sunlit Field*. New York: Crown, 1950.

McCaffrey, Lawrence J. "Forging Forward and Looking Back." In *The New York Irish*, edited by Ronald H. Bayor and Timothy J. Meagher, 213–33. Baltimore: Johns Hopkins University Press, 1996.

Rader, Benjamin G. *Baseball: A History of America's Game*. Urbana: University of Illinois Press, 1992.

Riess, Steven A. *City Games: The Evolution of American Urban Society and the Rise of Sports*. Urbana: University of Illinois Press, 1989.

Seymour, Harold. *Baseball: The Golden Years*. New York: Oxford University Press, 1960.

Spalding, A. G. *America's National Game*. New York: American Sports Publishing, 1911.

Spink, Alfred H. *The National Game.* 2d ed. St. Louis: National Game Publishing, 1911; Carbondale: Southern Illinois University Press, 2000.

Tiemann, Robert L., and Mark Rucker, eds. *Nineteenth Century Stars.* Cleveland: Society for American Baseball Research, 1989.

Ward, Geoffrey C., and Ken Burns. *Baseball: An Illustrated History.* New York: Knopf, 1994.

Untitled and uncredited material from *The Sporting News* and the *Gael* provided by the National Baseball Library.

★5★

Unreconciled Strivings:
Baseball in Jim Crow America

JULES TYGIEL

Andrew "Rube" Foster epitomized African American pride. A tall, imposing, right-handed pitcher, he had migrated from his native Texas to Chicago in 1902 to play for the Chicago Union Giants. When warned that he might face "the best clubs in the land, white clubs," he announced, "I fear nobody." Over the next decade, he established himself as perhaps the outstanding pitcher in all of baseball. In 1911, he formed his own team, the Chicago American Giants, and won a reputation as a managerial genius equal to his friend John McGraw. Nine years later, Foster, seeking to "keep colored baseball from control of the whites" and "to do something concrete for the loyalty of the Race," created the Negro National League. Foster criticized white owners for not letting African Americans "count a ticket [or] learn anything about the business" and called for a league dominated by black men. "There can be no such thing as [a black baseball league] with four or five of the directors white any more than you can call a streetcar a steamship," he asserted. Foster urged black fans: "It is your league. Nurse it! Help it! Keep it!" Yet, Foster's intense racial pride notwithstanding, he also made his ultimate goal clear. "We have to be ready," he proclaimed, "when the time comes for integration."[1]

Rube Foster and, indeed, the entire experience of blacks in baseball in early-twentieth-century America, exemplifies elements of Booker T.

68

Washington's call for the development of separate economic spheres so that his race might prepare itself for ultimate inclusion in American life. Yet, black baseball also captured what Washington's rival, W. E. B. DuBois, labeled the "twoness" of the African American experience. "One ever feels his twoness—an American, a Negro," wrote DuBois, "two souls, two thoughts, two unreconciled strivings; two warring ideals in one dark body, whose dogged strength alone keeps it from being torn asunder." The architects of black baseball embodied this dualism. They strove to create viable enterprises that served their communities and simultaneously might win a measure of respectability in the broader society. These ventures would prepare them for the day on which, according to DuBois's vision, it would be "possible for a man to be both a Negro and American, without being cursed and spit upon by his fellows, without having the doors of Opportunity closed roughly in his face."[2]

The essence of black professional baseball is far more elusive than that of its white counterpart. The major leagues always constituted the epitome and cultural core of mainstream baseball, but the formal Negro leagues represented no more than a segment of the black baseball experience. No leagues existed until 1920, and even during their halcyon days, official contests never constituted more than perhaps a third of the games played. Some of the strongest black teams and best players performed outside of the league structure. Top teams often boasted names like the Homestead Grays, Bachrach Giants, or the Hilldale Club, reflecting affiliations not to major cities but to people and smaller communities. The most popular attractions often involved exhibitions against white semiprofessional and professional teams. In all of these many guises and varieties, black baseball constituted a vital element of African American culture, while also dramatizing the contradictions and challenges of survival in a world dominated by whites.

Within the African American community, the officials, players, and teams of black baseball symbolized pride and achievement while creating a sphere of style and excitement that overlapped with the worlds of black business, politics, religion, and entertainment. During the baseball season, Negro League teams were a constant presence in the black community. Placards announcing the games appeared in the windows of local businesses along with advertisements featuring player endorsements and commands to "get those pretty clothes" for the "opening day . . . Fashion Parade."[3] In Kansas City, fans could purchase tickets in a number of locales where African Americans congregated, including the

Monarch Billiard Parlor, Stark's Newspaper Stand, the Panama Taxi
Stand, and McCampbell's and Hueston's Drug Store. The Elbon and Lincoln movie theaters would show pictures of the players, advertisements
for the games, and newsreel footage of the lavish opening-day ceremonies.[4]

Local businesses rallied around the teams. Some, like Herman Stark's
clothing store in Detroit, offered prizes to the first player to hit a home
run or get a hit in a Sunday or opening-day contest.[5] Several cities featured booster clubs, like the Hilldale Royal Rooters and Baltimore's
Frontiers Club, that supported their teams. The Kansas City Booster
Club, the most lavish of these organizations, included both black and
white merchants whose stores served the black community. Formed in
1926, the Kansas City Boosters organized the opening-day parade, sponsored banquets for the players, and staged beauty contests at the ball
game.[6] These businesses profited, in turn, from black baseball. "The cafes,
beer joints, and rooming houses of the Negro neighborhoods all bene-
fited as black baseball monies sometimes trickled, sometimes rippled
through the black community," writes Donn Rogosin. After the 1944
East-West All Star game in Chicago, reported Wendell Smith, "hot spots
were all loaded, and so were most of the patrons."[7]

African American baseball also provided one of the most popular features of black newspapers. As early as the turn of the century, the *Indianapolis Freeman* had discovered that baseball coverage attracted readers.
Sportswriter David Wyatt, who had played for the Cuban Giants and Chicago Union Giants from 1896–1902, reported on news of black baseball
from all over the country. The Indianapolis ABCs and other teams would
arrange matches by placing ads in the *Freeman*.[8] Other black weeklies
began covering the game more seriously after 1910. The *Philadelphia
Tribune* forged a close alliance with Ed Bolden's Hilldale Club. Bolden
advertised games in the *Tribune* and provided press releases and game
results. Beginning in 1914, the *Tribune* began to print box scores and in
1915 published Bolden's weekly column, "Hilldale Pickups."[9] Black
newspapermen, led by Wyatt, played key roles in the creation and promotion of the Negro National League in 1920. "Behind this opening
should be the concentrated support of every race man in Detroit," asserted the *Detroit Contender*. "If the league succeeds your race succeeds;
if the league fails, the race fails. . . . Our ability to put over large projects
will be measured largely by the way we handle this one."[10]

Owners and officials of black clubs often ranked among the most prominent figures in the African American community. Several team owners figured prominently in civil rights activities. Olivia Taylor, who inherited the Indianapolis ABCs from her husband, became president of the Indianapolis NAACP chapter in 1925.[11] Newark Eagle owner, Effa Manley, was an indefatigable campaigner against discrimination. In the years before she and her husband Abe purchased the ball club, Manley had achieved prominence in New York City as the secretary of the Citizen's League for Fair Play, which waged successful campaigns against Harlem businesses that refused to employ African Americans. In Newark, Manley served as the treasurer of the New Jersey chapter of the NAACP and on several occasions held ballpark benefits for the organization. At one event, the Eagles sold NAACP "Stop Lynching" buttons to fans. Manley also joined the Citizen's Committee to End Jim Crow in Baseball created by the Congress of Industrial Organizations in 1942.[12]

Black teams hosted numerous benefit games for African American charities and causes, raising funds for churches, hospitals, youth groups, and civil rights bodies. The Kansas City Monarchs staged benefits for the Negro National Business League and the Red Cross. The Newark Eagles regularly raised money to purchase medical equipment for the Booker T. Washington Community Hospital. During World War I, the Indianapolis ABCs and Chicago American Giants played games on behalf of the Red Cross, and in the 1920s, Hilldale played fund-raisers for war veterans. The first black baseball game at Yankee Stadium pitted the Lincoln Giants against the Baltimore Black Sox in a 1930 benefit for the Brotherhood of Sleeping Car Porters. The outbreak of World War II prompted additional efforts.[13]

The players themselves often had close ties to the cities in which they performed. Many teams recruited from the local sandlots and discovered some of their best players perched on their doorsteps. Hall of Fame outfielder Oscar Charleston, who grew up on Indianapolis's east side, served as a batboy for the ABCs before joining the squad as a player. He performed alongside Frank Warfield, "the pride of Indianapolis's West Side." The Homestead Grays discovered Josh Gibson playing semiprofessional baseball in Pittsburgh's Hill district. Memphis Blues pitching ace Verdell Mathis grew up within a short walk of Martin Field. Effa Manley's Eagles frequently found their best players—including Monte Irvin, Larry Doby, and Don Newcombe—in the Newark area.[14] The Birmingham Black Barons snatched fifteen-year-old Willie Mays from a local high school.

Willie Mays. From the private collection of Richard A. Johnson.

The players often made the Negro League cities their year-round homes and became fixtures in their communities. Those who did not have homes in the city often resided during the season at the finest black hotels. In an age when most mainstream hotels even in northern cities barred African Americans, each major city featured a showplace hotel where traveling athletes, entertainers, and members of the black elite lodged and congregated. These were the places, as poet Amiri Baraka describes Newark's Grand Hotel, where "the ballplayers and the slick people could meet."[15] In Detroit, the players stayed at the Norwood, which also housed the Plantation nightclub. In Baltimore, the Black Sox lived at the Smith Hotel, owned by the city's black Democratic political boss. Street's Hotel in Kansas City, located at Eighteenth and Vine Streets, was the place, according to its manager, that "everybody that came to KC stopped at."[16]

As a teenager in Newark, Baraka reveled in mixing with the postgame throngs at the Grand Hotel, where "everybody's super clean and high-falutin." Monte Irvin recalls that "to the fans, the hotel presented an opportunity to join the ballplayers' special circle."[17] This circle often included not just ballplayers but the entertainment royalty of black America—jazz musicians, dancers, actors and actresses, theater and movie stars, and boxers like Jack Johnson and Joe Louis. Indeed, a close bond formed between the itinerant athletes and performers. Entertainers often could be found at the ballparks, rooting for their favorite clubs and clowning around with their favorite players. The Mills Brothers loved to don Pittsburgh Crawford uniforms and work out with the club. When they appeared at team owner Gus Greenlee's Crawford Grille, Satchel Paige, a talented singer, would return the favor, joining them on stage for impromptu jazz sessions. In Memphis, where Martin Park bordered the Beale Street music district, bluesman B. B. King would set up near first base and sing as the fans filed in. Lena Horne, whose father was Gus Greenlee's right-hand man, appeared frequently at Negro League games. The New York Black Yankees, co-owned by dancer Bill "Bojangles" Robinson, attracted a parade of celebrities to games at Dyckman's Oval in Harlem. When Count Basie was in Kansas City on a Sunday, he headed out to see the Monarchs, "because that's where everyone else was going on a Sunday afternoon."[18]

The games themselves, particularly season openers and Sunday games, were festive occasions in the black community. As the *Chicago Defender* reported in 1923, fans would turn out for the first home game "like a lot of bees hidden away all winter . . . getting active when the sun shines."[19] The contests often marked the culmination of daylong celebrations. David Wyatt, a former player turned sports reporter, described the scene in Indianapolis in 1917: "The big noise, the mammoth street parade, swung into motion promptly at 10 o'clock upon Saturday. There were something like one hundred conveyances of the gasoline, electric or other propelling types in the line . . . occupied by persons of both races, some internationally known to fame. . . . [We] jammed the downtown district and went on our way rejoicing."[20] In Kansas City, the Monarchs' booster club organized an annual parade that snaked through the city's black district, arriving at the park in time for the opening ceremonies.[21] These ceremonies in most cities featured high school bands, color guards, and prominent black celebrities or politicans (black or white) to throw out the first pitch.

Indeed, as the African American citizenry in northern cities expanded in numbers and influence, baseball stadiums became a prime location for politicians courting the black vote. In Atlantic City in the 1920s, the Bachrach Giants were named for Mayor Henry Bachrach, who had brought an African American team up from Florida to entertain the resort town's growing population of black hotel workers. Playing at a converted dog track near the Boardwalk, the Bachrach Giants became a popular fixture and an advertisement for the mayor for the remainder of the decade. Indiana governor Harry Leslie, hoping to rebuild black support for the Republicans in the wake of the party's flirtation with the Ku Klux Klan, threw out the first pitch at the ABCs home opener in 1930.[22] Although attendance by governors proved rare, in the 1930s and 1940s, big-city mayors routinely kicked off the local black season. When Pittsburgh Crawfords' owner, Gus Greenlee, unveiled his new stadium in 1932, the mayor, city council, and county commissioner all attended. In 1935, Mayor Fiorello La Guardia performed the first-pitch honors at a Brooklyn Eagles–Homestead Grays game, and Cleveland mayor Harry L. Davis joined 8,000 fans at a match between the Crawfords and American Giants honoring Ohio State track star Jesse Owens. The mayors of Baltimore, Kansas City, and Newark all frequently appeared at opening games. The mayor of Newark, recalls Jerry Izenberg, could avoid the Eagles' home opener only "if he chose not to be re-elected."[23]

Opening-day and Sunday contests attracted a wide cross section of the African American community, dressed in their finest clothes. The Sunday spectacle, according to Newark resident Connie Woodruff, represented "a combination of two things, an opportunity for all women to show off their Sunday finery" and "a once a week family affair." People would arrive, according to Woodruff, "with big baskets of chicken, potato salad, all the things you would have on a picnic. . . . It was the thrill of being there, being seen, seeing who they could see."[24]

The Sunday games, asserted Black Yankees outfielder Charlie Biot, "were THE event of the week." Teams capitalized on the popularity of these contests by throwing their star pitchers and scheduling four-team doubleheaders. According to an intimate of Rube Foster, Foster commanded Negro National League affiliates in the 1920s that "no star twirler was used to the limit before a small Saturday crowd with the prospects of a good Sunday attendance." In Memphis in the 1940s, ace

Verdell Mathis became known as the "Sunday Feature," because he almost always hurled the first game of the scheduled doubleheader.[25]

This emphasis on Sunday games, however, also revealed the limitations of black baseball. The black professional game depended, as Janet Bruce has written, "on an impoverished people who had too little discretionary money and too little leisure time."[26] Since most blacks who could afford to attend games worked or searched for casual work six days a week, Sunday was often the only day they could attend games. Sunday matchups usually attracted between 4,000 and 8,000 fans; weekday contests drew a few hundred. As Foster noted, "There are only twenty-seven Sundays and holidays in the playing season. It is a proven fact that on Sundays only have clubs been able to play at a profit. The weekdays have on many occasions been a complete loss."[27] Since several states, most notably Pennsylvania, had "blue laws" prohibiting Sunday games, teams like the Hilldale Club lost these lucrative home dates. Teams that shared facilities with white major and minor league squads could only schedule home Sunday dates when the host club was on the road. A few Sunday rainouts could devastate a team's narrow profit margin.

Attempts to stage a World Series between the champions of the Negro National League and the Eastern Colored League in 1924 illustrated the problem. Since black fans in any city could not be expected to afford tickets for more than a few consecutive games, the ten-game series pitting the Hilldale Club against the Monarchs was played not just in Philadelphia and Kansas City but in Baltimore and Chicago as well. Three Sunday dates attracted an average of almost 7,000 fans a game. Two Monday games, including the finale to a tightly contested series, attracted crowds of 534 and 1,549. This pattern continued into the 1930s and 1940s. The Newark Eagles, for example, averaged 4,293 Sunday admissions in 1940, but only 870 on other days.[28]

These realities of black baseball exposed a great deal about the complex racial dynamics of America. As early as 1911, David Wyatt pointed out that "baseball can not live or thrive upon the attendance of colored only," and noted the necessity of scheduling weekday games against white teams. As Neil Lanctot demonstrates, the success of the Hilldale Club in the early 1920s stemmed from the availability of white opponents. Hilldale played almost two-thirds of its games against white semiprofessional and industrial teams.[29]

White baseball fans across the nation attended games that pitted black teams against white semiprofessional and professional squads, but most

whites had minimal exposure to top-level competition between black athletes. The daily press in most cities rarely covered constructive black activities of any kind. When several white papers deigned to mention the
1924 Negro World Series, the *Kansas City Call* observed, "Negro sport
has done what Negro Churches, Negro lodges, Negro business could not
do . . . shown that a Negro can get attention for a good deed well done,
and that publicity is no longer the exclusive mark of our criminals." But
such attention was unusual; in the 1930s and 1940s, Effa Manley discovered that "it was next to impossible to get much space in the white metropolitan dailies."[30] Reports of games that found their way into the white
press often lampooned the fans and festivities or referred to the players
as "duskies" and other racist terms.

White fans appear to have been more likely to attend all-black games
in the early years of the century. In 1907, a three-game series in Chicago
between the Indianapolis ABCs and the Lincoln Giants attracted 30,000
fans, some black, some white. "There was no color line anywhere; our
white brethren outnumbered us by a few hundred, and bumped elbows
in the grandstands . . . the box seats and bleachers," reported Wyatt. The
ABCs, Monarchs, Hilldales, and Lincoln Giants (who played in Harlem)
all reported substantial white attendance during these years.[31] During the
1920s, however, perhaps due to the more rigid segregation arising in
response to the Great Migration and 1919 race riots, white attendance
dropped to 10 percent or less. Efforts to bolster profits by attracting more
whites inevitably proved unsuccessful. In 1939, Effa Manley made a
strong effort to lure whites to Newark Eagles games, but the *Philadelphia
Tribune* reported in 1940 that "up in Newark . . . [one] would have seen
95 colored faces for every five white ones." Chicago reporter Fay Young
frequently criticized attempts to get more whites to the games. Although
the leagues had employed white promoters to bolster attendance at all-
star games in Chicago and New York in 1939, observed Young, the
32,000 fans in Chicago included only 1,500 whites, and "the white
people in New York didn't give a tinker's damn about Negro baseball."
Two years later, Young noted, the crowd of 50,000 people who attended
the East-West game "didn't have 5,000 white people out."[32]

Although whites rarely attended Negro League games, blacks in many
cities frequented major and minor league ballparks. Many African Americans, particularly those who read only mainstream newspapers, were more
aware of white baseball than the black alternative. "Scores of people in
Harlem . . . do not know there is a colored baseball club in the city,"

alleged the *Amsterdam News* in 1929. The *Philadelphia Tribune* reported that black children attending a Hilldale game in the 1920s "had heard of Cobb, Speaker, Hornsby and Babe Ruth and other pale-faced stars, but knew not that they had players of their own group who could hold their own with any stars of any league." Buck O'Neil recalled that as children in Florida he and his friends, unfamiliar with black baseball, emulated the intensely racist Ty Cobb and other major league players in their imaginary games.[33]

African American newspapermen repeatedly chided blacks for supporting organized white baseball. "It is bad enough to ride on Jim Crow cars, but to go into ecstasies over a Jim Crow sport is unforgivable," admonished the *Chicago Whip* in 1921. Two years later, a sportswriter in Washington, D.C., where African Americans avidly rooted for the Senators, asked, "Why then should we continue to support, foster and fill the coffers of a national enterprise that has no place or future for men of color, although they have the ability to make the grade?"[34] Wendell Smith offered a scathing critique of black fans in 1938:

> Why we continue to flock to major league ball parks, spending our hard earned dough, screaming and hollering, stamping our feet and clapping our hands, begging and pleading for some white batter to knock some white pitcher's ears off, almost having fits if the home team loses and crying for joy when they win, is a question that will probably never be settled satisfactorily. What in the world are we thinking about anyway?
>
> The fact that major league baseball refuses to admit Negro players within its folds makes the question just that much more perplexing. Surely, it's sufficient reason for us to quit spending our money and time in their ball parks. Major league baseball does not want us. It never has. Still we continue to help support this institution that places a bold "Not Welcome" sign over its thriving portal and refuse to patronize the very place that has shown that it is more than welcome to have us. We black folks are a strange tribe![35]

The presence of black fans at white games grated for many reasons. As a Kansas City minister commented about the patronage of white-owned businesses, "all of that money goes into the white man's pocket and then out of our neighborhood." The prevalence of segregated seating provoked additional irritation. In St. Louis, where fans had to sit in a separate area behind a screen, a black newspaper condemned fans who ignored the St. Louis Stars, but chose to "fork over six bits to see a game at Sportsman's Park . . . and get Jim Crowed in the bargain." In Kansas City, blacks faced segregated seating at minor league Blues games throughout the 1920s. When former major league catcher Johnny Kling bought the team in the 1930s, he ended this policy, but when the Yankees purchased the club in 1938, the organization reinstituted Jim Crow. Other ballparks, like Griffith Stadium, had no formal policy dividing the races, but African Americans always sat in specific areas of the outfield. "There were no signs," remembered one black Senators fan. "You just knew that was where you would sit."[36]

Many of these same ballparks regularly hosted Negro League and other black contests. After 50,000 fans attended the all-star extravaganza at Comiskey Park in 1941, Fay Young protested, "The East versus West game ought to make Chicago folk get busy and have a ballyard of their own. Why is it we have to 'rent' the other fellow's belongings?" But the cost of constructing a stadium fell beyond the limited resources of most team owners. Only a handful of teams—the Memphis Red Sox, the Pittsburgh Crawfords in the 1930s, and the Nashville Elite Giants—owned the stadiums they played in.[37] Most leased or rented facilities usually controlled by whites, often in white neighborhoods and governed by the unpredictable racial mores of the era.

The thorny issue of acquiring a place for black teams to play further illustrated the complex American racial dynamics. For the independent clubs of the early twentieth century, the ability to secure reliable access to a playing field often elevated the team from sandlot to professional level. After 1907, the Indianapolis ABCs held a lease to play at Northwestern Park, a small black-owned stadium in the city's African American district. The club advertised itself as one of the few black teams to "own their own park," and the ability to guarantee playing dates attracted a steady stream of frontline opponents. In the 1910s, Ed Bolden obtained the use of Hilldale Park in Darby, Pennsylvania, just outside Philadelphia. Connected by trolley to Philadelphia's African American area, Hilldale Park seated 8,000 fans, providing Bolden's Hilldale Club with a steady following.[38]

Hilldale Park was a curious affair, with several trees and tree stumps scattered through the outfield and a hazardous depression that ran across center field. Indeed, many of the ballparks left much to be desired as playing fields. Early teams in Newark performed at Sprague Stadium, hemmed in on one side by a laundry building so close to the infield that balls hit on its roof became ground-rule doubles. The Baltimore Black Sox played in what the *Afro-American* called "a sewer known as Maryland Park, which featured broken seats, holes in roof, nonworking toilets and weeds on the field."[39]

As the popularity of black baseball increased, however, teams began renting larger and better white-owned facilities from recreation entrepreneurs or major and minor league teams. Some parks were located in black neighborhoods, but others brought players and fans across town into white districts. When the White Sox abandoned 18,000-seat South Side Park in Chicago's Black Belt for the new Comiskey Stadium, Charles Comiskey's brother-in-law, John Schorling, refurbished the arena and offered it to Rube Foster's American Giants. After 1923, the Kansas City Monarchs leased Muehlebach Stadium, home of the Kansas City Blues of the American Association, another ballpark located in a black section. The Detroit Stars, on the other hand, played at Mack Park, situated amid a German working-class neighborhood. After Mack Park burned down in 1929, the Stars moved to a field in Hamtramck, a Polish community.[40]

Playing in a white-owned facility raised numerous problems for black teams and players. Many stadiums refused to allow African American players to use the locker rooms. When the Pittsburgh Crawfords or Homestead Grays played at Ammons Field or Forbes Field, the players had to dress and shower at the local YMCA. Some ballparks, like American Association Park in Kansas City, where the Monarchs played from 1920 to 1922, insisted on segregated seating, even for Negro League games.[41] The shift from a small black-owned arena to a larger white-owned one also raised the specter of racial betrayal. The 1916 move by the ABCs from Northwestern Park to Federal League Park posed a familiar dilemma. Switching to the new park placed the ABCs in a modern facility, comparable to many major league fields. However, as the *Indianapolis Freeman* complained, the relocation would transfer rent and concession money as well as jobs from blacks to whites.[42] When the Lincoln Giants moved their games from Olympic Stadium in Harlem to the more distant but attractive Protectory Oval, the *New York Amsterdam News* protested, "To see a good baseball game in which colored men engage you now have to travel miles out of the district."[43]

By the late 1930s and early 1940s, several major and minor league teams had discovered that renting their stadiums for Sunday Negro

League doubleheaders could be a lucrative proposition. In 1932, the New York Yankees began scheduling four-team doubleheaders at Yankee Stadium when the Yankees were on the road. In 1939, the Yankees even donated a "Jacob Ruppert Memorial Cup," named after the team's late owner, to the black club that won the most games at the stadium that year. By the end of the decade, the Yankees also rented out the ballparks of their Kansas City and Newark affiliates to the Monarchs and Eagles.[44] In 1939, the Baltimore Orioles, who had previously refused to allow the Elite Giants to use Oriole Park, accepted several Sunday dates. The Homestead Grays played regular Sunday dates at Griffith Stadium starting in 1940, averaging better than 10,000 fans a game. Even Shibe Park in Philadelphia, where blacks had rarely played previously, began scheduling Negro League games in the 1940s.[45]

These bookings marked important breakthroughs. They demonstrated the economic potential of black baseball fans—and their respectability as well. As the *Kansas City Call* commented in a 1949 editorial, "From a sociological point of view, the Monarchs have done more than any other single agent to break the damnable outrage of prejudice that exists in this city. White fans, the thinking class at least, can not have watched the orderly crowds at Association Park . . . and not concede that we are humans at least, and worthy of consideration as such."[46]

Perhaps the most significant area of racial controversy revolved around the white owners and booking agents who profited from black baseball. In 1917, David Wyatt derided "the white man who has now and in the past secured grounds and induced some one in the role of the 'good old Nigger' to gather a lot of athletes and then used circus methods to drag a bunch of our best citizens out, only to undergo humiliation, with all kinds of indignities flaunted in their faces, while he sits back and grows rich off a percentage of the proceeds."[47] Yet, as Wyatt well knew, few African Americans in the early twentieth century had the resources to underwrite a baseball enterprise. As *Pittsburgh Courier* columnist Rollo Wilson observed in 1933, "Mighty few teams have been entirely financed by Negro capital. . . . There have been many instances of so-called Negro 'owners' being nothing but a 'front' for the white interest behind him."[48] Before the 1930s, when the urban "numbers kings" began bankrolling Negro League franchises, economic survival almost always required either partial or complete white ownership or an alliance with white booking agents who controlled access to playing fields.

Both contemporaries and historians have frequently portrayed white booking agents as the Shylockian villains of black baseball. Operating in a universe in which few African American teams owned playing fields, these baseball entrepreneurs controlled access to the best ballparks and many of the most popular opponents. Nat Strong personified these individuals. A former sporting goods salesman, Strong, like the men who founded vaudeville, had glimpsed an opportunity to profit along the fringes of American entertainment. Recognizing the broad interest in semiprofessional baseball in the 1890s, Strong gained control of New York–area ball fields like Dexter Park in Queens that hosted these games. He rented out these facilities to white and black teams alike and gradually expanded his empire to include a substantial portion of the East Coast. In 1905, Strong formed the National Association of Colored Professional Clubs of the United States and Cuba, which booked games for the Philadelphia Giants, Cuban X Giants, Brooklyn Royal Giants and other top eastern black squads.[49]

Any team hoping to schedule lucrative Sunday dates at a profitable site had to deal with Strong, who systematically attempted to secure a monopoly over black professional baseball. Teams that defied Strong found themselves barred from the best bookings. When John Connors, the black owner of the Royal Giants, obtained a playing field in 1911 and attempted to arrange his own games, Strong blacklisted teams that dealt with Connors. Within two years, Strong had wrested control of the rebellious franchise from Connors.[50] Black teams also resented the fact that Strong paid a flat guarantee rather than a percentage of the gate, allowing him to reap the profits from large crowds. Behavior like this led former player and organizer Sol White to remark in 1929, "There is not a man in the country who has made as much money from colored ballplaying as Nat Strong, and yet he is the least interested in its welfare."[51]

The creation of the original Negro leagues in the 1920s occurred against this backdrop. Historians have usually accepted Rube Foster's descriptions of his Negro National League (NNL) as a purer circuit than the rival Eastern Colored League (ECL). Black owners predominated in the NNL; white owners, particularly Strong, prevailed in the ECL. Foster vehemently dismissed the ECL as a tool of Strong. But, the reality of the two leagues was more complex.

As Neil Lanctot has demonstrated, the key figure of the ECL was not Strong, but its president, Ed Bolden. Bolden, a black Philadelphia-area postal worker, had elevated the Hilldale Club of Darby, Pennsylvania, from a sandlot team into a frontline independent competitor. In 1918, when Strong had attempted to gain control of the Hilldale Club, Bolden sent an open letter to the *Philadelphia Tribune,* proclaiming, "The race people of Philadelphia and vicinity are proud to proclaim Hilldale the biggest thing in the baseball world owned fostered and controlled by race men. . . . To affiliate ourselves with other than race men would be a mark against our name that could never be eradicated."[52] Yet, five years later, Bolden allied with Strong to form the ECL. Bolden, heavily dependent on scheduling nonleague games at locales like Dexter Park, owned or controlled by Strong, recognized the benefits of amalgamation. "Close analysis will prove that only where the color line fades and co-operation instituted are our business advances gratified," wrote Bolden in 1925.[53]

If, as Foster and black sportswriters alleged, Strong "was the league and ran the league," his conduct certainly belied this accusation. The ECL failed, in no small measure, because Strong's Brooklyn Royal Giants refused to adhere to the league schedule. A traveling team with no home base, the Royal Giants frequently bypassed games with league opponents if offered more lucrative bookings. In 1924, the league commissioners voted the Royal Giants out of the ECL, but relented when Strong promised his team would play all scheduled games. His failure to adhere to this pledge greatly weakened the league.[54]

As Bolden noted, however, the Negro National League also had a "few [white] skeletons lurking in the closet."[55] The most visible white presence in the NNL was league secretary J. L. Wilkinson, the owner of the Kansas City Monarchs. Wilkinson represented the best in Negro League ownership, white or black. As Wendell Smith later saluted, he "not only invested his money, but his very heart and soul" in black baseball. But Wilkinson always remained conscious of the need to portray the Monarchs as a black institution. African Americans Dr. Howard Smith and Quincy J. Gilmore became the public faces of the Monarchs, attending league meetings and riding in the lead car at the opening game festivities.[56] In Detroit, first Tenny Blount and later Mose Walker fronted for white businessman John Roesink as owner of the Stars. Most significantly, Foster himself was not the sole owner of the Chicago American Giants. John Schorling, owner of Schorling Stadium, the team's home grounds, underwrote the American Giants and split all profits evenly with Foster. After the *Chicago Broad Ax* protested in 1912 that Schorling received proceeds that "should be received by the Race to whom the patrons of the game belong," Foster concealed Schorling's role. Nonetheless, other NNL owners remained suspicious of Schorling's influence, and when Foster became ill in 1926, Schorling assumed sole ownership of the team.[57]

Both the NNL and ECL collapsed with the onset of the Great Depression. By this time, a group of unorthodox, but highly successful, nonwhite businessmen wealthy enough to finance black professional baseball had arisen in many cities. Cuban Stars impresario Alejandro (Alex) Pompez pioneered this new breed of owner in the 1920s. Pompez, a Cuban American born in Florida, reigned as the numbers king of Harlem. The numbers game was a poor man's lottery. For as little as a nickel, individuals could gamble on hitting a lucky combination of three numbers and winning a payoff of 600 to 1. Since the true odds of winning were 999 to 1, considerable profits awaited a resourceful and reliable man who could oversee the operation. Pompez reportedly grossed as much as seven thousand to eight thousand dollars a day from his organization. In the 1920s, Pompez purchased Dyckman's Oval, a park and stadium in Harlem, and staged a variety of sports events including boxing, wrestling, and motorcycle racing. Pompez, who had strong connections in Cuba and a keen eye for baseball talent, formed the Cuban Stars to play at Dyckman's Oval. In 1923, they joined the ECL, one of only two black-owned clubs in the league. During the 1930s, he owned the New York Cubans. Pompez imported top Cuban players like Martín Dihigo and Luis Tiant Sr. to perform for his teams.[58]

The numbers operations run by Pompez and others were illegal but widely accepted in black America. In a world in which African Americans had few legitimate business opportunities, many of the most talented and resourceful entrepreneurs, men who, according to Richard Wright, "would have been steel tycoons, Wall street brokers, auto moguls had they been white,"[59] entered the numbers racket. Some, like Jim "Soldier Boy" Semler of New York or Dick Kent of St. Louis, were ruthless gangsters, prone to violence and intimidation.[60] Others, like Pompez and Gus Greenlee of Pittsburgh, although not averse to using strong-arm methods to expand and defend their empires, won reputations as community benefactors. Often these numbers kings turned a portion of their profits back into the black community through loans, charity, and investments.[61]

Their wealth, power, and influence within the black community notwithstanding, the numbers kings still had to make their way in a white-dominated world. Of the Negro National League teams of the 1930s and 1940s, only the Pittsburgh Crawfords owned and operated their own stadium. All teams still relied heavily on white booking agents for scheduling. Nat Strong had died in the early 1930s, but William Leuchsner, who ran Nat C. Strong Baseball Enterprises in the New York area, and Eddie Gottlieb, who operated out of Philadelphia, now ruled Strong's domain.[62] In the Midwest, where a new Negro American League formed in 1937, Abe Saperstein, better known as the founder of the Harlem Globetrotters, had succeeded Rube Foster as the preeminent booking agent. Saperstein even received 5 percent of the substantial gate at the East-West showcase.[63] These arrangements were not without benefits for Negro League teams. Gottlieb, for example, coordinated ticket sales and newspaper and poster publicity for events he booked, enabling teams to reduce their overhead and maintain fewer employees. The booking agents also negotiated reduced rental, operating, and insurance fees from major and minor league ballparks. The Homestead Grays reported that Gottlieb's intervention with the Yankees saved league owners ten thousand dollars in 1940.[64]

Nonetheless, many owners bridled at the influence of white booking agents and repeatedly sought to be free of them. According to Effa Manley, who owned the Newark Eagles with her husband, Abe, "[We] fought a . . . war against the booking agents from the first day [we] entered the picture . . . but [we] fought a losing battle. The tentacle-like grip of the booking agents proved impossible to break." Their resistance cost the Eagles their Yankee Stadium playing dates in 1939 and 1940. At the 1940 league meetings, the Manleys demanded the removal of Gottlieb as booking agent for Yankee Stadium. According to *Baltimore Afro-American* sports editor Art Carter, Effa Manley "assumed the position that the league was a colored organization and that she wanted to see all the money kept within the group." When Homestead Grays owner Cumberland Posey defended Gottlieb, Manley (who although she lived as a black woman later claimed to be white) denounced the Grays' owner as a "handkerchief head," a street slang variation on "Uncle Tom."[65] That same year, black sportswriters at the East-West game organized the American Sportswriters Association to protest Saperstein's domination of that event, and the Negro American League removed Saperstein as its official booking agent.[66]

These conflicts and debates over the role of whites in black baseball revealed not just the racial tensions that always existed in the age of segregation but the stake of African Americans in successful black-owned and -operated institutions. "Who owns the Grays?" reflected the *Washington Afro-American* in 1943. "It is a pleasure to inform the fans of

Washington that the Washington Homestead Grays are owned and operated by three colored gentlemen."[67] A scene at the opening game of the 1946 Negro League World Series captured this sense of pride. When heavyweight champion Joe Louis threw out the first pitch, he tossed a silver ball that had been awarded to the Cuban Giants, the first great black professional team, for winning a tournament in 1888. As James Overmyer writes, "With a sweep of his right arm, Louis, the greatest black athlete of his day, symbolically linked the earliest era of Negro baseball with its most recent high point."[68]

The World Series ceremony occurred at a critical juncture in the history of black baseball. In September 1946, Jackie Robinson was completing his successful first season in organized baseball. The response to Robinson revealed the fragile hold that all-black baseball held on the African American psyche. From its earliest days, the promoters of the African American game had made its transitional nature clear. In *The History of Colored Baseball* in 1906, Sol White advised the black ballplayer to take the game "seriously . . . as honest efforts and his will open an avenue in the near future wherein he might walk hand-in-hand with the opposite race in the greatest of all American games." In a remarkably prescient passage, White added, "There are grounds for hoping that some day the bar will drop and some good man will be chosen out of the colored profession that will be a credit to all, and pave the way for others to follow."[69] Rube Foster had another vision, wherein an all-black team would pierce the ranks of the white professional leagues, but the model of ultimate integration remained. The *Crisis*, the journal of the National Association for the Advancement of Colored People, left no doubt as to the ultimate purpose of the Negro leagues. "It is only through the elevation of our Negro league baseball that colored ballplayers will break into white major league ball," avowed the *Crisis* in 1938. Even as strong an advocate of "Race baseball" as Fay Young, who railed against white umpires, publicity men, and booking agents, joined the chorus. "We want Negroes in the major leagues if they have to crawl to get there," wrote Young in 1945.[70]

Most people involved with black baseball had few illusions as to what the impact of integration would be. Asked about the prospect of blacks in the major leagues in 1939, the manager of the Homestead Grays, Vic Harris, replied, "If they start picking them up, what are the remaining players going to do to make a living? . . . And suppose our stars—the fellows who do draw well—are gobbled up by the big clubs. How could

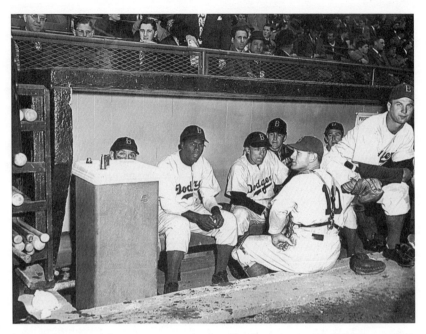

Jackie Robinson with his teammates in the Brooklyn Dodgers dugout, 1947. Courtesy of
The Sporting News.

the other 75 or 80% survive?" Black sportswriters like Sam Lacy "knew
[that integration] would have a devastating effect on black baseball."[71]
Joe Bostic wrote in 1942:

> Today, there are two Negro organized leagues, just on the thresh-
> old of emergence as real financial factors. . . . To kill [them] would
> be criminal and that's just what the entry of their players into the
> American and National Leagues would do. . . .
>
> Nor should money from the byproducts be overlooked such
> as the printers, the Negro papers and the other advertising media,
> which get their taste: the officials, scorekeepers, announcers, sec-
> retaries and a host of others. These monies are coming into Negro
> pockets. You can rest assured that we'd get none of those jobs in
> the other leagues, *even with a player or two in their leagues.* . . .
>
> In sum: From an idealist and democratic point of view, we
> say "yes" to Negroes in the two other leagues. From the point
> of practicality: "No."[72]

But for Lacy, Bostic, and others, "the idealistic and democratic point of view" won out. Less than three years after issuing his admonition, Bostic ardently pursued the policy he had condemned, confronting Branch Rickey with Negro League players Terris McDuffie and Dave Thomas and demanding a tryout with the Dodgers during spring training in 1945. Wendell Smith might criticize black fans for attending white games, but working alongside Rickey, he became one of the key architects of baseball integration. Sam Lacy acknowledged, "After Jackie, the Negro Leagues was a symbol I couldn't live with anymore." For these sportswriters, as James Overmyer points out, "covering baseball integration [was] the biggest story of their lives," and they pursued it wholeheartedly.[73]

Throughout black America, the focus shifted from the Negro leagues to the major leagues. The African American press reduced its coverage of the Negro leagues to make room for updates and statistics about Robinson and other black players in organized baseball. Advertisements appeared for special rail excursions to National League cities to see Robinson play. Even the Negro leagues themselves attempted to capitalize on Robinson's popularity. The cover of the 1946 Negro League yearbook featured Robinson rather than one of the established league stars. A program for the Philadelphia Stars in the late 1940s pictured Robinson in his Dodger uniform.[74]

Negro League fans voted with their dollars decisively in favor of integration. In 1946, Effa Manley found that "our fans would go as far as Baltimore" to see Robinson play for the Montreal Royals.[75] Once he joined the Dodgers and New York–area fans could see Robinson in eighty-eight games at Ebbets Field and the Polo Grounds, attendance plummeted for the Newark Eagles and New York Black Yankees. Other teams also felt the pinch. "People wanted to go to see the Brooklynites," recalled Monarch pitcher Hilton Smith. "Even if we were playing here in Kansas City, people wanted to go over to St. Louis to see Jackie."[76]

Occasionally critics raised their voices to protest the abandonment of black baseball. "Around 400 players are involved in the Negro version of the national pastime," warned Dan Burley in the *Amsterdam News* in 1948. "If there are no customers out to see them, they don't earn a living. In enriching the coffers of the major league clubs, we put the cart before the horse for no purpose."[77] But most commentators were less sympathetic. In response to Manley's complaints about declining fan support, the *Kansas City Call* cajoled, "The day of loyalty to Jim Crow anything is fast passing away. Sister, haven't you heard the news? Democracy is a-coming fast."[78] The Manleys sold the Eagles after the 1948 season. By the early 1950s, all but a handful of the Negro League clubs had disbanded.

As Burley, Manley, and others had predicted, the end of segregation would mean that fewer rather than more African Americans would earn their living from baseball in the latter half of the twentieth century. The failure of major league teams to hire black managers, coaches, and front-office personnel compounded this problem. The nearly universal celebration of Jackie Robinson's triumph notwithstanding, integration would produce negative as well as positive consequences.

Cultural critic Gerald Early sees the demise of the Negro leagues as the destruction of "an important black economic and cultural institution" that encompassed many of the best and worst elements of African American life. Blacks, writes Early, "have never gotten over the loss of the Negro Leagues because they have never completely understood the ironically compressed expression of shame and pride, of degradation and achievement that those leagues represented."[79] In the final analysis, the black baseball experience captured the "twoness" in the "souls of black folk" as well as the "dogged strength" that kept them "from being torn asunder."

Notes

The literature on black baseball is extraordinarily rich. The pioneering works in this field include Robert Peterson, *Only the Ball Was White: A History of the Legendary Black Players and All-Black Professional Teams* (Englewood Cliffs, N.J.: Prentice Hall, 1970); and Don Rogosin, *Invisible Men: Life in Baseball's Negro Leagues* (New York: Atheneum, 1983). An impressive body of team and community studies has supplemented these overviews. This essay relies heavily on Richard Bak, *Turkey Stearnes and His Detroit Stars: The Negro Leagues in Detroit, 1919–1933* (Detroit: Wayne State University Press, 1994); Janet Bruce, *The Kansas City Monarchs: Champions of Black Baseball* (Lawrence: University Press of Kansas, 1985); Paul Debono, *The Indianapolis ABCs: History of a Premier Team in the Negro Leagues* (Jefferson, N.C.: MacFarland, 1997); Neil Lanctot, *Fair Dealing and Clean Playing: The Hilldale Club and the Development of Black Professional Baseball, 1910–1932* (Jefferson, N.C.: MacFarland, 1994); James Overmyer, *Effa Manley and the Newark Eagles* (Metuchen, N.J.: Scarecrow Press, 1993); Rob Ruck, *Sandlot Seasons: Sport in Black Pittsburgh* (Urbana: University of Illinois Press, 1987). Two photographic histories of black baseball, Bruce

Chadwick, *When the Game Was Black and White: The Illustrated History of the Negro Leagues* (New York: Abbeville Press, 1992); and Phil Dixon and Patrick J. Hannigan, *The Negro Baseball Leagues: A Photographic History* (New York: Amereon House, 1992) were also very helpful, as was Jim Reisler, *Black Writers/Black Baseball: An Anthology of Articles from Black Sportswriters Who Covered the Negro Leagues* (Jefferson, N.C.: MacFarland, 1994). For those interested in learning more about the stars of black baseball, the oral histories of John Holway and the reference works of James A. Riley are indispensable.

1. On Rube Foster, see Peterson, 103–15; Rogosin, 33; Bruce, 31–32; Lanctot, 29; and Jules Tygiel, "Black Ball," in *Total Baseball*, 5th ed., ed. John Thorn et al. (New York: Viking, 1997), 435.

2. W. E. B. DuBois, *Souls of Black Folk* (New York: Vintage Books/Library of America, 1990).

3. Overmyer, 111; Lanctot, 23; Bruce, 44.

4. Bruce, 42, 29.

5. Bak, 135.

6. James H. Bready, *Baseball in Baltimore* (Baltimore: Johns Hopkins University Press, 1998), 174; Lanctot, 61; Bruce, 45–47.

7. Rogosin, 32–33; Reisler, 49.

8. Debono, 2, 44–48.

9. Lanctot, 23.

10. On Negro National League, see Debono, 49, 84; Bak, 71.

11. Debono, 101.

12. Overmyer, 15–17, 59, 215.

13. Overmyer, 5, 59–60, 167–68, 174; Bruce, 45; Lanctot, 176.

14. Debono, 74; Stephen J. Ross, *Black Diamonds, Blues City: Stories of the Memphis Red Sox* (University of Memphis, 1997) (film); Overmyer, 86.

15. Imamu Amiri Baraka, *The Autobiography of LeRoi Jones/Amiri Baraka* (New York: Freundlich Books, 1984), 35.

16. Bak, 126; Bready, 166; Bruce, 42.

17. Baraka, 35; Overmyer, 66.

18. James Bankes, *The Pittsburgh Crawfords: The Lives and Times of Black Baseball's Most Exciting Team* (Dubuque, Iowa: William C. Brown, 1991), 104–5; Ross; Chadwick, 54; Overmyer, 112; Bruce, 44.

19. Bruce, 3.

20. Debono, 73.

21. Bruce, 44–45.

22. Chadwick, 50; Debono, 180.

23. Overmyer, 34, 64, 97; Riesler, 99–100; Ruck, 157; Bready, 181; Bruce, 47.

24. Overmyer, 63.

25. Chadwick, 55; Peterson, 113; Ross.

26. Bruce, 58.

27. Charles E. Whitehead, *A Man and His Diamonds: A Story of the Great Andrew (Rube) Foster, the Outstanding Team He Owned and Managed and the Superb League He Founded and Commissioned* (New York: Vantage Press, 1980), 180.

28. Lanctot, 112–20; Overmyer, 107.

29. Lanctot, 40, 62–63.

30. Lanctot, 121; Overmyer, 113–14.

31. Debono, 22, 42; Lanctot, 62; Bruce, 44–45.

32. Overmyer, 166; Riesler, 60, 61.

33. Lanctot, 184; Ross.

34. Lanctot, 183–84.

35. Reisler, 36–37.

36. Bruce, 29, 51–52; Lanctot, 184; Brad Snyder, senior thesis, Duke University, 1994, 4.

37. Reisler, 61; Dixon and Hannigan, 176.

38. Debono, 20; Lanctot, 20, 23.

39. Lanctot, 60; Overmyer, 104–5; Bready, 167.

40. Lanctot, 37; Bruce, 52–53; Bak, 57, 186.

41. Bankes, 25; Bruce, 51.

42. Debono, 66–67.

43. Lanctot, 99.

44. Overmyer, 122.

45. Bready, 175; Snyder, 2–9; Bruce Kuklick, *To Every Thing a Season: Shibe Park and Urban Philadelphia, 1909–1976* (Princeton, N.J.: Princeton University Press), 146–47.

46. Chadwick, 121.

47. Bruce, 11.

48. Ruck, 116.

49. On Nat Strong, see Lanctot, 29, 62.

50. Lanctot, 29.

51. Overmyer, 269.

52. Lanctot, 73–74.

53. Lanctot, 66.

54. Bruce, 31; Lanctot, 145, 162.

55. Lanctot, 96.

56. Ruck, 221; Bruce, 212–22.

57. Bak, 55–57, 202; Lanctot, 37–38; Peterson, 113–14.

58. Overmyer, 10, 272–77; Bankes, 91–92.

59. Rogosin, 104.

60. Bankes, 94.

61. Overmyer, 9–10; Ruck, 149–50.

62. Overmyer, 268–69.

63. Bruce, 90.

64. Overmyer, 135, 139.

65. Overmyer, 134, 138–39.

66. Bruce, 90; Lanctot, 95. '

67. Snyder, 2–24.

68. Overmyer, 204.

69. Dixon and Hannigan, 241–42; Peterson, 59.

70. Dixon and Hannigan, 242; H. B. Webber and Oliver Brown, "Play Ball!" *Crisis* 45 (May 1938): 137; Bruce, 111.

71. Reisler, 16, 13.

72. Reisler, 80–81.

73. Reisler, 13; Overmyer, 244.

74. Overmyer, 108–9; Debono, 121; Chadwick, 165; Dixon and Hannigan, 252.

75. Overmyer, 235.

76. Bruce, 116.

77. Reisler, 143.

78. Bruce, 116.

79. Geoffrey C. Ward and Ken Burns, *Baseball: An Illustrated History* (New York: Alfred A. Knopf, 1994), 413.

★6★

Before Joe D: Early Italian Americans in the Major Leagues

LAWRENCE BALDASSARO

When Joe DiMaggio died on 8 March 1999, news of his death was on the front pages of all the major newspapers and was the lead story on the network newscasts. Cable networks broadcast tributes and documentaries, and *Newsweek* put his picture on its cover. Very few figures in American life could generate such a response. More than fifty years after his final baseball game, Joe DiMaggio was still a cultural icon, someone who transcended the world of baseball.

No Italian American athlete, in any sport, achieved as much enduring fame as Joe DiMaggio. But even before DiMaggio made his major league debut in 1936, many other Italian Americans had paved the way by playing big league baseball. Several had notable careers, and two are enshrined in the Baseball Hall of Fame. Rather than attempt an overview of the entire span of Italian American participation in baseball, this essay will focus on those athletes who made significant contributions to the game before the appearance of DiMaggio. In many ways, their stories reflect the general experience of the Italian Americans of their time.

By the early 1880s, what had previously been a trickle of Italian immigrants to the United States suddenly turned into a flood tide. Over the next forty years, more than four million Italians immigrated, most of them unskilled laborers from the rural southern regions, and they all came in search of the American Dream. Those immigrants encountered an ambiguous reception. On the one hand, they were welcomed as part of the urban labor force needed to build a rapidly expanding nation. At the same time, like other southern and eastern European immigrants, the Italians were viewed with suspicion and often hostility both by those who feared that the newcomers posed a threat to their job security and by those who saw these "different" outsiders as a threat to an established American way of life.

While many, if not most, first-generation immigrants held on to their Old World ways, their children inevitably found themselves torn between their parents' traditional culture and the "American" culture they encountered outside the home. For them, the answer to the stigma of being outsiders was to find a way to become less different, to assimilate into the larger culture that found their differences to be unsettling, if not unacceptable.

Especially for second-generation Italian Americans, baseball provided one avenue of entry to mainstream society, either as fans or as participants. Italians came to America at a time when baseball was already well established as the national pastime, and when journalists and social workers were touting the game as a means of acculturating the new immigrants to American values.

Like the German and Irish who had preceded them, the children of Italian immigrants naturally gravitated to the American game. As one contemporary observer pointed out in 1906, "the children [of Italian immigrants] almost immediately become Americans. The boy takes no interest in 'Boccie.' . . . Like any other American boy, he plays marbles, . . . and, when there is no policeman about, baseball."[1] But it was to be a long time before Italian Americans appeared in the major leagues in numbers that even approached their percentage of the American population.

What's in a Name? Abby, Ping, and Babe

Since name changes were so common among immigrants, no one can identify with absolute certainty the first Italian American to play in the big leagues. Without question, however, the first to have a significant major league career was Ed Abbaticchio. His story is atypical in that, unlike most of the early Italian American ballplayers, he did not come from a working-class background. His father had immigrated in 1873 to Latrobe, Pennsylvania, where he became a successful businessman and landowner. And, unlike most children of immigrant families, Ed

Ed Abbaticchio. National Baseball Hall of Fame Library, Cooperstown, N.Y.

Abbaticchio attended college, receiving a Master of Accounts degree in 1895 from St. Mary's College in North Carolina.

In spite of his educational training, which would suggest that he was preparing for a career in business, Abbaticchio chose to play professional baseball. For the son of Italian immigrants, baseball was a most unlikely and unpromising career choice in the 1890s. Nevertheless, after playing semiprofessional ball in Greensburg, Pennsylvania, Abbaticchio began his major league career with a brief three-game stint with the Philadelphia Phillies at the end of the 1897 season.

However, even before he appeared in his first major league game with the Phillies, he had already made his debut as a professional athlete —as a football player. In 1895, Latrobe fielded what is generally acknowledged as the first professional football team in the country. Ed Abbaticchio was its star fullback and kicker. When he began his major league baseball career in 1897, he became the first two-sport professional athlete.[2]

After appearing in twenty-five games for the Phillies in 1898, Abbaticchio spent the next five seasons playing minor league baseball in Minneapolis, Milwaukee, and Nashville. In 1903, he returned to the major leagues, starting at both shortstop and second base for the Boston Nationals in the National League for three seasons. Then, he suddenly "retired" from baseball after the 1905 season.

According to a *Pittsburgh Post* story of 2 January 1905, Abbaticchio's father offered to turn his hotel over to his son on condition that he never play baseball again: "His father has always been opposed to his playing in the big leagues and has stipulated that the hotel will revert to him if the well-known short stop ever again dons a league uniform." Regardless of the accuracy of that story, Abbaticchio did in fact retire from baseball after the 1905 season to run the hotel, in spite of efforts by Boston and New York Giants manager John McGraw to sign him.

Abbaticchio announced that if he were to play again, it would only be for the Pittsburgh Pirates, apparently for business reasons. State law required that the owner of a liquor license could not reside outside the state for more than three consecutive months. By playing for the Pirates, Abbaticchio could stay near his hotel and retain his liquor license.

So anxious were the Pirates to secure the rights to Abbaticchio that in 1907 they sent three frontline players to Boston in what would today be considered a blockbuster deal. What is even more remarkable is that the Pirates also gave him what was at the time the extraordinary salary of five thousand dollars.[3] That was one thousand more than the salary of Honus Wagner, the Pirates' star shortstop who had led the National League in hitting in 1900, 1903, 1904, and 1906.

Abbaticchio's salary for 1908 remained at five thousand dollars, but not because he hadn't lived up to Pittsburgh's expectations in 1907. He was the Pirates' starting second baseman, forming the double play combination with Wagner, and drove in eighty-two runs, tying "the Fly-ing Dutchman" for second place in the National League.

Abbaticchio was the regular second baseman again in 1908, but his offensive production slipped; he hit .250—the league average was .239—and drove in sixty-one runs. The following year, the Pirates won the World Series, but Abbaticchio lost his starting job at second and became a role player, playing in only thirty-six games. In 1910, after appearing in three games for the Pirates, he returned to the Boston Nationals, playing in only fifty-two more games. When his career was over, Abbaticchio continued to run his hotel in Latrobe until 1932, when he retired to Florida. He died in Fort Lauderdale on 6 January 1957.

Ed Abbaticchio played in an era when major league rosters were filled with the names of players of Irish and German descent. His teammates on the 1908 Pirates team bore names like Shannon, Clarke, O'Connor, Kane, Leach, and Mueller. From his early days in professional baseball, his multisyllabic Italian name posed problems for sportswriters. From at least his time in Nashville, they were abbreviating his name to both "Abby" and "Batty." While not exceptional in themselves, those are nick-names that obviously mask Abbaticchio's Italian origins and may indicate that some compromise of his ethnic background was a necessary condi-tion of his acceptance in professional baseball. At the very least, they suggest a need to anglicize Abbaticchio's identity at a time when fans and the media were not yet accustomed to seeing Italian surnames in the box score.

Apart from abbreviating his name, however, the press paid little at-tention to Abbaticchio's ethnicity. There were occasional references to his Italian background, but for the most part, his nationality was ignored. However, on 7 June 1903 (Abbaticchio's first season with the Boston Nationals), the *Boston Sunday Journal* ran a story under the headline "Boston May Contribute to Italian Supremacy in Baseball." The article began by posing the question: "Does the entrance of an Italian into baseball presage another great ethnological movement such as has taken place in the American labor world?" Noting that while a decade earlier, "the large majority of laborers seen in the city streets were Irish," but now "the majority are Italians," the writer posed yet another question: "Will the Italians supplant the Irish on the diamond as they have sup-planted them with the pick and the shovel?"

The writer then revealed his real concern with the broader implica-tions of "Batty's case." The Italians, he concluded, are "the most clannish of all the nationalities that emigrate to the United States," and since they are the most reluctant to give up allegiance to their native land, they are the hardest to assimilate into American life.

Though the story was ostensibly about the implications of Abbaticchio's arrival for the baseball world, the issues and questions it raised reflected the nativist concern with the rapidly increasing numbers of immigrants who, it was feared, threatened not only to take jobs away from earlier immigrants but also posed a threat to accepted social mores. The writer's concerns about an Italian infiltration of baseball would prove to be unfounded. Ed Abbaticchio's arrival was not the beginning of a trend but a relatively isolated case. By the end of the twenties, only twenty-one Italian Americans had appeared on major league diamonds.

The first Italian American after Abbaticchio to have a significant major league career chose to mask his ethnic identity behind a pseudonym. He played under the unlikely name of Ping Bodie, but he was born as Francesco Pezzolo, the son of immigrant parents. In the 1870s, his parents had immigrated to New York City, where his father worked on the Brooklyn Bridge. By 1876, they had moved to California, settling for a while in the booming gold-mining town of Bodie (the apparent source of his pseudonym) before moving to San Francisco, where Francesco was born on 8 October 1887.

After setting a Pacific Coast League record (and gaining national attention) in 1910 by hitting the then-remarkable total of thirty home runs in a 212-game schedule, Pezzolo (playing as Ping Bodie) made his major league debut in 1911 with the Chicago White Sox. The right-handed-hitting outfielder hit .289 and finished third in the American League with ninety-seven runs batted in.

Bodie hit .294 in 1912 but then slipped to .265 and .229 the next two years and found himself back with the Seals in 1915. But in 1917, he returned to the majors, this time with Connie Mack's Philadelphia Athletics. He hit .291 in 148 games, led the Athletics in RBIs with seventy-four (sixth best in the National League), and his seven home runs were only two fewer than the number hit by league leader Wally Pipp of the Yankees.

Impressed by his performance, the New York Yankees bought Bodie from Mack, who was cleaning house in one of his cost-saving campaigns. The New York press eagerly welcomed Bodie, who by then had established a reputation as both a hard-hitting outfielder and a colorful character. A *New York Times* story on 8 March 1918 reported that Bodie was a "baseball character" who "will be an attraction with New York baseball fans," and concluded that the Yankees "have never had a player of such individuality." That, of course, was two years before Babe Ruth came to town.

The Sporting News commented on 18 March that "Bodie may not be a Speaker or a Cobb, but he can hammer the old apple." Bodie was indeed no Tris Speaker or Ty Cobb in the field. With his squat body—he stood five feet, eight inches tall and weighed 195 pounds—Bodie was no sleek ballhawk. (He did have a strong arm, however, and led the American League in outfield assists in 1917.) Bodie was variously described in the press as stout, rotund, and even roly-poly.

Yet, in his nine seasons in the majors, he stole eighty-three bases and hit seventy-two triples, numbers that suggest he had some speed. But it was a failed stolen base attempt that inspired sportswriter Bugs Baer to write this memorable line: "Ping had larceny in his heart, but his feet were honest."[4]

In his first two years with the Yankees, Bodie played in 91 and 134 games and hit .256 and .278, respectively. When it was announced in January 1920 that Babe Ruth had been sold to the Yankees, Bodie reportedly said: "I suppose this means I'll be sent to China."[5] But 1920 proved to be his best year with New York; he hit .295 in 129 games.

Bodie's name will forever be linked with that of Babe Ruth because of one of the most frequently quoted lines in baseball lore. Ping was Ruth's roommate, at least for one year, before the Babe decided to room by himself. When a reporter asked Bodie what it was like to room with the freewheeling Ruth, who rarely spent time in his hotel room when on the road, Ping replied: "I don't room with the Babe, I room with his suitcase."[6]

Bodie was not the only link Ruth had with Italian Americans in New York. By then, the large Italian immigrant community had become fascinated with baseball, probably due more to Ruth's immediate historical impact and his enormous popularity than to the presence of Bodie in the Yankee lineup. It was from them that one of Ruth's enduring nicknames was born; he became the "Bambino," the Italian word for "babe."

When Bodie was traded to the Red Sox near the end of the 1921 season, he refused to report. Instead, he spent the next seven seasons playing in the Pacific Coast, Western, and Texas Leagues. He finished his career in 1928 by hitting .348, at the age of forty-one, for the San Francisco Missions of the PCL. When he finally left baseball, he became

·an electrician on Hollywood movie sets, where he worked for thirty-two years. He died in 1961, one year after retiring at the age of seventy-three.

Though obviously not in the same league as the Babe on or off the field, Ping Bodie was quite a celebrity in his own right; his *Sporting News* obituary called him "one of the most colorful characters the game has ever produced." Bodie was well aware of his popularity with fans, even when he played for Connie Mack in Philadelphia. When Mack asked him to take a pay cut before the 1918 season, Bodie was reported as saying: "Now I ain't bragging or anything like that, but I got to admit I'm the only real ball player Connie's got. I and the Liberty Bell are the only attractions left in Philadelphia."[7]

Long before Yogi Berra and Phil Rizzuto came along, Bodie was well known for his colorful approach to the English language and has even been credited with adding some new terms to the baseball lexicon. The ball was not only an apple but a "stitched apricot" and a "spheroid"; he didn't just hit the ball, he "whaled the onion" and "rammycackled the old persimmon." A home run was a "four-ply swat." And when someone asked Bodie, then in his seventies, if he thought he could still hit, he replied: "Give me a mace and I'll drive the pumpkin down Whitey Ford's throat." Bodie has even achieved a quirky place in literary history as (reportedly) a major inspiration for Jack Keefe, the brash, eccentric ballplayer who is the protagonist of Ring Lardner's classic book of fictional letters, *You Know Me Al* (1916).[8]

Why did Bodie choose to play under an assumed name? As the Abbaticchio case demonstrates, Italian surnames were perceived as foreign and difficult; they did not trip off the Anglo-Saxon tongue as easily as Tinker, Evers, and Chance. For many Italian Americans, it was more desirable to conceal their ethnic identity so as to appear more American and therefore acceptable and mainstream. The bias against "odd" names was so blatant that in a story that appeared on 12 May 1918, *New York Tribune* reporter Wood Ballard could write of Bodie: "Ping needs a stage name. Pezzolo wouldn't look well in a box score." Not only would it not "look well," it would likely be inaccurate. Franceto Sanguenitta Pezzola, Francis Stephano Pezzolo, and Francisco Luigi Pizzola are just a few of the many variations that have appeared in print over the years. For the record, the proper form is Francesco Stefano Pezzolo.[9]

It is ironic that the first of what was to be a large number of Italian American players to have an impact in New York, with its huge Italian population, played under an assumed name. To add to the irony, even though Ping Bodie abandoned his family name, he was proud to think of himself (mistakenly) as the first Italian to play in the big leagues. In *The Sporting News* obituary, Bodie is quoted as acknowledging that his father had been angry about the name change "because I became a national figure and the first player of Italian descent to reach the majors." Bodie's claim is particularly curious since his major league career began in 1911, only one year after Ed Abbaticchio's ended. Perhaps Bodie simply didn't recognize other players as Italians from their names. When Babe Pinelli, who was playing for the Detroit Tigers in 1920, asked Bodie, "What's the idea of claiming you're the only Italian ballplayer in the big leagues?", Bodie replied, "I am." At which point Pinelli said, "What do you think I am, a Chinaman?"[10]

Apart from his role as one of the first baseball "characters," Bodie holds a special place in Italian American baseball history as the first in a long line of major league players of Italian descent from the San Francisco area. The list includes Hall of Famers Ernie Lombardi, Tony Lazzeri, and Joe DiMaggio. At least seventeen Italian Americans from the San Francisco area broke into the majors prior to 1950.

Except for Joe Giannini (a shortstop who appeared in one game for the Boston Red Sox in 1911), Babe Pinelli was the first San Francisco native to follow Bodie to the majors. Unlike Bodie, Pinelli did not play under a pseudonym, but he did abbreviate his birth name. Born Rinaldo Angelo Paolinelli, he became Ralph Pinelli in order to accommodate the media bias of his time. "I shortened it to Pinelli when I began to play ball and my name began to appear in box scores," he explained in his autobiography: "Pinelli was easier for sports writers."[11]

When Pinelli was ten years old, his father, an immigrant who ran a fruit and vegetable store, was crushed by a telephone pole during the 1906 earthquake. In order to help his mother support the family of three sons and a daughter, he left school and worked at various jobs. He also earned a reputation as a tough kid on the streets; he had, in his words, "firecrackers in my blood" (8). More than anything, though, he loved to play baseball.

A diminutive third baseman, Pinelli alternated between the Pacific Coast League and the majors between 1917 and 1921, playing for both the White Sox and Tigers. After hitting .339 with fifty stolen bases for the Oakland Oaks in 1921, he was signed by Cincinnati, where he had the unenviable task of replacing third baseman Heinie Groh, a favorite of the city's large German fan base. But Pinelli himself had support in

Cincinnati from the local Italian population, which formed the Pinelli Rooters fan club; its slogan was "Viva Pinelli." Pinelli stayed with the Reds until his major league career ended in 1927.

Always known as a slick fielder, Pinelli was renowned as the master of the hidden-ball trick. In his eight-year career in the majors, he hit for a .276 average. His best season came in 1924, when he hit .306 in 144 games and stole twenty-three bases. That year, he became the first Italian American to receive consideration for the Most Valuable Player award, finishing twelfth in the National League with seven votes.

Throughout his playing career, Pinelli struggled with the "firecrackers" in his blood. He stood five feet, nine inches and weighed 165 pounds, but he was a fiery player who, on occasion, fought with teammates as well as opposing players. One of his fights was with Bob Smith, a reserve infielder for the Boston Braves, who taunted Pinelli from the dugout, calling him a "dago." That was not the only time Pinelli heard that epithet. "From 1922 to 1925 I was the only Italian in the National League," he wrote in his autobiography. "I'd taken a riding from the bench jockeys and I'd had to keep my fist cocked" (73).

When, near the end of his playing days in the major leagues, Pinelli thought about becoming an umpire, he realized that in order to succeed, he would have to learn to control his temper. When Pinelli told Bill Klem of his future plans, the legendary umpire offered this piece of advice: "Get rid of that chip on your shoulder" (77).

After his big league career ended in 1927, Pinelli played in the Pacific Coast League through 1932. The year after he ended his playing career, he got the chance to prove he could heed Klem's advice when he was hired by the PCL, thus beginning "the transition from fiery player to self-controlled umpire" (95). After two seasons in the Coast League, Pinelli became the first Italian American umpire in major league history when he was hired by the National League in 1935. He would remain in the big leagues for the next twenty-two years.

His ability to control his temper was tested early and often. One of the testers in his first year was none other than Babe Ruth, who was winding up his career with the Boston Braves. Pinelli recalled that when Ruth came to bat in the first inning, he greeted the umpire with the same "Hi ya, Wop" salutation he had used when they played against each other in the American League. "As I was the only Italian in the American League at the time," Pinelli wrote, "'Wop' seemed to him appropriately distinguishing."[12] Then, when Pinelli called him out on strikes in his first

at bat, Ruth came at the rookie ump. "He bulged with wrath," Pinelli
wrote. "He started with 'Wop' and called me everything" (116). But
Pinelli had learned to control the firecrackers and walked away.

Pinelli went on to have a distinguished career as an umpire, winning the respect of players and managers with his evenhanded, and even-
tempered, demeanor. So cautious was he in ejecting people from games
that he earned the nickname of "the Soft Thumb." Over a span of
twenty-two years and some 3,400 games, Pinelli never missed a single
umpiring assignment. On 9 October 1956, his career ended in historic
fashion; in his very last game as a home plate umpire, he called Don
Larsen's perfect game in the sixth game of the World Series.[13]

If Abbaticchio was the pioneer and Bodie the first Italian American
to capture public attention, it was Pinelli who had the greatest long-term
impact because of his exemplary role as umpire. As an umpire, he became
the first Italian American to assume a role of responsibility and authority
in the world of major league baseball. By performing that job with dignity and skill, he gained respect and conveyed a positive image of his
ethnic group to everyone involved with big league baseball.

The First Italian Superstar

By the mid-twenties, no more than thirteen players identifiable as Italian Americans had ever played in the major leagues. (Of those, five barely
had time for a cup of espresso with "careers" ranging from one to three
games.) But the changing demographics of the population spurred baseball executives to expand the ethnic makeup of their rosters. Prior to
the 1920s, baseball games were attended mostly by relatively affluent
white-collar workers who had the leisure time to attend games that were
played primarily on weekday afternoons. In the twenties, a higher standard of living and the curtailment of blue laws that had prohibited Sunday games resulted in a broadening of the fan base. Now people from all
social classes were going to ball games, including the working-class children and grandchildren of immigrants.[14]

Baseball executives sought to capitalize on the broader fan base by
recruiting players who would appeal specifically to ethnic fans. John
McGraw, manager of the New York Giants, tried unsuccessfully in the
twenties to develop Jewish stars who would appeal to the large Jewish
population of New York.[15]

The Yankees were more successful in their efforts to find—and market

Tony Lazzeri. National Baseball Hall of Fame Library, Cooperstown, N.Y.

—a hero for the largest Italian American community in the United States. Ironically, they found him on the opposite coast. Like Bodie and Pinelli, Tony Lazzeri was a native of San Francisco. Born in 1903, Lazzeri left school at the age of fifteen to work as a boilermaker's assistant. Four years later, in 1922, he began his professional career in the Pacific Coast League.

In 1925, he hit 60 home runs and drove in 222 runs (in 197 games) for the Salt Lake City Bees. He joined the Yankees in 1926, stepping right into the starting lineup, and was a key member of the famed 1927 "Murderer's Row" Yankees, thought by many to be the greatest team of all time. In his rookie year, he hit 18 homers (third in the American League behind Ruth and Al Simmons) and drove in 114 runs (trailing only Ruth in the American League). In each of the next four years, he hit over .300, reaching a career high of .354 in 1929. His lifetime average over fourteen years was .292. From 1926 to 1937, Lazzeri was seventh in the American League in total home runs and sixth in runs batted in, averaging ninety-six RBIs per year. On 24 May 1936, he became the first player in major league history to hit two grand slams in one game, and he set the still-standing American League record with 11 runs batted in. Lazzeri was also a power hitter with speed; three times he finished in the top five in stolen bases.

At five feet, eleven inches and 160 pounds, Lazzeri surprised observers with his power; his work as a boilermaker's assistant had given him tremendous strength in his forearms. Like Pinelli, Lazzeri was a tough kid from the tough streets of San Francisco. "It was always fight or get licked," recalled Lazzeri, "and I never got licked."[16] But, unlike Pinelli, Lazzeri did not get into scraps as a major leaguer. On the field he was a no-nonsense, hard-nosed player, but he was mild-mannered and quiet, well liked and respected by both teammates and opponents.

Lazzeri, in fact, was so quiet that one reporter wrote that interviewing him was "like trying to mine coal with a nail file and a pair of scissors." The familiar anecdote of Lazzeri's cross-country drive from San Francisco to the Yankees' spring training camp in Florida in 1936, during which he and teammates Joe DiMaggio and Frank Crosetti hardly spoke, was confirmed by Crosetti in a phone interview: "We didn't say much on the whole drive. The three of us were quiet."[17]

But there was also a mischievous side to Lazzeri, who was a notorious locker room prankster. Babe Ruth was one of his favorite targets. In addition to nailing the Babe's shoes to the floor of his locker, Lazzeri liked to "doctor" Ruth's eyedrops. When Ruth came into the clubhouse after a long night on the town, he would clear his eyes with the drops, saying, "These are what makes the Babe hit." But Lazzeri had already emptied the solution from the bottle and filled it with water.[18]

In spite of his outstanding career, Lazzeri remains one of those unfortunate ballplayers, like Fred Merkle and Bill Buckner, who are remembered primarily, and unfairly, for a single lapse. Lazzeri's moment of infamy came in his rookie year of 1926. In the seventh inning of the seventh game of the World Series, Lazzeri came to bat with the bases loaded and the Yankees trailing the Cardinals, 3-2. St. Louis manager Rogers Hornsby went to the mound and brought in the veteran Grover Cleveland Alexander to face Lazzeri. (Both Lazzeri and Alexander, incidentally, suffered from epilepsy.) On a 2-1 count, Lazzeri hit a vicious drive down the left field line that was just foul. (Some reports say it would have been a home run, others a double. Either way, it would have given the Yanks the lead.) Then, on the next pitch, Lazzeri struck out swinging, ending the threat.

Lazzeri's moment of failure is even immortalized on Alexander's Hall of Fame plaque, which reads, in part: "Won 1926 world championship for Cardinals by striking out Lazzeri with bases full in final crisis at Yankee Stadium." This quotation, with its reference to the "final crisis," also perpetuates the misconception that Lazzeri's strikeout ended the Series when, in fact, the Yankees had two more innings to come from behind.

By comparison, his performances in later World Series games are all but forgotten. In the fourth and clinching game of the 1932 Series against the Cubs, Lazzeri hit two home runs. (That Series is best remembered for Ruth's "called" home run off of Charlie Root in game three.) In the second game of the 1936 Series, Lazzeri again came to the plate with the bases loaded and this time hit a grand slam in an 18-4 Yankee victory over the Giants.

His contemporaries thought of Lazzeri as anything but a loser. Referring to the strikeout against Alexander, Yankees manager Miller Huggins said: "Anyone can strike out, but ballplayers like Lazzeri come along once in a generation." And General Manager Ed Barrow later wrote of Lazzeri's impact as a rookie in 1926, the year of his fateful strikeout: "He was the making of that ball club, holding it together, guiding it, and inspiring it. He was one of the greatest ballplayers I have ever known." As impressive as his offensive statistics are, they tell only part of the story of Lazzeri's significance to the Yankees; he was widely considered one of the smartest of ballplayers. Legendary sportswriter Red Smith wrote of Lazzeri that "in all his time with the Yankees there was no one whose hitting and fielding and hustle and fire and brilliantly swift thinking meant more to any team."[19]

Both as a productive player and as an ethnic hero, Lazzeri was everything Yankee officials could have hoped for. He was idolized by Italian fans, who would chant his nickname of "Poosh-'Em-Up," a tag he earned for his ability to advance runners with his timely hitting. Some opposing players, on the other hand, were less benevolent toward Lazzeri's Italian heritage. In a 1927 article in *Baseball Magazine*, F. C. Lane noted that "opposing catchers and coaches try to get Lazzeri's goat by calling him Dago and Wop."[20]

It was not just in New York that Lazzeri drew Italian fans. Noting the large number of Italians who came to see their hero, Lane reported that "Yankee management have capitalized this popularity of his, during the season, with a whole series of Lazzeri Days at various ballparks. . . . Moreover, Lazzeri has been the guest of honor at no fewer than five banquets in various cities of the circuit." One of those banquets took place in September 1927 at New York's Hotel Commodore and was attended by a thousand guests. The *New York Times* reported: "Speeches lauding the brilliant work of the popular infielder and his exemplary conduct both on and off the field rang through the grand ballroom."[21]

In 1938–39, Lazzeri ended his playing career as a part-time player for the Cubs, Dodgers, and Giants. He then managed in the minor leagues (Toronto, Portsmouth, and Wilkes-Barre) through 1943 before retiring to San Francisco. It was there that he died in 1946, at the age of forty-two, from a heart attack.

If ever a player was destined to play in the shadow of his teammates, it was Lazzeri. Though he was one of the most productive hitters on one of the most powerful teams of all time, he was overshadowed by Ruth and Gehrig, the most awesome duo in baseball history. Nevertheless, his fame was duly noted by contemporary writers, some of whom betrayed the ethnic stereotyping common at the time even as they were complimentary. During Lazzeri's rookie year, *The Sporting News* referred to him as "the walloping wop"; the next year the same publication called him the "popular Wop." And in an anonymous entry in the 1933 edition of *Who's Who in Major League Baseball,* the writer noted: "Though of Italian paternity this great keystone guardian chatters little Neapolitan" and quoted teammate Frank Crosetti's assessment of Lazzeri's spoken Italian: "Tony's wop is terrible."[22]

Crosetti, also of San Francisco, had joined Lazzeri in the Yankees infield in 1932. (The Yankees had bought his contract from the San Francisco Seals for seventy-five thousand dollars, a hefty price tag in the midst of the Depression.) Together they formed the Yankees double play combo between 1932 and 1937, the longest consecutive streak of any pair of Yankee middle infielders. Crosetti, who finished his career with a lifetime batting average of .245, played for the Yankees for seventeen years. He then went on to serve as their third base coach from 1948 to 1968—he appeared as a player or coach in 122 World Series games—thus setting the all-time record for service in a Yankee uniform.

The First MVP

Yet another native of the San Francisco area became the most famous Italian American to play in the big leagues between Lazzeri and DiMaggio. Ernesto Natali "Ernie" Lombardi was born in Oakland, California, in 1908, the son of Italian immigrants who operated a grocery store. After hitting .377, .366, and .370 in consecutive years for Oakland in the Pacific Coast League, the right-handed slugger was acquired in 1931 by the Dodgers, who hoped Lombardi's presence would attract more Italian fans to Ebbets Field.[23]

Lombardi was traded the following year to Cincinnati, where he played for the next ten seasons and hit over .300 in seven of those years. His highest average came in 1935 when he hit .343; he hit .333 and .334 the following two seasons. Then, in 1938, he became the first catcher, and the first Italian American, to win a batting title with a .342 average.[24] That same year, Lombardi (who caught both of Johnny Vander Meer's back-to-back no-hitters) also became the first Italian American to win a Most Valuable Player Award.

Lombardi was six feet, three inches tall and weighed 230 pounds, but his most distinctive physical feature was his large nose, which earned him the nickname of "Schnozz." Despite his size, he was an able catcher with a strong and accurate arm. His lack of mobility, however, was an obvious liability; he holds the major league record for most years leading the league in passed balls (ten).

Lombardi's slowness afoot was legendary. Infielders routinely played exceptionally deep, knowing they had plenty of time to throw him out, both because he was slow and because he hit the ball so hard. He once told Dodger shortstop Pee Wee Reese, "It was five years before I learned you weren't an outfielder." Lombardi, who used an interlocking golf-style grip on the bat, was also known for his screaming line drives. Giants pitcher Carl Hubbell once said, "I thought he might hurt me, even kill me, with one of those liners."[25]

In 1942, the Reds sold Lombardi to the Braves. He hit .330, winning his second National League batting title (though by current standards, his 309 times at bat would be too few to qualify for the title). He then spent the last six years of his career with the New York Giants. Over his seventeen-year career, Lombardi hit over .300 ten times and compiled a .306 lifetime average, played in five All-Star games and two World Series, helping lead the Reds to the pennant in 1939 and 1940. No less an authority than Ted Williams has called Lombardi "one of the greatest batters of all time."[26]

But, like Lazzeri, Lombardi became the victim of a single World Series play that haunted him for the rest of his life. Unlike Lazzeri's strikeout, however, Lombardi's lapse did not come at a crucial moment. It was the tenth inning of the fourth game of the 1939 World Series, and the Reds were already down three games to none to the Yankees. Ironically, Lombardi's moment of infamy involved two other prominent Italian American players. The score was tied 4-4 when Joe DiMaggio came to the plate with Frank Crosetti on first and Charlie Keller on third. When DiMaggio hit a single to right, Crosetti scored the go-ahead run. When the right fielder bobbled the ball, Keller rounded third and headed for home. As Lombardi applied the tag, Keller bowled him over, leaving the catcher momentarily stunned. DiMaggio, seeing Lombardi lying on the ground and the ball a few feet away, headed for home. Before Lombardi could recover, DiMaggio slid across home with the final run in a 7-4 victory. In other words, DiMaggio's run was meaningless, but Lombardi became the goat and never lived down that one moment, which became known as "Ernie's Snooze."[27]

His lumbering slowness, his large nose, and his generally ungainly appearance, together with the stigma of "Ernie's Snooze," turned Lombardi into something of a comic figure and robbed him of due recognition by the press—if not by his peers—which treated him more as a pathetic than heroic figure. But it was his failure to gain admission to the Hall of Fame that hurt him the most. As the years passed, he became increasingly bitter and despondent and even attempted suicide in 1953. In 1986, nine years after his death, the Veterans Committee voted Ernie Lombardi into the Hall of Fame.

1936—The Italians Arrive

While no more than thirteen Italian Americans had ever played in the majors by 1926, no fewer than twenty-three were playing in the big leagues in 1936. In many ways, the 1936 season was a watershed year for

Italian American participation in major league baseball, and not just because it marked the sensational rookie season of Joe DiMaggio. Several other Italian players were receiving media attention.

In a 1936 story entitled "Viva Italia," Dan Daniel acclaimed the arrival of several Italian American players in the majors. "This surely is Italy's year," he proclaimed. "Italy," he wrote, "finally has invaded baseball with a bang." In addition to Lazzeri, Crosetti, DiMaggio, and Lombardi, several of the players mentioned in his story would have notable careers, including Gus Mancuso, Zeke Bonura, Tony Cuccinello, Cookie Lavagetto, Phil Cavarretta, and Dolph Camilli. Daniel noted just how remarkable this "invasion" was at the time. "The time was when it was considered an oddity for any club to have an Italian ballplayer." For a team to have two (Lazzeri and Crosetti) in the lineup "was considered phenomenal or bizarre, according to . . . the manner in which your psychology responded to the invasion of baseball by the sons of immigrants from Europe." According to Daniel, the exploits of DiMaggio, Lazzeri, and Crosetti "have intrigued Italians all over the country" and "have established in every city visited by the Yankees . . . a new school of fans."[28]

By 1936, Italian Americans had arrived—not only in numbers but in achievement. Of the top thirty-two batting averages in the National League, six belonged to Italian Americans. Three players (Mancuso, Camilli, and Lombardi) received MVP votes in the National League and two (DiMaggio and Bonura) in the American League.[29]

Nevertheless, stereotypical media portrayal continued through the thirties. In the 1936 edition of *Who's Who in the Major Leagues,* for example, players of Italian heritage were almost always identified as such, whereas ethnic references were almost nonexistent for other players. Ernie Lombardi was "one of numerous Italians who won major league renown," Lazzeri was "the lanky Italian," and DiMaggio "the giant Italian." A Willard Mullin cartoon in 1936 depicted Lazzeri, Crosetti, and DiMaggio as the "Three Musketeers from Frisco" singing "Oh, the miners came in '49, th' wops in '51."[30]

Two of the more common adjectives applied to Italian ballplayers were "fiery" and "colorful," as if they were code words signaling the common perception of Italians as hot-blooded and temperamental. Dan Daniel, in his "Viva Italia" story of 1936, characterized Italians as an "agile race, a sturdy, enduring and durable people, quick to learn and aggressive to the highest degree." And, in a 1939 *Sporting News* article, Frederick Lieb wrote of pitcher Italo Chelini, "his hot Italian blood gets him in trouble."[31]

The most significant event of 1936, of course, was the arrival of Joseph Paul DiMaggio, the much-heralded rookie from San Francisco who had hit in sixty-one consecutive games in the Pacific Coast League at the age of nineteen. DiMaggio was one of five sons of parents who emigrated in 1902 from Sicily. Giuseppe DiMaggio expected his sons to be fishermen, like himself, but baseball was a strong attraction to the children of immigrants living in San Francisco. The two oldest brothers, Tom and Michael, did become fishermen, but the other three all became major league ballplayers. A year after Joe's arrival, he was joined in the majors by older brother Vince, a strikeout-prone outfielder who played for five different teams between 1937 and 1946. Then, in 1940, both were joined by younger brother Dominic, a sparkling center fielder for the Red Sox who hit .298 over eleven years. But it was Joe who became one of the most celebrated athletes of all time.

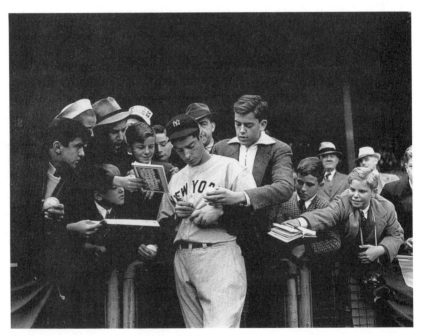

Joe DiMaggio, early in his career, surrounded by adoring fans. National Baseball Hall of Fame Library, Cooperstown, N.Y.

DiMaggio quickly became the undisputed leader of the great Yankee teams that appeared in ten World Series during his thirteen-year career, winning nine of them. He was chosen three times as the American League's Most Valuable Player, and he holds what many consider to be the most remarkable baseball record of all, a fifty-six-game hitting streak set in 1941. In 1969, on the occasion of major league baseball's centennial, he was selected as the greatest living ballplayer. Whereas Lazzeri played in the shadow of Ruth and Gehrig, it was DiMaggio who cast the shadow on his Yankee teams.

But before DiMaggio became an American hero, he was an ethnic hero, the most important hero Italian Americans have had. To a nation of immigrants accustomed to facing prejudice and the poverty of the Depression, he came to symbolize the fulfillment of America's promise. As Frank Deford wrote soon after DiMaggio died, "curiously, long before his death DiMaggio had been forgotten for what matters most in his legend—that he was a significant ethnic figure. Not quite as Jackie Robinson was, nor as Roberto Clemente, but as the first great American star of Italian heritage. Twenty-five thousand Italian-Americans came out to Yankee Stadium that day in 1936 when DiMaggio made his debut."[32]

Not even Joe DiMaggio was totally immune from stereotypical depiction. In the years prior to World War II, sportswriters liked to remind readers of DiMaggio's ethnicity. He may have been the best player in baseball, but his first name often appeared in print as Giuseppe—as if to suggest that, for all his greatness, he was somehow not quite an authentic American hero. His picture appeared on the cover of the 1 May 1939 issue of *Life* magazine, but the story by Noel Busch, while meant to be flattering, contained strong evidence that DiMaggio's ethnic background made him something less than an All-American.

Acknowledging DiMaggio as "baseball's no. 1 contemporary player," Busch noted that "Italians, bad at war, are well-suited for milder competitions" (63). DiMaggio may be blessed with great natural talent as an athlete, but off the field he displays the traits of "shiftlessness" and "idleness" (64). Busch also seemed surprised by DiMaggio's relatively high level of assimilation, judged, apparently, by the writer's general perception of Italian Americans: "Although he learned Italian first, Joe, now 24, speaks English without an accent and is otherwise well-adapted to most U.S. mores. Instead of olive oil or smelly bear grease he keeps his hair slick with water. He never reeks of garlic and prefers chicken chow mein to spaghetti" (66).

DiMaggio overcame the stereotypical depiction of him as an "ethnic" ballplayer both by his achievements on the field and by his military service in World War II. By enlisting in the army in February 1943 to fight against the Axis powers, which included his parents' homeland, he established his credentials as an assimilated American. Following the war, media portrayals of DiMaggio as an Italian ballplayer faded, and he was depicted more and more as a great American hero.

Unlike Lazzeri, DiMaggio became a national hero whose appeal was not limited to New Yorkers or to Italian Americans. The son of Sicilian immigrants and a high school dropout who had no desire to be a fisherman like his father, he became not only the most famous athlete of his time but one of the most admired men in America. He was, in fact, the great American hero of his time, one who was immortalized by Hemingway in *The Old Man and the Sea* in 1952. By the time songwriter Paul Simon posed the question, "Where have you gone, Joe DiMaggio?" in his 1968 song "Mrs. Robinson," the Yankee Clipper had become a symbol of a more heroic and noble time.

In Joe DiMaggio, the Italian American ballplayer not only entered the mainstream of American popular culture, he dominated it as few have before or since. He came to symbolize the fulfillment of America's promise. And the myth was only enhanced when, in 1954, this olive-skinned, slick-haired son of a Sicilian fisherman married Marilyn Monroe, the golden goddess of postwar America who was perceived by many as the feminine manifestation of the American Dream. By carefully guarding both his privacy and his image until the time of his death, DiMaggio retained an aura of mystery that only added to his enduring mystique.

DiMaggio, who played from 1936 to 1951, was a link between early Italian American players, like Lazzeri, and the more numerous "second generation" that came to the big leagues in the late thirties and forties. Yogi Berra, Phil Rizzuto, Vic Raschi, and Billy Martin (born Alfred Pesano), for example, were all key figures on Yankee teams that continued to dominate major league baseball throughout the forties and fifties. And their crosstown rivals, the Brooklyn Dodgers, also featured several prominent Italian Americans, including Carl Furillo, Ralph Branca, Cookie Lavagetto, and Roy Campanella, the son of an Italian American father and an African American mother. Like Berra, Campanella won the Most Valuable Player Award three times and is enshrined in the Hall of Fame.

There have been any number of outstanding Italian American major leaguers since the era of DiMaggio: Rocky Colavito, Ron Santo, Tony Conigliaro, Joe Torre, Ken Caminiti, and Mike Piazza, just to name a few. For all of them, the way was paved by those who played prior to World War II, when a player's ethnicity was still a matter of note.

After the war, however, things were different. As others have pointed out in this volume, references to the ethnic heritage of players of European descent became much less common after the war. Both DiMaggio and Hank Greenberg, the great Jewish star, went from being ethnic heroes to national heroes.[33] And the number of Italian Americans in major league baseball began a slow but steady decline as other economic opportunities opened up, thanks to the GI bill and the postwar economic boom. But for much of the first half of the twentieth century, baseball provided a window on the American Dream, engendering in second-generation youth an awareness of those ideals that the arbiters of mainstream culture identified as "American" and providing a bridge between the customs of their immigrant parents and the world they found outside the home.

Baseball provided a shortcut to assimilation for only a relative handful of Italian Americans. However, the visible success of ballplayers like Lazzeri and DiMaggio undoubtedly served as a source of ethnic pride for many in the Italian community and inspired hope that they too could prosper in America. Sociological implications aside, there is no question that Italian Americans have played a significant role in major league baseball, so much so that today the names of DiMaggio, Berra, and Rizzuto are as much a part of baseball lore as those of Ruth, Wagner, and Cobb.

Notes

1. John Foster Carr, "Coming of the Italian," *The Outlook* 82 (24 February 1906): 429.

2. Abbaticchio played football against another early two-sport star, Christy Mathewson, who was a fullback and kicker with the Pittsburgh Stars in 1900. Recalling those days, Abbaticchio later said: "I played against Matty when we both were fullbacks. What a ballplayer that fellow was!" (*Fort Lauderdale Daily News,* 13 May 1952.) Also see Stan Grosshandler, "Two-Sport Stars," in John Thorn and Pete Palmer, eds., *Total Baseball,* 3d ed. (New York: Harper Collins, 1993), 237–43.

3. At the time, the average major league salary was under $2,500. See

Robert Frederick Burk, *Never Just a Game: Players, Owners and American Baseball to 1920* (Chapel Hill: University of North Carolina Press, 1994), 160.

4. Quoted in *The Sporting News,* 27 December 1961.

5. Robert Creamer, *Babe: The Legend Comes to Life* (New York: Penguin, 1983), 213.

6. Creamer, 222

7. *New York Times,* 8 March 1918; Creamer, 147; *The Sporting News,* 27 December 1961.

8. *The Sporting News,* 27 December 1961.

9. The proper form of Bodie's Italian name was confirmed in a letter to me (21 July 1999) from his nephew, Joseph Pezzolo (the son of Bodie's brother, Jack), who cited both his grandmother's notebook, in which she had written the names and birth dates of her children, and his grandfather's mortgage in the name of Joseph Pezzolo.

10. Frank Graham, "Hidden Ball King: Pinelli," *Baseball Digest* 7, no. 11 (November 1948): 53.

11. Babe Pinelli, as told to Joe King, *Mr. Ump* (Philadelphia: Westminster Press, 1953), 11. Subsequent references will be cited in the text.

12. Here Pinelli's recollection is faulty. In both years he played in the American League (1918 and 1920), Ping Bodie was also in the league.

13. Two other Italian Americans played prominent roles in Larsen's perfect game. The Yankees catcher was Yogi Berra and the Giants pitcher was Sal Maglie, who gave up only five hits in the complete game, 2-0 loss.

14. Steven A. Riess, *Touching Base: Professional Baseball and American Culture in the Progressive Era* (Westport, Conn.: Greenwood Press, 1980), 39.

15. Peter Levine, *Ellis Island to Ebbets Field: Sport and the American Jewish Experience* (New York: Oxford University Press, 1992), 109.

16. *San Francisco Star Chronicle,* 11 December 1930.

17. Frank Graham, *The New York Yankees, 1900–1946* (New York: G. P. Putnam's Sons, 1946), 115; Frank Crosetti, telephone interview, 4 September 1998.

18. Dario Lodigiani, telephone interview, 6 March 1999. Lodigiani, another San Francisco native, was Lazzeri's roommate when the latter was the player-manager for Toronto in the International League in 1940.

19. Mike Shatzkin, ed., *The Ballplayers* (New York: William Morrow, 1990), 609; Edward Grant Barrow and James M. Kahn, *My Fifty Years in Baseball* (New York: Coward-McCann, 1951), 145; Red Smith, column of 9 August 1946, repr. in *Red Smith on Baseball* (Chicago: Ivan R. Dee, 2000), 17.

20. F. C. Lane, "A Great Natural Ball Player Is Tony Lazzeri," *Baseball Magazine* 40 (December 1927): 305.

21. Lane, 305; *New York Times,* 9 September 1927.

22. *The Sporting News,* 8 March 1926 and 16 June 1927; Harold Johnson, ed., *Who's Who in Major League Baseball* (Chicago: Buxton, 1933), 256.

23. *The Sporting News,* 29 January 1931.

24. "King" Kelly, a catcher, won the National League batting title in 1884 and 1886. However, in both years, he caught in fewer than half the games in which he appeared. Lombardi caught in all 129 of his games. In 1926, Eugene "Bubbles" Hargrave hit .353, but had only 326 official times at bat, and the batting title is credited to Paul Waner, who hit .336.

25. *The Sporting News,* 15 October 1977.

26. Quoted in Lee Allen, *Cooperstown Corner: Columns for "The Sporting News," 1962–1969* (Cleveland: SABR, n.d.), 61.

27. While written accounts of the incident suggest that Lombardi lay senseless as DiMaggio scored, film of the game shows that Lombardi did recover the ball and lunged toward home to apply the tag, but DiMaggio eluded the tag with a hook slide away from the catcher's outreached hand.

28. Daniel M. Daniel, "Viva Italia," *Baseball Magazine* 57, no. 2 (July 1936): 347.

29. Another player to receive MVP votes was Frank Demaree, whose birth name is listed in several printed sources as Joseph Dimaria (see Hy Turkin and S. C. Thompson, *The Official Encyclopedia of Baseball* [New York: Barnes and Co., 1951]; and Thorn and Palmer). However, on both his American League questionnaire (filled out by Demaree himself) and his Hall of Fame questionnaire (filled out by his widow), his nationality is listed as German-Irish.

30. *The Sporting News,* 21 May 1936.

31. Daniel, 349; *The Sporting News,* 28 October 1939.

32. Frank Deford, "Our Nation Turns Its Lonely Eyes to You," CNNSI.com, 8 March 1999.

33. For an overview of this topic, see G. Edward White, *Creating the National Pastime: Baseball Transforms Itself, 1903–1953* (Princeton, N.J.: Princeton University Press, 1996), ch. 8.

★7★

From Pike to Green with Greenberg in Between: Jewish Americans and the National Pastime

STEVEN A. RIESS

American Jews have not been among the most prominent ethnic groups in the production of high-quality baseball players.[1] Nonetheless, Jews have contributed in significant ways to the history of American baseball. There was a Jewish professional ballplayer even before the first professional league was organized, and a few, particularly Hank Greenberg and Sandy Koufax, achieved great prominence. Jews were among the early owners of professional baseball teams, and their representation in baseball's inner circles today exceeds their representation in society as a whole. Furthermore, Jewish journalists played an important role in popularizing the national pastime, and Jewish novelists have been among its most eminent critics.[2] This essay examines the Jewish contribution to the national pastime, primarily on the playing field. I argue that the Jewish encounter with baseball reflected their experience with the broader culture, particularly their migration from urban slums to suburbia and the problems of acculturation, assimilation, and anti-Semitism.

German Jews in the National Pastime

Most Jews living in the United States in the nineteenth century were of German origin, part of the large mid-century German migration. They came to America for economic betterment and brought with them skills, education, some capital, and pride in their native culture. German Jews were largely emancipated, modern Jews, whose leisure patterns were not very different from gentile Germans, although they were stereotyped as unathletic and physically unfit. However, in actuality, Jewish Americans were notable contributors to the rise of American sport even before the Civil War. The first noted athletes were Anglo-Jewish prizefighters like Barney Aaron, American lightweight champion in the 1850s. However, the second generation made significant contributions in upper-middle-class sports like track and field and football and made sport a cornerstone at the Young Men's Hebrew Association by the mid-1870s. The rise of overt anti-Semitism at recreational areas and metropolitan men's clubs in the 1880s encouraged German Jews to form their own athletic and country clubs.[3]

There were just six major league Jewish baseball players in the nineteenth century, including Lipman Pike and Nate Bertonstock, who both played in the National Association of Professional Base Ball Players (NA) in its first year. Pike was a Brooklynite of Dutch descent who averaged over .300 in ten seasons in the early professional leagues and was a manager for three years. In 1866, Pike became one of the first professional ballplayers as a twenty-dollar-a-week second baseman for the Philadelphia Athletics. He later starred with the New York Mutuals and the Brooklyn Atlantics and, in 1871, played for and managed Troy (NA). Pike played in all of the NA's five seasons, batting .321, and then in 1876 moved to St. Louis in the new National League. The following season, he managed Cincinnati and led the NL in homers with four. Francis Richter, editor of *Sporting Life*, selected him for his 1870–80 all-star team.[4]

Jews were much more active in the business side of early professional baseball than on the playing side. This reflected the strong entrepreneurial tradition Jewish immigrants brought to the United States. The first Jewish sports entrepreneur was probably John M. Brunswick, who established a billiard manufacturing company in the 1840s. German Jewish businessmen became very involved in early professional baseball, partly as an investment but also to gain acceptance in their communities and to show their civic-mindedness. They were similar to the Jewish artisans and nickelodeon operators who later built up the motion picture industry. Both enterprises were originally low-status businesses avoided by men of old wealth, who preferred more conservative and prestigious investments. There were German Jewish owners in southern cities like Atlanta, Augusta, Birmingham, Houston, Macon, Mobile, and New Orleans, and there were several in the majors, most notably Cincinnati, which had a prominent Jewish community. They included Nathan Menderson, the team president in 1880, clothier Aaron Stern, who owned the team from 1882 to 1890, and Louis Kramer, a founder and later president (1891) of the American Association. The Jewish baseball connection there resumed in 1902 when Mayor Julius Fleischmann, heir to a yeast manufacturing empire, led a syndicate that purchased the Reds.[5]

German Jewish major league magnates at the turn of the century included the Frank brothers in Baltimore (1901–2), immigrant Barney Dreyfuss, who owned franchises in Louisville and Pittsburgh from 1888 until 1932, and Andrew Freedman, a New York Tammanyite who owned the Giants (1895–1902). Freedman was born in New York in 1860 and graduated from City College with a law degree. He made a fortune in the real estate business, abetted by his political contacts, including membership on Tammany's finance committee, as treasurer of the national Democratic Party, and as Boss Richard Croker's close friend and confidant.[6]

Freedman was one of the most unpopular owners in baseball history. He fought with fans, ballplayers, umpires, and sportswriters, underpaid his players, and went through sixteen managers in eight years. Freedman's fellow owners were frightened by his political clout, felt he was hurting baseball's public image, and believed he was ruining the lucrative New York market. The Giants owner was subjected to considerable anti-Semitism. During an 1898 home game against the Baltimore Orioles, ex-Giant Ducky Holmes responded to his old teammates' derision: "Well, I'm glad I'm not working for a sheeny any more." Freedman demanded that umpire Tom Lynch kick Holmes out of the game, but Lynch said he had heard nothing. Freedman then took the Giants off the field, forfeited the game, and returned the fans' money. The league fined Freedman and suspended Holmes for ten games.[7]

Freedman used his clout and connections to keep the American League out of New York in 1901 when it proclaimed itself a major league. He controlled most potential ballpark sites through leases or options and got the Interborough Rapid Transit Company to change its mind about subsidizing a ballpark near one of its new stations. Later that year, he tried unsuccessfully to establish a national baseball trust to make baseball operate more efficiently. He proposed that the NL create a cartel that could move franchises and shift reserved players wherever they would best promote profits. The Giants would get a 30 percent share, with 12 percent for each of Freedman's allies: Brush of Cincinnati, Soden of Boston, and Robison of St. Louis. The other four teams, who were to divide the remaining 34 percent, blocked the plan.[8]

On 7 July 1902, John McGraw jumped from the Baltimore Orioles (AL) to manage the Giants for a four-year, $11,000 contract. McGraw built the Giants into one of the best teams in the majors, abetted by Freedman's purchase of a majority interest in the Orioles, after which McGraw moved four star players to the Giants. The Orioles could no longer field a competitive team, and the AL forfeited the franchise. Later that year, Freedman sold the Giants for $125,000 to John Brush. He was tired of fighting other owners, journalists, and his players and disappointed at the team's unprofitability, continuing poor play, and public criticism. Freedman returned to his business interests, including the building of the New York subway.[9]

There continued to be Jewish owners in the NL but none in the American League after 1902. Besides Dreyfuss, there was Judge Emil Fuchs in Boston (1923–36), Sydney Weil in Cincinnati (1929–33), and advertising executive Albert D. Lasker, a major Cubs stockholder in the World War I era. He was largely responsible for the creation of the commissioner system and the hiring of Judge Kenesaw M. Landis in 1920. Dreyfuss died in 1932 and was succeeded by son-in-law Bill Benswanger who, from 1936 until the team was sold in 1946, was the only Jewish owner in major league baseball.[10]

Baseball and the Eastern European Jew

The two million eastern European Jewish immigrants who arrived in the United States between 1882 and 1914 were quite different from their German compatriots. They came from a premodern world, looked and dressed differently, spoke Yiddish, and were strictly orthodox. Their presence encouraged growing anti-Semitism and nativism in the late nineteenth century, and many German Jews blamed them for causing discrimination. Nonetheless, they helped their coreligionists adjust to life in urban America and sustain their Judaic heritage through such institutions as the Hebrew Immigrant Aid Society and settlement houses like New York's Educational Alliance.[11]

The eastern Europeans were stereotyped as weak, unhealthy, physically

unfit, and unaccustomed to "manly" labor. They arrived with no famili-
arity with sports, which they considered strange "Yankee" institutions
that were a waste of time, if not, like boxing, immoral. Russian Jews had
little free time or discretionary income. They came to America to escape
the czar, work hard, and take care of their families. Their little free time
was spent socializing with family or friends at home or at a coffee shop
or possibly attending the Yiddish Theater. The newcomers were particularly bemused by baseball, an activity in which youths and young men
wearing short pants try to hit a ball with a stick and run around in circles.
Immigrants made fun of newcomers, like Jake (Yekl) the Tailor, protagonist of an Abraham Cahan novelette, because he was a sports fan.[12]

Eastern European parents exerted pressure on sons against playing
sports because they were too dangerous, distracted them from study or
work, and Americanized children at the cost of the traditional culture.
Entertainer Eddie Cantor remembered that the worst thing a parent or
grandparent could call a child was "you baseball player, you."[13] In 1903,
an immigrant father wrote to the *Forward* about his opposition to baseball: "It makes sense to teach a child to play dominoes or chess. However,
what is the point of a crazy game like baseball? The children can get
crippled. When I was a boy we played rabbit, chasing each other, hide and
seek. Later we stopped. If a grown boy played rabbit in Russia, they
would think he had lost his mind. Here in educated America adults play
baseball. They run after a leather ball like children. I want my boy to
grow up to be a *mensch*, not a wild American runner. But he cries his head
off." Editor Cahan agreed that many parents had a problem with their
boys playing ball, but advised, "Let your boys play baseball and play it
well, as long as it does not interfere with their education or get them into
bad company. Half the parents in the Jewish quarter have this problem.
Chess is good, but the body needs to develop also. . . . Baseball develops
the arms, legs, and eyesight. It is played in the fresh air. The wild game
is football—the aristocratic game in the colleges. Accidents and fights
occur in football, but baseball is not dangerous."[14] Four years later, the
Forward printed an article entitled "Der iker fun di base-ball game, erk-
lert far nit keyn sports layt" ("The Fundamentals of Baseball Explained
to Those Unfamiliar with Sports").[15]

Parents could not stop boys from loving baseball. Youngsters growing
up on the Lower East Side of New York or the Near West Side of Chicago
identified baseball with America and wanted to become acculturated.

They read about baseball and their heroes in newspapers and cheap magazines and debated about it in their free time. However, they rarely went to games and had limited opportunity to play "hardball" because their neighborhoods did not have enough space. Kids probably were first exposed to baseball by playing punchball, stoopball, or stickball in crowded alleys where they made up ground rules to adjust to their space. George Burns and his pals adapted baseball to their crowded Lower East Side streets: "Our playground was the middle of Rivington Street. We only played games that needed very little equipment, games like kick-the-can. . . . When we played baseball, we used a broom handle and a rubber ball. A manhole cover was homeplate, a fire hydrant was first base, second base was a lamp post, and Mr. Gitletz, who used to bring a kitchen chair down to sit and watch us play, was third base. One time I slid into Mr. Gitletz; he caught the ball and tagged me out."[16]

These boys seldom attended professional games because children's tickets cost at least fifteen cents and a round-trip on the trolley was another ten cents. Boys could get a pass by retrieving balls hit out of the park or helping to clean the stands before a game. Some begged passes from a ballplayer or sneaked in. Occasionally, teams gave away free tickets to youth groups to demonstrate their civic-mindedness. In the 1890s, when the Dodgers played at Brownsville's Eastern Park, neighborhood lads like Morris Raphael Cohen walked to the park to watch through a knothole in the fence. Two decades later, Al Schacht, a future major leaguer of Russian background, watched Giants games for free from Coogan's Bluff that overlooked the Polo Grounds. Young Harry Golden attended games there after delivering pretzels. He arrived around ten o'clock and lounged about the clubhouse until game time, running errands for players.[17]

Youth workers like settlement house personnel and schoolteachers wanted Jewish boys to participate in baseball to acculturate. Syndicated columnist Hugh Fullerton, an ardent advocate of baseball's ability to promote Americanization and teach sportsmanship and team play, published a letter from Chicago settlement house workers in a Bohemian Jewish neighborhood: "We consider baseball one of the best means of teaching our boys American ideas and ideals." Chicago's youth agencies tried to use baseball to rectify urban problems. The public school system in 1904 made adult-supervised ballplaying a central part of physical education in the elementary grades.[18]

Jewish Major Leaguers

There were only five Jews in the majors in the 1900s and eleven in the
1910s. They were probably mainly German Jews like Erskine and Sam
Mayer of Atlanta. Contemporary sportswriters were puzzled by their
absence, especially given their visibility in boxing. In 1903, journalist
Barry McCormick noted, "He [the Jew] is athletic enough and the great
number of Jewish boxers show that he is adept at one kind of sport
at least".[19] The absence of Jews reflected the social conditions among
second-generation eastern European Jews who lived in crowded neighborhoods where they did not get enough experience playing baseball.
They could not compete with lower-middle-class and upper-lower-class
youth who lived where there were ample baseball fields used by highly
skilled sandlot teams and played in competitive interscholastic, intercol-
legiate, and semipro leagues. Jewish young men fared better at sports that
fit in with their tough inner-city environment, especially boxing, where
there were already Jewish world champions, and sports like basketball and
track that required little space. The Jewish absence also reflected parental
opposition. In 1919, when Joseph Gilbert showed his father a letter from
Connie Mack giving him a chance to play for the Philadelphia Athletics,
his father told him, "Joe, ballplayers are bums. If you want to play ball,
go ahead. But you'll have to move out of the house. You can't live here
anymore." He didn't move out.[20]

The rare Jewish ballplayer who made the major leagues encountered
a lot of discrimination. They were badly treated by veterans, who were
often anti-Semitic and, even if not, were worried these newcomers could
take their jobs, lower wages, and force a decline in the status of baseball.
Not surprisingly, Jewish ballplayers often changed their names to avoid
anti-Semitism. One-third of the Jewish major leaguers active between
1900 and 1921 played under pseudonyms, including all five Cohens, who
became Bohne, Cooney, Corey, Ewing and Kane.[21]

Fans, players, and the media taunted Jewish players. In 1908, *The
Sporting News* reported the following public reaction in New York to Giants rookie Buck Herzog, who the weekly mistakenly thought was Jewish: "The long-nosed rooters are crazy whenever young Herzog does anything noteworthy. Cries of 'Herzog! Herzog! Goot poy, Herzog!' go up
regularly, and there would be no let-up even if a million ham sandwiches
suddenly fell among these believers in percentages and bargains."[22] A
1910 book of sports humor noted, "In looking over the list of names

comprising the American and National Leagues we fail to discover any of those well worn Semitic cognomens, such as Moses, Abraham, Ikey, Solomon, Aaron, etc., or the tribe of numerous 'Skys.' Something wrong. Is the work too arduous?"[23]

Early-twentieth-century Jewish major leaguers were not usually from inner-city Jewish slums but from localities where youths had more opportunities to play ball and become more fully assimilated. Al Schacht, the "Clown Prince of Baseball," was a Manhattanite whose family moved in the early 1900s to the more spacious Bronx, where he could play ball in school yards, city streets, and empty lots that made "the Bronx much like a wilderness." Just one-third of Jewish major leaguers active before 1964 came from New York City, even though about one-half the Jewish American population in 1920 lived there. Birthplaces included Atlanta, Georgia, Hamburg, Arkansas, and Metropolis, Illinois.[24]

Negative stereotypes about Jews were bolstered by the apparent Jewish involvement in the 1919 World Series fix and its cover-up. *The Sporting News* on 9 October 1919 crudely referred to suspicions about the integrity of the World Series between the White Sox and the Reds: "There are no lengths to which the crop of lean-faced and long-nosed gamblers of these degenerate days will go." One week later, after Hugh Fullerton had questioned the integrity of certain White Sox, *The Sporting News* asserted that there had been no cheating, although "a lot of dirty, long-nosed, thick-lipped, and strong smelling gamblers butted into the World Series."[25]

When the story of the fix emerged after the 1920 season, it was widely believed that the notorious Arnold Rothstein was behind the fix. A protégé of Big Tim Sullivan, the number two man in Tammany Hall in the early 1900s, Rothstein was, by the 1910s, the preeminent gambler in New York. In 1919, he reputedly arranged the sale of the controlling share from the Brush family for $1.1 million to Tammanyite Charles Stoneham, a close friend and partner with Rothstein and John J. McGraw in Havana's Oriental Racetrack.[26]

Historians believe that one of Rothstein's associates, former Jewish featherweight champion Abe Attell, met with the fix's ringleaders and presented Rothstein with a plan to fix the Series. Rothstein turned the proposal down, but Attell went ahead anyhow, negotiating with the players on his own, giving the impression that Rothstein was backing him. In the meantime, Rothstein probably financed Boston bookmaker Sport Sullivan's plot to fix the Series. Rothstein reputedly won $350,000 betting on the Series. F. Scott Fitzgerald modeled his character Meyer Wolfsheim in *The Great Gatsby* after Rothstein, reflecting the conventional wisdom that he was the fixer.[27]

The fix provided fodder to Jew-haters like Henry Ford, who fanned the growing flames of anti-Semitism by blaming underworld Jews for the Black Sox scandal. Ford's *Dearborn Independent* published articles in September 1921 entitled "Jewish Gamblers Corrupt American Baseball" and "The Jewish Degradation of American Baseball." According to Ford, "If fans wish to know the trouble with American baseball, they have it in three words—too much Jew."[28] Furthermore, "the Jews are not sportsmen. . . . The Jew saw money where the sportsmen saw fun and skill. The Jews set out to capitalize rivalry and to commercialize contestant zeal. . . . If it [baseball] is to be saved, it must be taken out of their hands until they have shown themselves capable of promoting sports for sports sake." The scandal exemplified to bigots how Jews were insidiously destroying the inner fabric of American society by ruining the national pastime (not to mention motion pictures and Wall Street) and thereby subverting American institutions and undermining American morality.[29]

Charles Comiskey's efforts to cover up the fix and protect his interests were abetted by his Jewish colleagues. Team secretary Harry Grabiner kept a diary that recorded Comiskey's machinations, and attorney Alfred Austrian tried to divorce Comiskey from the bad publicity by arranging for Ed Cicotte, Joe Jackson, and Lefty Williams to confess to the grand jury. Austrian subsequently arranged for outgoing State's Attorney Mac-Clay Hoyne to purloin the confessions before the trial. The absence of that incriminating testimony enabled the eight indicted players to be ruled not guilty. Comiskey hoped that if the players were found innocent, they would be returned to his team, but Commissioner Kenesaw M. Landis banned them from baseball despite the verdict. In 1924, Jackson sued for back pay, but Austrian conveniently discovered the confessions, and Jackson lost his case.[30]

A few teams in the 1920s, mainly the Giants and Dodgers, made a concerted effort to find a first-rate Jewish ballplayer. Jews then made up about one-third of New York City's population, and the Polo Grounds' Washington Heights community was fast becoming a Jewish neighborhood. However, the Yankees made no such effort, even though its Grand Concourse neighborhood in the Bronx soon became heavily Jewish. In 1926, baseball writer Frederick C. Lane published an article in *Baseball Magazine* entitled "Why Not More Jewish Ballplayers?" He quoted Eddie

Reulbach, a former great Chicago Cubs pitcher: "If I were a magnate in Greater New York at least, I would send scouts all over the United States and Canada in an effort to locate some hooked-nose youngster who could bat and field. Then I would ballyhoo him in all the papers. The Jewish people are great spenders and they could be made excellent fans. You could sell out your boxes and your reserved seats any time in Greater New York."[31]

Late that season, the Giants purchased the minor league contract of Mose Solomon, an outstanding athlete from Columbus, Ohio, who hit forty-two homers and batted .429 to lead the Southwestern League. However, the "Rabbi of Swat" played only two late-season games, making three hits in eight at bats, and was sent back to the minors. His short tenure may have been related to manager John McGraw's anti-Semitism. McGraw wanted him to stay in New York for the World Series, for which he was ineligible to play and would not be paid. Solomon disregarded McGraw's warnings that if he left he would not be brought back in 1924 and instead joined Portsmouth of the National Football League.[32]

In 1926, the Giants promoted second baseman Andy Cohen to the majors, the first Cohen to play under his real name. "The Great Jewish Hope" was advertised as a son of the ghetto but was born in Baltimore and grew up in Waco, Texas. Cohen's cigar-making father, an eastern European immigrant, had himself been a good enough ballplayer to have had a tryout with the Baltimore Orioles. The University of Alabama star had a brief stay with the Giants and then was sent down to Buffalo of the International League, where he was the all-star shortstop, batting .353. Cohen started the 1928 season at the Polo Grounds, replacing superstar second baseman Rogers Hornsby, who was traded to the Boston Braves because of his unpopularity with teammates and his gambling problems. Cohen immediately became a big hero, attracting lots of Jewish fans, including many first-timers. On Opening Day, thirty thousand spectators, many Jewish, saw Cohen drive in three runs and score two more in a 5-2 victory. After the game, fans carried him off the field. An anonymous parody entitled "Cohen at the Bat" concluded, "There may be no joy in Mudville, but there's plenty in the Bronx." Cohen performed capably in 1928, batting .274, and earned a 53 percent raise to $11,500, probably more than his statistics merited. He hit .294 the following season, but was sent back to the minors. Andy encountered substantial anti-Semitism and was called "Cocky Kike" and "Stupid Hebe." At one game in Louisville, when a heckler kept calling him "Christ Killer," Cohen got sick of the name calling: "I took a bat and went to the stands and looked up at him and said, 'Yeah, come down here and I'll kill you, too.'" Some observers felt he was under too much pressure, carrying the aspirations of the Jewish people in major league baseball, though Cohen relished the challenge.[33]

Despite the ballyhooed effort to discover Jewish ballplayers, there were only fourteen in the major leagues in the 1920s. The most famous today is Moe Berg, a second-generation Russian Jew who grew up on the Lower East Side, graduated from Princeton, and played fifteen years in the majors. Berg took photographs during a 1934 baseball tour of Japan that some biographers incorrectly claimed were used eight years later to plan General Doolittle's air raid on Tokyo. During World War II, he was sent to Switzerland to investigate Werner Heisenberg and Nazi research into the atomic bomb. Berg was authorized to kill him if necessary.[34]

The low Jewish representation in the majors substantially increased in the 1930s. The number of Jewish major leaguers increased to twenty-four in the 1930s and remained fairly steady at twenty-two in the 1940s. In 1936 alone, there were twelve Jews on major league rosters. Jewish youths by then had become well assimilated, were staying longer in school, and their families had moved out of the slums into less densely populated, more prosperous areas where there was more space to play baseball. Historian Peter Levine also suggests that many successful Jewish athletes were children of sports fans who supported their sons' sporting ambitions and were happy they could get a job during the Depression. The growing number of Jewish players in the mid-1930s was similar to the simultaneous growing success of Italian and Polish ballplayers for the same reasons. Their success was visible both in numbers and in quality, reflected by the first Polish (Al Simmons, 1930), Jewish (Buddy Myer, 1935) and Italian (Ernie Lombardi, 1938) batting champions.[35]

From the 1920s onward, baseball dominated the summers of Jewish youth. Talking about baseball, playing catch, and attending Dodgers games were a great means to socialize with buddies and, as the future baseball writer Roger Kahn found, terrific moments to bond with fathers. Jewish men (and women) not only read about baseball but, especially after the Depression, could afford to attend games. Thursday in Brooklyn was Ladies' Day, and admission for women into Ebbets Field was just ten cents. May Abrams, the wife of Dodgers outfielder Cal Abrams, remembered that when growing up in Brooklyn, even outside, you could hear radio broadcasts in the afternoon: "In the summer, everybody had their windows open. You could hear the ball game coming out of every apartment. . . . You sat on the stoop and, whether you wanted to know about baseball or not, you had no choice"[36]

These fans idolized Jewish major leaguers. They read about them in the daily press, saw them in their neighborhoods, held special days honoring them, and invited them to synagogue groups. The players were expected not to play on High Holidays and to speak out against overt anti-Semitism. On 25 April 1933, there was an ugly scene at Washington's Griffith Stadium after Ben Chapman, a noted anti-Semite, slid hard into second baseman Buddy Myer. A fistfight ensued, followed by a near riot among hundreds of spectators. Journalist Shirley Povich reported that Chapman "cut a swastika with his spikes on Myer's thigh."[37] Later that summer in Toronto, when Harbord, a Jewish team, was playing for the city championship, supporters of the rival St. Peter's nine unfurled a large swastika and shouted, "Heil Hitler." A fight broke out lasting well into the evening and expanding into the surrounding neighborhoods. Brawls at parks that divided rival ethnic groups were hardly limited to inner-city Toronto.[38]

Anti-Semitic major leaguers aimed loathsome words at Jewish fans and players. At the 1935 World Series between the Cubs and Tigers, umpire George Moriarty stopped the game to chastise the Cubs for their anti-Semitic bench jockeying. Commissioner Kenesaw M. Landis fined him $250 for halting the game. Moriarty later wrote that the Cubs had "crucif[ied] Hank Greenberg for being a Jew" and scorned umpire Dolly Stock as a "Christ-killer."[39] Greenberg noted in his autobiography, "How the hell could you get up to home plate every day and have some son of a bitch call you a Jew bastard and a kike and a sheenie . . . without feeling the pressure. If the ballplayers weren't doing it, the fans were."

Anti-Semitism was even a bigger problem in minor league towns, where Jews were often unknown. When Cal Abrams in the late 1940s played in the South, fans asked him if he was a Baptist Jew or a Methodist Jew. Several major leaguers, notably Buddy Myer, Andy Cohen, Hank Greenberg, and especially Al Rosen, were considered "tough Jews" who got into fights and beat up malicious anti-Semitic players.[40]

Hank Greenberg was the preeminent Jewish athlete in the first half of the twentieth century and the first elected to the Baseball Hall of Fame. Hank was a huge, powerful first baseman at nearly six feet, four inches and 215 pounds, hardly the stereotyped effete Jew. He batted .313 during his career, won four home run titles, had a .605 slugging percentage,

Hank Greenberg. *Boston Herald* photo.

fifth highest in major league history, and led the Tigers to four pennants and two world championships. Hank drove in the third most RBIs ever in one season, 183 in 1937, hit fifty-eight homers one year later, and won the MVP Award in 1935 and 1940. Greenberg grew up in the Bronx in an observant middle-class Romanian immigrant family that owned a textile business. He preferred sports to school: "The Jewish women on my block . . . would point me out as a good-for-nothing, a loafer, and a bum who always wanted to play baseball rather than go to school. Friends and relatives sympathized with my mother because she was the parent of a big gawk who cared more for baseball . . . than school books." The only one of four siblings not to graduate college, he remembered, "I was Mrs. Greenberg's disgrace."[41]

Jewish Americans followed Greenberg's exploits on and off the field. He became an important role model because of his great play and his character. During the end of the 1934 pennant race, with the Tigers closing in on the AL championship, Greenberg agonized whether or not to play on the Jewish High Holidays. Greenberg went to synagogue the day before Rosh Hashanah and, after receiving a supportive theological interpretation by a rabbi, played the next day. He stroked two home runs to win the game 2-1. However, he did not play on Yom Kippur. Journalists widely praised his decision, and poet Edgar Guest complimented him in the *Detroit Free Press:*

Come Yom Kippur—holy fast day world wide over to the Jew
and Hank Greenberg to his teaching and the old tradition true,
Spent the day among his people and he didn't come to play.
Said Murphy to Mulrooney, "We shall lose the game today!
We shall miss him in the infield and shall miss him at the bat,
But he's true to his religion—and I honor him for that."[42]

Greenberg felt the weight of being *the* Jewish hero: "After all, I was representing a couple of million Jews among a hundred million gentiles and I was always in the spotlight. . . . I felt a responsibility. I was there every day and if I had a bad day every son of a bitch was calling me names so that I had to make good. . . . As times went by I came to feel that if I, as a Jew, hit a home run, I was hitting one against Hitler."[43] Greenberg was one of the first ballplayers to join the army, early in 1941, and served longer than any other major leaguer. He rose to the rank of captain, with service in Asia. Hank was traded in 1947 to the Pittsburgh Pirates, who made him the first one-hundred-thousand-dollar player. He subsequently became a very successful baseball executive under Bill Veeck, serving as Cleveland Indians general manager (1948–57) and Chicago White Sox vice president (1959–61).[44]

The pressing issue in baseball during Greenberg's career was the integration of baseball. Jewish Americans were in the forefront of this movement, which reflected their own concerns about civil rights and discrimination in America. In the 1930s, Jewish Communists like Lester

Rodney were among the most outspoken white advocates for ending the color line. Jewish journalists like Shirley Povich and Walter Winchell spoke out against prejudice in baseball. Then, in the early 1940s, it was reported that Ike and Leon Levy were going to buy the hapless Philadelphia Phillies and hire Eddie Gottlieb, a prominent promoter of African American sports, as general manager. There was speculation Gottlieb would then bring in Negro League stars to man the roster. All this was opposed by National League President Ford Frick, who "wanted neither Jews nor blacks in the majors."[45]

After World War II, mainstream Jewish organizations like the American Jewish Committee and the Anti-Defamation League sought to end all forms of bigotry against all Americans, including racism in sports. In 1944, Isadore Muchnick, a Jewish city councilman in Boston (who represented a predominantly white district), pressured the local franchises to desegregate by threatening to pass a law banning Sunday baseball. He arranged a Red Sox tryout in April 1945 for Jackie Robinson and two other African Americans. While this turned out to be a sham, it helped bring Robinson to Branch Rickey's attention. Once integration was achieved, Hank Greenberg stood up for Robinson because "I had feelings for him because they had treated me the same way." Furthermore, Jewish sportswriters like Roger Kahn continued to speak out against prejudice in the national pastime.[46]

The conditions of major league baseball during the war gave rise to the All-American Girls Professional Baseball League, which included four Jewish players. The most outstanding was Tiby Eisen of Los Angeles, who played nine years, making the all-star team in 1946 when she led the league in triples and stole 128 bases. She gained a measure of celebrity, and her picture was printed in all the Jewish newspapers.[47]

Greenberg's successor as the preeminent Jewish ballplayer was Al Rosen, born in Spartanburg, South Carolina, and reared in Miami, Florida, whose outstanding nine-year career was cut short by injuries. The star third baseman won the MVP Award in 1953 by a unanimous vote, just missing the Triple Crown, coming in second in batting by .001 percentage points. Like Greenberg, he fought anti-Semitism with his fists (he led the league one season in being hit by pitches), and respected his faith by not playing on the High Holidays. He also went into the baseball business after retirement, serving as president of the Yankees and the San Francisco Giants.[48]

The number of Jewish players remained steady in the 1950s at twenty and rose slightly to twenty-three in the 1960s. This was far better than the steep drop in Jewish players in pro football and basketball and the virtual disappearance of Jews from boxing. Anti-Semitism was still a problem, even among the Brooklyn Dodgers. Cal Abrams in 1951 was leading the NL in batting, but manager Chuck Dressen rarely started him, claiming that Abrams was playing over his head. Abrams reportedly was often forced off the team bus and rode with the equipment manager because of his religion.[49]

The premier Jewish athlete in this era was Sandy Koufax, a Brooklyn youth whom the Dodgers signed in 1954 for fourteen thousand dollars after his sophomore year at the University of Cincinnati. Since he was a bonus baby, the Dodgers had to keep him on their roster for the next two years although he rarely played. Sandy's first several seasons were mediocre; he suffered from poor control except for momentary flashes, as in 1959 when he struck out eighteen Cubs. Koufax has claimed that manager Walt Alston retarded his progress as a starter because he was anti-Semitic. He came into his own in 1961 when he won eighteen games and led the NL in strikeouts. Over the next five years, he was as dominant as any pitcher in baseball history ever was, compiling a record of 111-34, leading in ERA every year and strikeouts in three (including 382 in 1965, then a major league record). Koufax pitched four no-hitters, including a perfect game in 1965, won three Cy Young Awards and a MVP Award in 1963, leading the Dodgers to three pennants and two world championships. He sat out the first game of the 1965 World Series against the Twins because it was played on Yom Kippur. In 1966, he staged a joint holdout with teammate Don Drysdale and negotiated a contract for $130,000. He retired after the 1966 season at the height of his prowess, at the age of thirty-one, having just won twenty-seven games, because of traumatic arthritis in his elbow. His record was 165-87 with an ERA of 2.76. Koufax was a hero and a symbol of Jewish pride, but he was the last player whose Jewish identity drew substantial attention. He did not have to contend with the burden of previous major leaguers, who had to fight virulent anti-Semitism; by Koufax's time, it had become a minor threat to American Jewry.[50]

The number of Jewish ballplayers dropped slightly, to nineteen, in the 1970s, and then fell to merely ten in the 1980s, the fewest since the 1910s. Jews had not suddenly lost their interest in sports or their

Sandy Koufax. Courtesy of the Sports Museum of New England.

athletic skill. There was a significant rise in Jewish participation in more elite sports, particularly golf, tennis, and swimming, tied to Jewish economic success, the suburban migration, and structural assimilation among third-generation Jewish Americans. Athletically gifted Jewish athletes grew up in families that stressed education rather than sports and were not so consumed by baseball to make the sacrifices necessary to play at the major league level, which was now recruiting African American and Latin American ballplayers. Aspiring ballplayers like Art Shamsky did not have the same kind of encouragement and motivation the previous generation had.

There were a growing number of players who had only one Jewish parent, like 1960s players Bo Belinsky and Dave Roberts, which reflected the rapidly escalating rate of intermarriage among Jewish Americans. The changing American religious mosaic was also reflected by players with Jewish or partly Jewish backgrounds practicing other religions, like Bob Melvin and Jon Perlman, and even ballplayers converting to Judaism, like Elliott Maddox and Joel Horlen. There was still the occasional anti-Semitic episode, such as the crude jokes certain Yankees aimed at teammate Kenny Holtzman.[51]

There has recently been a resurgence of Jewish ballplayers. There were eighteen players of Jewish backgrounds in the majors in the 1990s. In 1995 alone, there were twelve, as many as there ever had been in any single season. This trend has some staying power; there were eleven Jews on major league rosters in 2001. The names have changed. Besides family names like Levine, there have recently been Jewish players named Amaro and Bautista and players of color like Micah Franklin. In part, this reflects the high proportion of intermarriage among American Jews which is over 50 percent. A few Jewish players come from metropolitan New York, Philadelphia, and Chicago, but most are from California and Florida, where, like other American players, they play year-round. They are mainly suburbanites, whose baby boomer parents support their baseball ambitions, especially since major leaguers began averaging one-million-dollar-plus incomes. The most outstanding current Jewish player is Shawn Green, the number one drafted player a few years ago by Toronto, who was recently traded to the Dodgers, who signed him to a six-year eighty-four-million-dollar contract, making him at the time the highest paid position player. He was born in a Chicago suburb to a father who coached sports but grew up primarily in California. He has been quite active in Jewish affairs and actually demanded that he be traded to a team where there is a large Jewish community.[52]

Jewish American Off-the-Field Contributions to Baseball

The entrepreneurial role of Jews in the national pastime that was so evident at the turn of the century virtually disappeared by the Depression, ironically the very time when Jewish ballplayers were making their mark. Jewish participation in the business of major league baseball, a significantly anti-Semitic enterprise, reached its nadir in 1946 when Bill Benswanger sold the Pittsburgh Pirates, then the only Jewish-owned team in major league baseball. There had been no Jewish owners in the American League since 1902, when the Baltimore franchise was taken over by the league. In 1946, the only Jews financially involved in any big league team that year were minor partners of Bill Veeck's syndicate that had just purchased the Cleveland Indians. After Veeck sold the Indians in 1949, a number of Jews, including Hank Greenberg and Nat Dolin, were important investors in the team. However, they were not allowed into other owners' private clubs where league meetings were held. Moreover, they were barred from a Phoenix hotel where the league held its annual conference one year.[53]

The next team to have significant Jewish participation was Baltimore, where, in 1954, beer baron Zanvyl Krieger shared control of the new Baltimore Orioles franchise, which had formerly been the St. Louis Browns. In 1965, the team was sold to a competing Jewish brewer, Jerry Hoffberger, and shortly thereafter, Jewish entrepreneurs purchased several other clubs. Since then, Jewish ownership of big league franchises has grown significantly. From the early 1960s through the mid-1990s, ten clubs had Jews in controlling or significant ownership positions, including Jerry Reinsdorf of the Chicago White Sox, Walter Haas of the Oakland Athletics, and Bob Lurie of the San Francisco Giants. There are currently three major league teams owned by Jews. The Jewish visibility in the major leagues has recently been capped by the rise of Milwaukee Brewers owner Bud Selig to the commissionership, where he has to deal with Donald Fehr, successor to Marvin Miller as director of the Major League Players Association. Miller became head of the moribund organization in 1966 and shaped it into possibly the most powerful union in the United States. His efforts led to the breaking of the reserve clause in 1976, which enabled average salaries to rise from $45,000 in 1975 to $1.4 million in 1999.[54]

Jews have also been significant contributors to baseball in the field of communications. Many novelists, journalists, and broadcasters who might not have been diamond stars could use their particular talents to be part of the national pastime, although Albert Von Tilzer composed "Take Me Out to the Ball Game" in 1908, before he had ever seen a major league game. The first noted Jewish sportswriter was Jacob C. Morse, sports editor of the *Boston Globe*, who in 1888 wrote one of the first histories of the game, *Sphere and Ash: A History of Baseball.* Early Jewish baseball writers included Dan Daniel, who wrote about baseball for over fifty years beginning in 1909, and Shirley Povich of the *Washington Post*, who wrote about baseball from the late 1920s until his recent death. Postwar baseball writing was heavily influenced by such gifted wordsmiths as Roger Kahn, Dick Young, Milt Gross, Leonard Koppett, and Jerome Holtzman. Jews were also very prominent broadcasters, more as commentators like Dick Schapp and Howard Cosell, than as play-by-play announcers like Mel Allen.[55]

Jewish American novelists often wrote about baseball, which, according to baseball historian Peter Bjarkman, "is, after all, a perfect shiksa—mysterious, foreign, and altogether unintelligible to Old World parents; enticing, exotic, and full of endless pleasures for its new and fanatic devotee." Baseball references often appeared in fiction, starting with Abraham Cahan's *Yekl: A Story of the New York Ghetto* (1896). Allen Guttmann has argued that there has been a disproportionate Jewish literary production on sporting subjects, particularly baseball, which best epitomized American culture, traditional values, beliefs, and aspirations. Second-generation Jewish American writers saw baseball as part of assimilation and a means to measure acculturation. The most outstanding works include Malamud's *The Natural* (1952), Mark Harris's *Bang the Drum Slowly* (1956), Philip Roth's *The Great American Novel* (1975), and Eric Rolfe Greenberg's *The Celebrant* (1983), considered by literary scholar Eric Solomon as the greatest American baseball novel.[56]

Conclusion

The Jewish American experience in baseball has faithfully mirrored the history of Jews in the United States. Jews had little success on the diamond until the 1930s because they mainly lived in crowded inner-city neighborhoods that lacked the wide-open spaces needed for baseball, and their immigrant parents were worried the sport would harm their children. Yet, their sons looked to baseball as a means of becoming real Americans and escaping Old World values and behavior and maybe achieving social mobility. By the 1930s, Jewish Americans were very acculturated, and certain athletically gifted young men, especially those living away from the original areas of settlement, became professional ballplayers who were role models trying to counter negative stereotypes and anti-Semitism. Still, compared with contemporary Poles and Italians, Jews remained under-represented in the major leagues, reflecting their greater success at traditional routes of social mobility. Nonetheless, Jewish Americans have strongly identified with the national pastime, often vicariously as entrepreneurs and communicators, fields of traditional Jewish achievement.

Notes

1. While there have been over 14,000 major leaguers, only about 138 can be identified as Jewish by religion or ethnicity. For estimates of the number of Jewish major leaguers, see Peter C. Bjarkman, "Six-Pointed Diamonds and the Ultimate Shiksa: Baseball and the American Jewish Immigrant Experience," in *Cooperstown Symposium on Baseball and the American Culture*, ed. Alvin L. Hall (Westport, Conn.: Meckler, 1991), 343; and Peter Levine, *Ellis Island to Ebbets Field: Sport and the American Jewish Experience* (New York: Oxford University Press, 1992), 100–1. Such lists always seem to include players who were thought to be Jewish but were not, such as Jake Atz, Johnny Kling, or Benny Kauff, while excluding a few who were actually Jewish, like Moxie Manuel, who played for the Chicago White Sox in 1907. Determining the Jewish ethnicity of ballplayers is an inexact science, especially for players whose names were not Jewish-sounding or who had a gentile father and a Jewish mother. While there are individual player files and extensive records on ethnicity at the National Baseball Library in Cooperstown (Lee Allen Files), the data are incomplete for the earlier players. For a nearly definitive listing of Jewish ballplayers, see David Spaner, "From Greenberg to Green: Jewish Ballplayers," in *Total Baseball*, ed. John Thorn et al. (New York: Macmillan, 1997), 179–80. Spaner personally contacted ballplayers or relatives if he were uncertain about their ethnicity to inquire if they identified themselves as Jewish by religion or ethnicity. Even with Spaner's excellent research, there are some problems. He identified Brad Ausmus as Jewish, but most current lists no longer do. Furthermore, his "Jewish Baseball Register" singled out four recent players who had some Jewish ancestry but practice other religions: Mike LaCoss, Jon Perlman, Ryan Karp, and Doug Johns (178). My position is that conversion by the individual is a greater signal of unidentifying from one's birth group than the parents' conversion or choice not to raise the child in their ancestral faith (and culture). See also www.yap.cat.nyu.edu/Jewishsports, an excellent new source established by the American Jewish Historical Society.

2. On Jewish American sport history see Steven A. Riess, ed., *Sports and the American Jew* (Syracuse: Syracuse University Press, 1998); Levine; Bernard Postal, Jess Silver, and Roy Silver, *Encyclopedia of Jews in Sport* (New York: Bloch, 1965), hereafter cited as *EJS*. See also the special issues on Jewish American sport in *American Jewish History* 74 (March 1985) and 83 (March 1995).

3. Daniel Stern was a founding member of the New York Athletic Club (NYAC) and won the first American amateur walking championship in 1876, while Lon Meyers of Richmond was the preeminent nineteenth-century American runner, holding every national record from fifty yards to the mile. Lucius Littauer starred in football for Harvard and coached there in 1881. On the YMHA movement, see Benjamin Rabinowitz, *Young Men's Hebrew Association*

(1854–1913) (New York: Jewish Welfare Board, 1948), 11–12, 53, 62, 75, 78, 85.

4. Spaner, 172.

5. Steven A. Riess, *Touching Base: Professional Baseball and American Culture in the Progressive Era*, 2d rev. ed. (Urbana: University of Illinois Press, 1999), 56, 187; Riess, *Sports and the American Jew*, 11–12.

6. Riess, *Touching Base*, 72, 98.

7. Riess, *Touching Base*, 71–74; *Dictionary of American Biography* (hereafter cited as *DAB*), s.v. "Freedman, Andrew"; *Biographical Dictionary of American Sports: Baseball* (hereafter cited as *BDAS*), s.v. "Freedman, Andrew"; David Q. Voigt, *American Baseball*, vol. 1, *From Gentlemen's Sport to the Commissioner System* (Norman: University of Oklahoma Press, 1966), 184.

8. Riess, *Touching Base*, 74.

9. Riess, *Touching Base*, 74–75; Charles C. Alexander, *John McGraw* (New York: Oxford University Press, 1999), 82–93; Harold Seymour, *Baseball*, vol. 1, *The Early Years* (New York: Oxford University Press, 1960), 317–22; *New York Times*, 14 January and 20 January 1902.

10. *EJS*, 28–29, 39–40, 56; Riess, *Touching Base*, 67–69; *DAB*, s.v. "Lasker, Albert D."; John Gunther, *Taken at the Flood: The Story of Albert D. Lasker* (New York: Harper & Bros., 1960), 98–125; Stanley Frank, *The Jew in Sport* (New York: Miles, 1936), 75–91.

11. Leonard Dinnerstein, *Anti-Semitism in America* (New York: Oxford University Press, 1994), 53–54; Howard Sachar, *A History of Jews in America* (New York: Knopf, 1992), 98–102, 125–26.

12. "Jewish Physique," *American Hebrew* 86 (27 December 1909): 200; Charles S. Bernheimer, *Russian Jews in the United States* (Philadelphia: J. S. Winston, 1905), 35; Riess, *Touching Base*, 47–48; Abraham Cahan, *Yekl: A Tale of the New York Ghetto* (New York: Appleton, 1896), 6.

13. Quoted in Louis I. Howe, *World of Our Fathers* (New York: Harcourt, Brace, Jovanovich, 1976), 182.

14. Irving L. Howe and Kenneth Libo, *How We Lived, 1880–1930* (New York: R. Marek, 1979), 51–52.

15. Ande Manners, *Poor Cousins* (New York: McCann and Geoghegan, 1972), 278; Gunther Barth, *City People: The Rise of Modern Urban Culture* (New York: Oxford University Press, 1980), 150f.

16. George Burns, *The Third Time Around* (New York: Putnam, 1980), 9–10. See also William C. Smith, *Americans in the Making* (1939; reprint, New York: Arno Press, 1970), 111–16.

17. Morris R. Cohen, *The Autobiography of Morris Raphael Cohen* (Boston: Beacon Press, 1949), 80–81; Rick Marazzi, "Al Schacht: 'The Clown Prince of Baseball,'" in *Baseball Annual: An Annual of Original Research*, ed. Peter Levine

(Westport, Conn.: Meckler, 1986), 34–35; Harry Golden, *The Right Time: An Autobiography* (New York: Putnam, 1969). See also Howe, 182–83, 259, 161.

18. *Atlanta Constitution,* 18 July 1909 (quote); *Chicago Tribune,* 14 May 1905.

19. *Cincinnati Enquirer,* 17 November 1903.

20. Riess, *Sports and the American Jew,* 16–31; Spaner, 178 (quote).

21. Spaner, 172; Levine, 100; Riess, *Touching Base,* 189–91; Erwin Lynn, *Jewish Baseball Hall of Fame: A Who's Who of Baseball Stars* (New York: Shapolsky, 1986); Bjarkman, 343; Joseph Gerstein, "Anti-Semitism in Baseball," *Jewish Life* 6 (July 1952): 21–22; *The Sporting News,* 13 June 1897.

22. G. Edward White, *Creating the National Pastime: Baseball Transforms Itself, 1903–1953* (Princeton, N.J.: Princeton University Press, 1996), 250.

23. Irving Leitner, *Baseball: Diamonds in the Rough* (New York: Abelard-Schuman, 1972), 205.

24. Marazzi, 34–35 (quote). Data on birthplaces taken from *The Baseball Encyclopedia* (New York: Macmillan, 1969).

25. *The Sporting News,* 9 October and 16 October 1919. On the history of the Black Sox scandal, see Eliot Asinof, *Eight Men Out: The Black Sox and the 1919 World Series* (New York: Holt, Reinhart and Winston, 1963); Victor Luhrs, *The Great Baseball Mystery: The 1919 World Series* (South Brunswick, N.J.: A. S. Barnes, 1966); Harold Seymour, *Baseball,* vol. 2, *The Golden Age* (New York: Oxford University Press, 1971), 294–339.

26. Riess, *Touching Base,* 76; Alexander, 208–10.

27. Riess, *Touching Base,* 259 n. 118; Leo Katcher, *The Big Bankroll: The Life and Times of Arnold Rothstein* (New York: Harper, 1959), 148.

28. Quoted in David A. Nathan, "Anti-Semitism and the Black Sox Scandal," *NINE* 4 (December 1995): 97.

29. Quoted in Arnd Kruger, "'Fair Play for American Athletes': A Study in Anti-Semitism," *Canadian Journal of the History of Sport and Physical Education* 9 (May 1978): 55; Roderick Nash, *The Nervous Generation, 1917–1930* (Chicago: Rand McNally, 1970), 130–32; Levine, 116–18; Nathan, 94–100.

30. Seymour, 2: ch. 14; Bill Veeck, *The Hustler's Handbook* (New York: Putnam, 1965), 252–99; Donald Gropman, *Say It Ain't So, Joe! The True Story of Shoeless Joe Jackson,* rev. ed. (New York: Carol, 1992). This edition includes the Jackson confession to the grand jury, correspondence between Jackson and Comiskey, and excerpts from Jackson's 1924 lawsuit for back pay.

31. Frederick C. Lane, "Why Not More Jewish Ballplayers?" *Baseball Magazine* 36 (January 1926): 341. The first Jewish Yankees were Phil Cooney (Cohen) in 1905, Guy Zinn in 1911–15, Ed Schwarz in 1914, and then Jimmy Reese (Hymie Solomon) in 1930–32, whose ethnicity was not well known. When he was in the Pacific Coast League, he played in a celebrity game against the Jewish battery of Harry Ruby, the songwriter, and minor leaguer Ike Danning. Danning

called out the signals in Yiddish, and so when Reese came to bat, he knew the pitches in advance and rapped out four hits. See Spaner, 172.

32. Marc Lee Raphael, *Jews and Judaism in a Midwestern Community: Columbus, Ohio, 1840–1975* (Columbus: Ohio Historical Society, 1979), 333; Louis Jacobson, "Will the Real Rabbi of Swat Please Stand Up?" *Baseball Research Journal* 18 (1989): 17–18.

33. Andy Cohen interview, Baseball Files, Weiner Oral History Library, American Jewish Committee, New York Public Library; Levine, 113–14; Tilden G. Edelstein, "Cohen at the Bat," *Commentary* 76 (November 1983): 53–56; Hank Greenberg, *Hank Greenberg: The Story of My Life* (New York: *Times* Books, 1989), xv (quote).

34. Louis Kauffman, *Scholar, Athlete, Spy* (Boston: Little, Brown, 1974); Nicholas Davidoff, *The Catcher Was a Spy: The Mysterious Life of Moe Berg* (New York: Vintage, 1994), 87–95, 135, 169–217; Vivian Grey, *Moe Berg: The Spy Behind Home Plate* (Philadelphia: Jewish Publication Society, 1996).

35. Riess, *Touching Base,* 192; Levine, 91–92, 101. Computed from Lee Allen Notebooks, National Baseball Library, Cooperstown, N.Y.; *Baseball Encyclopedia*; Spaner, 179–80; Bjarkman, 343.

36. Roger Kahn, *The Boys of Summer* (New York: Harper and Row, 1972), 37; Elli Wohlgelertner, "Interview: Calvin R. Abrams and May Abrams," *American Jewish History* 83 (March 1995): 113.

37. Spaner, 171; quote is cited in Stephen H. Norwood and Harold Brackman, "Going to Bat for Jackie Robinson: The Jewish Role in Breaking the Color Line," *Journal of Sport History* 26 (spring 1999): 131.

38. Spaner, 171. On conflicts between Jews and Poles in Chicago's West Side, see Frederick M. Thrasher, *The Gang: A Study of 1,313 Gangs in Chicago,* abr. ed. (Chicago: University of Chicago Press, 1960), 133–34, 138.

39. George Moriarty to A. B. Chandler, 19 April 1945, Chandler Papers, University of Kentucky, Lexington, Ky., quoted in Jules Tygiel, *Baseball's Great Experiment: Jackie Robinson and His Legacy* (New York: Oxford University Press, 1983), 182; see also Spaner, 177.

40. Greenberg, 116 (quote), 52–53, 82–84, 102–4, 106–7, 190–91; Levine, 123, 126–29, 131; Jack Torry, *Endless Summer: The Fall and Rise of the Cleveland Indians* (South Bend, Ind.: Diamond Communications, 1995), 2, 5–6. For an insightful interview of a Jewish player's struggle in the minors in the 1940s and his time with the Dodgers in the early 1950s, see Wohlgelertner, 109–22, which includes discussions of anti-Semitism or the appearance of it. The published interview was drawn from the Cal Abrams Interview, Weiner Library.

41. *BDAS,* s.v. "Greenberg, Hank"; *Detroit Jewish Chronicle,* 12 April 1933, quoted in Levine, 133. See also the excellent documentary *The Life and Times of Hank Greenberg,* prod. Aviva Kempner, 1999.

42. Greenberg, 57–62; Levine, 132–43, 136 (poem).

43. Greenberg, 138.

44. Greenberg owned 20 percent of the stock in the Indians when he left the club. Torry, 23.

45. Norwood and Brackman, 121–22; Bruce Kuklick, *To Every Thing a Season: Shibe Park and Urban Philadelphia* (Princeton, N.J.: Princeton University Press, 1991), 146; Shirley Povich, *All These Mornings* (Englewood Cliffs, N.J., 1969), 129–30 (quote), cited in Norwood and Brackman, 125. See Norwood and Brackman, 115–35 for a very thorough examination of the role of Jewish Americans in the effort to integrate baseball.

46. Greenberg, 191; Tygiel, 34–35, 37, 43–44; Norwood and Brackman, 124–25.

47. Spaner, 174.

48. Rosen also fared very well after leaving the diamond, becoming a stockbroker and eventually president of the San Francisco Giants. I strongly suspect that former Jewish ballplayers did markedly better after retirement than their peers because of their education, entrepreneurial tradition, and family support, which reflected the overall Jewish occupational success in the United States. See Torry, 25, 29. Spaner listed Lou Boudreau as a "Jewish" player. Boudreau's mother came from a religiously observant family, but he mainly lived with his French American father after his parents separated and grew up in a small Illinois town. Boudreau was a seven-time all-star shortstop and Hall of Famer who was the Cleveland Indians player/manager at the age of twenty-four. Spaner, 175.

49. Computed from data in Spaner, 179–80. On Abrams's experience, see Wohlgelertner, 115.

50. Sandy Koufax and Ed Linn, *Koufax,* (New York: Viking, 1966); Spaner, 175–76; Levine, 243–47; *BDAS*, s.v. "Koufax, Sandy." Koufax's primary sport was originally basketball, for which he earned a scholarship to Cincinnati. Actor Lou Gossett, who played basketball in college, said that when he grew up in New York, Koufax was the best player he ever faced.

51. Data on ballplayers computed from Spaner, 179–80. For a discussion of the decline in Jewish success on the diamond, see Levine, 235–47. On the continuing anti-Semitism in major league baseball, see Spaner, 177. The number of players active in the 1970s would be twenty if we add Mike LaCoss, whose father was Jewish (Marks), but he took his stepfather's name and practiced another religion. Among players who started in the 1980s, Jon Perlman and Bob Melvin also followed other religions. These three players were all listed by Spaner as Jewish, but I don't see any identification with their Jewish heritage. Spaner, 178; www.Jewishsports.com.

52. Spaner's list includes Ausmus, Melvin, Perlman, and Karp. Computed from Spaner, 179–80. On Green, see *Chicago Tribune,* 23 February 2000.

53. Greenberg, 207–8; Norwood and Brackman, 130. On the possible

anti-Semitism of Branch Rickey, see Riess, *Sports and the American Jew*, 40–41, 55 n. 29.

54. James E. Miller, *The Baseball Business: Pursuing Profits and Business in Baltimore* (Chapel Hill: University of North Carolina Press, 1990), 35, 60, 97, 100–2; Benjamin G. Rader, *Baseball: A History of America's National Game* (Urbana: University of Illinois Press, 1992), 194, for salaries. For a historical listing of baseball team owners, see James Quirk and Rodney Fort, *Pay Dirt: The Business of Professional Team Sports* (Princeton, N.J.: Princeton University Press, 1990), 391–408. On current Jewish owners, see www.Jewishsports.com.

55. Riess, *Sports and the American Jew*, 55–56. To compare Jewish leadership in the majors with the NFL and the NBA, see 29, 55.

56. Bjarkman, 308–14, 313 (quote); Walter Lee Harrison, "Six-Pointed Diamond: Baseball and American Jews," *Journal of Popular Culture* 15 (September 1981): 112–18; Eric Solomon, "Jews, Baseball, and the American Novel," *Arete* 1 (spring 1984): 43–66; Eric Solomon, "Jews and Baseball: A Cultural Love Story," in *Ethnicity and Sport in North American History and Culture*, ed. George Eisen and David K. Wiggins (Westport, Conn.: Prager, 1994), 75–102; Eric Solomon, "Eric Rolf Greenberg's *The Celebrant*: The Greatest (Jewish) American Baseball Novel," in Riess, *Sports and the American Jew*, 256–83; Harlan Henry, "'Them Dodgers Is My Gallant Knights': Fiction as History in *The Natural* (1952)," *Journal of Sport History* 19 (fall 1992): 110–29; and Mark Harris, "Horatio at the Bat, or Why Such a Lengthy Embryonic Period for the Serious Baseball Novel," *Journal of Sport Literature* 3 (spring 1988): 1–18; Allen Guttmann, "Becoming American: Jewish Writers on the Sporting Life," in Riess, *Sports and the American Jew*, 241–55.

★8★

Diamonds out of the Coal Mines:
Slavic Americans in Baseball

NEAL PEASE

On 13 May 1958, a sunny afternoon in Chicago, Stan Musial came to bat as a pinch hitter for his St. Louis Cardinals in the sixth inning of a close game with the Cubs in Wrigley Field. An established star of the first rank and defending batting champion of the National League, the durable Musial rarely came off the bench despite his thirty-seven years. The only reason he was not in the lineup that day was that his manager, Fred Hutchinson, had hoped that his first baseman would collect his next hit in front of his home fans in Sportsman's Park, but the game situation dictated otherwise. When he laced a 2-2 curveball to left field for a double, the son of a Polish immigrant and his Slovak American wife became the eighth player to amass three thousand major league hits. The pitcher who surrendered the milestone blow was a twenty-two-year-old right-hander named Moe Drabowsky who, according to Musial, "had me beat on at least one point. He'd actually been born in Poland."[1] This memorable at bat, matching the young Pole against the greatest of all players of east European ancestry, stands as an apt symbol of an era when athletes of Slavic origins reached the peak of their influence in professional baseball, a development that started slowly, built gradually during the opening decades of the twentieth century, and crested during and directly after the Second World War. Along with Ike, Elvis, and the Chevy, muscular sluggers whose forebears hailed from the other side of

142

the Iron Curtain became emblematic of American culture of the fifties, the good old days of baseball's popular memory.

To a greater extent than with some other ethnicities, tracing the Slavic presence in the history of baseball can be a tricky business. In the first place, of course, Slavs are not one nation, but a group of related peoples speaking similar but distinct Slavonic languages and making up most of the population of Europe east of the regions of German and Italian settlement. By convention, the Slavs are subdivided into three branches clumping their separate nationalities by degree of kinship: east Slavs (Russians, Ukrainians, and Belorussians); west Slavs (Poles, Czechs, and Slovaks); and south Slavs (Serbs, Croats, Slovenes, Bulgarians, and Macedonians).[2] At the same time, many non-Slavs inhabit this area as well, notably Hungarians, Romanians, Greeks, Albanians, Estonians, Latvians, and Lithuanians. Furthermore, until World War II decisively transformed the ethnic complexion of east and central Europe by genocide, refugee flight, and forced expulsions of minorities by newly installed Communist regimes, its population was a complex intermixture that included millions of Germans and most of the world's Jews. Consequently, knowing that a ballplayer's ancestral roots lie in, say, Slovakia is no reliable sign of his Slovak identity, as opposed to more homogeneous lands such as Ireland or Italy. Slavic surnames are a surer indicator, but even their usefulness is reduced or even obscured altogether by intermarriage, anglicization, or the once-common practice of shortening or changing names to accommodate journalists or to fit in a box score. For example, the average fan might be forgiven for not suspecting that the player he knew as Cass Michaels had been born Casimir Kwietniewski, or that Bingo Binks, Tony Piet, Whitey Witt, Pete Appleton, and Ray Mack were christened, respectively, Binkowski, Pietruszka, Witkowski, Jablonowski, and Mlckovsky.

The initial appearance of a Slavic player in a major league took place in 1872, when Oscar Bielaski, an American-born outfielder of Polish extraction, made his debut with his hometown Washingtons of the National Association, but his modest career was an early anomaly. Until the final decade of the nineteenth century, only a handful of east European immigrants entered the United States, dwarfed by the more substantial numbers of English and then Irish and Germans, who firmly established themselves as the leading ethnic elements in the formative era of baseball. For the most part, the first Slav arrivals were Czech farmers who settled in the Midwest or Croat fishermen from Dalmatia who transferred their livelihood to the Pacific coast.[3] Apart from their scarcity, these Slavic pioneers were slow to take up baseball for other reasons. The Czechs brought with them to the New World their native institution of the Sokol, or "Falcons," a fraternal patriotic and exercise society, and other Slavs developed their own variants of the organization both in Europe and in emigration. However, Slavic cultures had little tradition of team athletics, regarding games as childish pursuits not worthy of adult attention.[4] Nor had they much ancestral exposure to bat and ball sports. While Russian lore included the folk game *lapta,* and Poles had played *palant,* a diversion with surface resemblances to one-old-cat, neither had a wide following nor could be considered a true antecedent of baseball.[5]

Not surprisingly, these original east European immigrants took no interest in the definitively American sport, and not until their sons began to come of age around the turn of the century did a scattered few Slavic names start to pop up on major league rosters. This second generation, born in the United States in the 1880s as baseball was cementing its status as the national pastime and generally eager to absorb American culture, adopted the game as their own and once in a while broke into the professional ranks. The first Slavic player to become a genuine standout in baseball was Ed Konetchy, a first baseman of Czech background from Wisconsin who collected more than two thousand hits for six teams in the National and Federal Leagues from 1907 to 1921. While little remembered today, Konetchy was better than more famous contemporaries at his position, such as Frank Chance and Hal Chase. In his peak years with the Cardinals at the outset of his career, he was, by the reckoning of *Total Baseball,* the best position player in the National League in 1910 and among the top five in two other seasons. Unusually tall and bulky for his time, Konetchy was known as "Big Ed," the first Slavic ballplayer, and hardly the last, to make an impression for sheer size.

Although only an occasional Slav could be found on American ballfields at this time, millions more had begun pouring into Ellis Island as part of the high tide of emigration from southern and eastern Europe that occurred over the twenty-five years that preceded the outbreak of the First World War in 1914. While most Slavs lived as subject and sometimes oppressed minorities in the Russian, German, Austrian, and Ottoman empires, few came to these shores as political refugees. For the most part, theirs was a migration *za chlebem,* in the Polish phrase, "for bread," a mass exodus of poor, uneducated, unskilled peasants fleeing economic privation. By 1910, more than four million Slavs and their descendants had taken residence in the United States, establishing the nucleus of the future American Slavic community before the coming of restrictive immigration laws after the war. More than half of this diaspora was Polish, with Slovaks and south Slavs comprising the next highest shares; by virtue of their numbers, Polish Americans would become the predominant nationality among Slavic ballplayers. The new arrivals found a niche as menial laborers and over time clustered in the industrial cities of the northeast and Great Lakes, such as Chicago, Buffalo, Detroit, and Milwaukee. In the near term, a plurality of them flocked to the mines and blast furnaces of Pennsylvania, where they formed the backbone of the booming industries of coal, iron, and steel.[6]

Out of this grueling Pennsylvania setting emerged the brothers Coveleski, Harry and Stanislaus, born into a Polish mining family in Shamokin, who both made it to the major leagues as pitchers. The older Harry hit the bigs first and gained brief notoriety as the "Giant Killer" when he defeated New York three times down the stretch of the epic National League pennant race of 1908.[7] However, Stan had by far the better career. A spitballer with excellent control, Coveleski ranked among the finest hurlers in baseball during his prime, roughly from 1917 to the mid-1920s. He was by all odds the top pitcher in the American League in 1920, the season he won three World Series games for Cleveland, and maybe again in 1925, when he led in earned run average and winning percentage. He finished with 215 victories, and upon his belated selection for the Hall of Fame in 1969 he became, and seems likely to remain, the Slavic player of earliest vintage to gain enshrinement at Cooperstown.

Looking back on it as an old man, Coveleski told Lawrence Ritter that the most remarkable aspect of his ballplaying career was that it happened at all. In a poignant and well-known passage from *The Glory of Their Times,* he describes his dreary beginnings as one of many Polish kids in Shamokin working the mines twelve hours a day, six days a week, at a nickel an hour: "I never played much baseball in those days. I couldn't. Never saw the sunlight. Most of the year I went to work in the dark and came home in the dark. I would have been a natural for night baseball. Never knew the sun came up any day but Sunday."

Seeking amusement after his shift, the boy became adept at throwing stones at makeshift targets in the dusk, leading to his chance discovery and an escape out of Shamokin and into baseball and celebrity. Ever after, the cheerless memories of the anthracite fields haunted Coveleski and motivated him with a sense of professional desperation. As a major league veteran, he saw any rookie pitcher as a threat to hand him a one-way ticket home to drudgery, and imagined the hotshot saying, "Back to the coal mines for you, pal!"[8]

Coveleski came closer to expressing a general principle than he may have realized when he stressed the unlikelihood that a Slavic American of his generation and circumstances might make his living on the diamond. In that era, Slavs occupied the bottom rungs on the white socioeconomic ladder and toiled at the hardest, most dangerous, and least desirable jobs. In the main, baseball did not recruit from the lowest social orders. Learning the game required leisure time, space, and surplus physical energy to expend for enjoyment, luxuries in short supply in the industrial slums and mining towns. In addition, Slavic youths rarely advanced far in the educational system, so they missed the opportunities for participation and coaching offered by school teams. Nor were they encouraged toward baseball by their immigrant parents, who still looked down on sports as frivolous and disreputable. For their recreation, Slavic males preferred relaxation in taverns and ethnic clubs, and their first noted athletes engaged in sports such as boxing that drew from the urban underclass, like the Polish middleweight champion Stanley Ketchell. Meanwhile, baseball continued to fill its rosters with players of German or Irish stock who stood a step or two above the Slavs in the social hierarchy.[9]

Gradually, this began to change as the result of a variety of forces that introduced Slavic Americans to baseball on an ever-widening scale. A central part of the agenda of Progressive Era reformers was to uplift the lives of the tenement dwellers and their children by the construction of parks, playgrounds, and recreational programs. They considered baseball a natural and uniquely effective means of assimilating immigrants and schooling them in American values, as did factory owners who established company teams and leagues for their largely hyphenate workforce.[10]

More important, second-generation Slavic youths loved the game and left their elders and community leaders no choice but to provide them the chance to learn and play it. Responding to the pressures from their sons and mindful of their organizational need to attract younger members, the ethnic Sokol societies expanded their Old World focus on calisthenics and gymnastics to include American sports, especially baseball. In addition, urban Roman Catholic parishes that tended Polish flocks began to found athletic clubs that prominently featured the national pastime while giving it the respectability imparted by the blessing of the Church, and

Slavic American businessmen started to sponsor neighborhood teams for purposes of advertising and creating good will.[11]

Because of this largely spontaneous growth at the grassroots level, during the first two decades of the new century, a hodgepodge of Polish and Czech American teams and leagues—fraternal, parochial, amateur, semipro—had mushroomed in the cities of the northeastern quadrant. At their best, they played the game at an accomplished level. In 1908, the Royal Colts, a Chicago Polish nine, capped an unbeaten season with a shutout victory over Rube Foster's Leland Giants, a flagship black team. Within a few years, another Polish American squad, the Kosciuszko Reds, had established themselves as the perennial kingpins of the thriving sand-lot competitions in Milwaukee and became the darlings of the city's heavily immigrant south side.[12] The success of Slavic American athletes at America's game stirred pride within their communities and produced a paradoxical but logical effect: while baseball indeed acted as an agent of assimilation and acculturation of foreign newcomers, at the same time it also reinforced a sense of ethnic identity and solidarity. In 1913, the organized Polonia of Chicago set up its own local baseball league to guard its youth against absorption into the Anglo world by the lure of sport. More and more, baseball became part of the fabric of life in the centers of Slavic settlement. Czech and Polish amateur and semipro contests in the Windy City drew large crowds and extensive mention in the ethnic press, sometimes even in the mainstream papers. Sensing a potentially lucrative new market, major league teams began hunting for players of east European heritage to pull Slavic fans into their ballparks.[13]

With a little more luck, Bunny Brief might have been remembered as the first marquee Slavic American baseball hero. As it was, he carved out a place for himself as a minor league legend. Born as Anthony Bordetzki, or maybe Grzeszkowski, depending on the source, but at any rate into an indisputably Polish household in Michigan, this first baseman-outfielder came up short in four cracks at the big time and never reached that level again after the age of twenty-four. As compensation, Brief emerged as the first great power hitter of the minors, winning eight home run titles, mostly with Kansas City and Milwaukee of the American Association. He gained recognition as the "Babe Ruth of the bush leagues" while the genuine Bambino was revolutionizing the game in New York. Brief did, in fact, become a fan favorite in ethnic Milwaukee while playing for the Brewers of the AA and retired in 1928 with a record total 340 minor league round-trippers and a fistful of other association batting marks. However, the Slavic breakthrough into the majors still proved elusive. In 1923, when *The Sporting News* famously proclaimed the openness of baseball to all except the black race by reciting a litany of ethnic epithets for the welcome nations—"the Mick, the Sheeney, the Wop," and so on—the list mercifully omitted any mention of the Polack or the Bohunk, perhaps because there were still so few of them. As late as 1925, the big league rookie crop included only one player of Polish descent out of more than one hundred.[14] The first bountiful crop of Slavic American talent, sown in the dusty urban diamonds of the immigrant districts, would require time to ripen and harvest.

The earliest prize graduate of this sandlot training school was Aloys Szymanski, who led his Right Laundry team to the Milwaukee amateur championship as a teenage prodigy in 1920. Already a local celebrity known as the "Duke of Mitchell Street," the main thoroughfare of his Polish neighborhood, he entered pro ball in short order. Feeling a need to adopt a simpler occupational nom de guerre, he borrowed the name of a Milwaukee hardware store, and as Al Simmons he rose through the minors and arrived in the outfield of Connie Mack's Philadelphia Athletics by 1924. Skeptics doubted the right-hander's chances to make the grade when they saw his unorthodox hitting style of striding toward third base as he swung, an offense against textbook form but common practice on the sandlots where he had picked up the game. Nevertheless, "Bucketfoot Al" stuck around for two decades, won two American League batting titles in consecutive years with marks of .381 and .390, and belted ninety-two home runs over the three seasons he patrolled Shibe Park's left field for the brilliant A's dynasty of 1929–31 that fell one game shy of becoming the first team to win three straight World Series crowns.[15]

Looking at his career in retrospect, one suspects that Simmons's standing in the pantheon of baseball can be easily overrated. He had his best years and posted his gaudiest numbers in a hitter's park in a hitter's era in the limelight of national attention as a member of a storied championship team. He may have been only the fourth best player on that A's juggernaut behind the formidable trio of Mickey Cochrane, Jimmie Foxx, and Lefty Grove, and he went into decline after being sold away from Philadelphia and after reportedly dulling his abilities with drink. Still, in his prime, Simmons plainly ranked as one of the foremost hitters in the American League, and *The Sporting News* bestowed on him its

Most Valuable Player Award in 1929. While always reluctant to single out any ballplayer as his favorite among the hundreds he managed, Connie Mack is on record as having hinted that Simmons might have been the one he would choose. He entered the Hall of Fame in 1953, the first player of Slavic background to gain baseball's highest accolade. Moreover, Simmons took pride in his Polish ancestry at a time when many preferred not to call attention to their immigrant roots, and as a veteran he made a point of offering friendly tips to a promising kid named Musial as a gesture of ethnic fellowship.[16]

When Al Simmons first reported to the A's, Slavic American players were still scarce in the bigs; by the time he hung them up in 1944, they were a substantial and growing segment of the major league population. During the intervening twenty years, the network of local youth, amateur, and semipro teams that served urban Slavic communities and surfaced their best athletes reached its zenith. In Chicago, the metropolis of Polish settlement in America, recreational centers and bowling parlors catering to Polonia provided a new source of sponsorship of baseball programs, and the fraternal societies and Catholic parishes continued to expand their leagues. By the end of the 1920s, scores of Polish nines were in operation in that city.[17] Just to the north, Polish teams bearing such names as St. Cyril's and Ryczek Morticians took turns ruling the Milwaukee sandlots; the South End Stars contingent that won the municipal American Legion championship six years running from 1928 through 1933 was featured in "Ripley's Believe It or Not" on the apparently unbelievable grounds that it was composed of all Polish youngsters but one.[18] In addition, other Slavic groups—Slovaks, Ukrainians, Carpatho-Rusyns—followed in the footsteps of the Poles and Czechs and began to form teams and leagues of their own in Chicago, the Pennsylvania coal fields, and elsewhere.[19]

As before, baseball continued to perform the dual function of fostering ethnic cohesion while simultaneously helping to integrate the hyphenates into American life. In gritty Johnstown, Pennsylvania, for example, in the years between the world wars, predominantly Slavic and Hungarian youth baseball teams excelled in regional competition. They became heroes in their own immigrant neighborhoods and, what is more, their exploits won the admiration of the wider community. When the established residents of the city took to lauding the athletes as "our Johnstowners," it marked one of the first times they expressed social acceptance of the roughhewn east Europeans in their midst instead of looking down their noses at them.[20] While their sandlot feeder system was reaching its fullest flowering—indeed, in large part related to it—Slavic Americans were also beginning slightly to raise their status in U.S. society. Although still blue-collar, they were no longer low man on the white working-class totem pole, but one or two ranges higher: the very stratum, in other words, that played baseball most avidly, and from which baseball traditionally recruited.[21]

Because of these developments, during the Depression decade of the 1930s, players of Slavic descent quietly started to enter the major leagues in unprecedented numbers. By 1931, *The Sporting News* took notice and alerted readers that the Poles and Italians had risen as threats to dethrone the Irish, at long last, as the reigning ethnic element in the game.[22] By 1941, the year of American entry into World War II, Polish Americans accounted for nearly 10 percent of major leaguers, roughly double their share in the white population as a whole.[23] The Slavic influx grew yet stronger during the war, as the departure of veteran players to the armed forces opened many vacancies in the bigs for the emerging generation of athletes of east European parentage. By and large, this Slavic cohort that exploded into pro ball had been born shortly before or after the armistice of 1918; reflecting shifting patterns of habitation, lots of them still came from the coal country of Pennsylvania, but many more now hailed from the industrial Great Lakes region, or even points farther west, than from the eastern seaboard. As always, most of them were Poles. Among other Polish American players who carved out substantial careers, Steve Gromek, Dave Koslo, and Whitey Kurowski debuted in 1941; Hank Borowy in 1942; Cass Michaels and Eddie Stanky in 1943; and Jim Konstanty and Ed Lopat in 1944. However, also at this time, Slavs of other backgrounds than Polish started to crack the majors in appreciable strength. During this same stretch in the early 1940s, Wally Judnich and Johnny Pesky, of Croatian origin, made their rookie appearances, as did Andy Pafko (Slovak) and Andy Seminick (Ukrainian).

From the start, the unquestioned gem of this wartime class of Slavic American ballplayers was a native of the steel mill town of Donora, Pennsylvania, born in modest circumstances into the family Musial and christened Stanislaus, in ancestral fashion, later anglicized to Stanley. The young Musial was of mixed Slavic heritage, but always considered himself Polish, and grew up in a largely Polish milieu. In Donora, the surname was pronounced "MEW-shil," closer to the original Polish usage than the trisyllabic rendition by which he would become famous. He was discovered by a scout for the St. Louis Cardinals while playing for the semipro Donora Zincs.[24] Initially signed as a pitcher, the left-hander converted to the outfield as a minor leaguer, jointly owing to a shoulder injury and his manifest precocity as a hitter. After an auspicious September call-up in St. Louis in 1941, he led the Cardinals to a trio of pennants and two World Series titles in his first three full seasons. Spraying doubles and triples out of a peculiar, severely closed stance—he eyed the pitcher, observers said, from behind his shoulder as if peeking around a corner—the "Donora Greyhound" quickly established himself as the premier player of the wartime National League before departing in 1945 for a hitch in the Navy.

Upon his peacetime return, Musial resumed his brutalization of

Stan "the Man" Musial. Courtesy of the Sports Museum of New England.

National League pitching and, if anything, just got better. He collected his second Most Valuable Player trophy in 1946, when the Cardinals took another World Series, and added a third two years later as a reward for one of the more impressive individual seasons in NL history. Raising his line drive power to a new level in 1948, he more than doubled his home run output to thirty-nine, one short of the league high, and missed a triple crown by that narrow margin while leading the circuit in nearly every other significant batting category. In effect, the new Musial converted fifteen singles per season into homers, and blossomed as a hitter capable of averaging .340 while slamming thirty or more round-trippers, year in, year out. After shifting into his late-forties prime, he acquired the nickname "Stan the Man," conferred, according to legend, by admiring but fearful Brooklyn fans in Ebbets Field, who groaned every time "that man" strode to the plate to punish their Dodgers.

With Musial at his splendid postwar peak, the infusion of Slavs into the major leagues that had mounted steadily over the past two decades kept on unabated for several more years. While overshadowed by the dramatic breaking of the color line, the cumulative result of this constant infiltration of athletes of Polish and east European background into baseball was that their numbers and visibility within the sport reached a historic apex during the 1950s.[25] Although nostalgia recalls the era as the heyday of Willie, Mickey, and the Duke, Slavic players and their achievements gave it much of its character and color. Jim Konstanty made an impact as one of the most spectacular and influential one-year wonders in the annals of the game in 1950 when he came out of nowhere to win the National League Most Valuable Player Award as a relief pitcher for the surprise pennant-winning "Whiz Kids" Phillies, lending enhanced glamour to the traditionally secondary role of the bullpen ace. An otherwise forgettable journeyman pitcher, Bob Kuzava, saved the clinching games of consecutive World Series for the Yankees in 1951–52. The 1953 Cardinals started a quartet of Poles—Steve Bilko, Ray "Jabbo" Jablonski, Rip Repulski, and, of course, Musial—known collectively as the "Polish Falcons."[26]

Beyond that, the image of the burly, leadfooted Slavic slugger, usually a first baseman, became fixed in memory as an icon of fifties ball, a one-dimensional game that eschewed speed and strategy and relied on the home run. Walt "Moose" Dropo, a hulking Serb American first sacker who drove in 144 runs as a rookie in 1950 but stole all of five bases over an in-and-out thirteen-year career, has been called "the embodiment of his era."[27] Bilko, Joe Collins, Andy Seminick, Stan Lopata, and Bill "Moose" Skowron also fit the mold. The best of this beefy type was Ted Kluszewski, "Big Klu," who bashed 171 homers over a four-year span for Cincinnati and inspired his team to adopt sleeveless uniforms so he could flex his massive biceps. Because they were so conspicuous and, no doubt, because they conformed to the entrenched notion of the "Polack" as a stolid lummox, plodding in more ways than one, these brawny specimens came to be seen as the standard model for all Slavic ballplayers. Never a man to be daunted by blanket ethnic stereotyping, Casey Stengel rated Poles behind blacks and Italians as hitters since "the Polish player is sometimes slow and sluggish swinging the bat."[28]

All the same, the decade produced its share of graceful Slavic middle infielders, such as Tony Kubek, the American League rookie of the year for 1957. And an excellent argument can be made for the dual proposition that Bill Mazeroski was both the finest Slavic ballplayer to break in during the 1950s and, very possibly, the most outstanding defensive genius the game has known. A fixture at second base for Pittsburgh for seventeen campaigns, Mazeroski won the 1960 World Series for the Pirates with one of the most fabled home runs ever struck, but he was never more than ordinary with the bat. However, in the field he had no peer, and his proficiency at the double play was dazzling. By the reckoning of *Total Baseball*, three times he ranked among the five top players in the National League solely due to his artistry with the glove. Until his induction into the Hall of Fame in 2001, few hot stove topics of debate could generate so much passion among horsehide cognoscenti as discussion of the pros and cons of Mazeroski's qualifications for Cooperstown despite his lack of the stellar offensive credentials that are the expected prerequisite.[29]

The fifties also embraced the careers of the only two significant foreign-born Slavic major leaguers, one nearing the end of the line, the other just starting out. Over the years, a total of fifteen players and one manager have made the bigs in the United States after emigrating from their native soil in the lands of modern Czechoslovakia, Poland, and Russia. Several of these were not Slavs but Russian Jews, and most left no discernible mark on the sport. Indeed, the best east European–born ballplayer may well have been Victor Starffin, who departed Russia as a child after World War I and became a renowned pitcher for the Yomiuri Giants of Japan, perhaps the greatest of all *Gaijin* and a luminary of the Japanese Hall of Fame. The first Slavic immigrant to serve a notable tenure in American pro ball was Elmer Valo, a Slovak from Ribnik, Czechoslovakia, who broke in with the A's in 1940. Although never quite a star, Valo was a hustling, popular outfielder much appreciated by the notoriously caustic fandom of Philadelphia for his willingness to challenge the walls of Shibe Park in pursuit of fly balls, and he lasted in the majors for twenty seasons. At about the time age finally began to catch up with Valo, Moe Drabowsky came up as a rookie pitcher with the Cubs some eighteen years after his parents had the lucky foresight to vacate the village of Ozanna, Poland, for the New World shortly before the outbreak of the Second World War. Drabowsky clocked in seventeen workmanlike campaigns for eight different teams and after his retirement, paid a return trip to his homeland in 1987 to help organize the first Polish Olympic baseball squad. The highlight of his career was a spectacular relief outing that won the opening game of the 1966 World Series, propelling his Baltimore Orioles to a sweep against the Dodgers, but he is most often recalled as the moundsman who gave up Stan Musial's three thousandth hit.

Through it all, Musial had continued to reign as the dominant Slavic player of the 1950s, just as he had in the forties. Combining performance, consistency, and longevity as few before or since, he became the National League counterpart of his contemporary, Ted Williams of the Red Sox—the venerable senior star who still outshone all but a handful of his younger rivals. Musial shed his Cardinals #6 uniform for the last time in 1963 with a .331 average, 475 home runs, and seven batting championships to his credit. At the time, he held the lion's share of NL offensive records, including most lifetime hits. Although his Slavic origin was hardly a secret—Polish Americans celebrated him as their own, he traveled to Poland occasionally once his playing days were over, and the Polish government honored him as the first foreigner to receive its highest award for athletic achievement—Musial was never pigeonholed as a "Polish" ethnic star in the same sense that Hank Greenberg was closely identified with Jews or the young Joe DiMaggio with Italians. His name was not instantly recognizable as Polish to many, he played his entire career in a city that did not qualify either as a media center or as one of the hubs of Polish American life, and his equable, unassuming personality did not command attention so readily as that of, say, the tempestuous Williams. Also, like DiMaggio, he gradually acquired the status of an idol in the public eye, a consummate professional who transcended ethnicity and came to represent baseball itself. He retired as the most universally respected figure in the game, with his induction into Cooperstown the most foregone of conclusions.

Not least, Musial entered the sport a few crucial years after Greenberg and DiMaggio, and over the course of his lengthy career, ethnicity began to matter less to baseball, and perhaps to American society, and baseball began to matter less to Slavic ethnics. As a general principle, the distinction between groups of European descent, still taken very seriously before World War II, seemed to fade with the passage of time and the increasing effects of assimilation. Within baseball itself, the admission of black players radically diminished the perception and importance of white ethnicity; Bill James exaggerates, but not by much, when he states that once the blacks came in, "everybody else was just white."[30] Old patterns of life among Slavic Americans also started to change as well. Growing numbers of them, in the main the grandchildren of the Ellis Island immigrants, rose into the middle class and moved to the suburbs, leaving room for new, frequently darker-skinned occupants of their historic city enclaves. This process broke down the cohesiveness of the various urban institutions—parish, club, factory, neighborhood—that had nourished the local Slavic baseball teams and leagues, and the sandlot programs that had trained two generations of apprentice professionals steadily withered away. Reflecting their more suburban and affluent constituency, the Slavic fraternal societies that had been mainstays of baseball within the community turned away from team sports in favor of white-collar diversions such as golf.[31] The salad days of America's game played with an east European accent had come and gone.

By the dawn of the 1960s, the quantity and, perhaps, the relative quality of Slavic American players within the world of baseball had begun to slip from the lofty levels of the fifties. The ever-expanding entry of blacks and Hispanics into the major leagues, often as the brightest stars in the sport, reduced the number of roster slots available to Polish Americans and their Slavic ethnic cousins and started to crowd them out of their accustomed place on the tables of league leaders. Out of Slavic ballplayers who debuted in the sixties, Mickey Lolich won three games in the 1968 World Series for his champion Detroit Tigers, and relief pitcher Ron Perranoski showed a knack for helping the Dodgers and Twins to reach postseason competition, but with one signal exception none of them ranks among the outstanding contributors of the decade.

That exception, of course, was Carl Yastrzemski, a third-generation Polish American from Long Island who first played ball alongside his father for their town team, the Bridgehampton White Eagles, and arrived in Boston in 1961 to replace none other than Ted Williams in left field of cozy Fenway Park.[32] He swung violently out of a tense, tightly coiled left-handed stance, making him the third in the line of great Polish hitters to use an idiosyncratic approach at the plate, behind Simmons and Musial. The young Yastrzemski performed well enough, claiming a batting title in his third year, but these achievements failed to satisfy Red Sox diehards, who doubted his ability to fill the shoes of the demigod Williams and saddled him with their frustrations over his downtrodden team as it struggled to avoid the American League cellar. This all changed in 1967, the stirring season of Boston's "Impossible Dream," when Yastrzemski captured the Triple Crown, a feat duplicated since by no major leaguer. More to the point, at least for the duration of the September stretch drive of a tight four-team battle for the AL crown, he was, in the judgment of Williams himself, "the greatest player who ever lived" as he lashed the undermanned Red Sox to an improbable pennant, their first in over twenty years.[33] A runaway choice as league MVP, he put an exclamation point on his epic campaign by swatting three home runs in the subsequent World Series.

By now a certified Boston hero, Yastrzemski followed up with a few seasons of only slightly lesser brilliance and continued as an effective player through the 1970s. The enduring mental image of the later Yastrzemski is his pop-up that sealed a bitter playoff defeat at the hands of the archrival Yankees in 1978; fewer recall that he also hit a home run to give the Red Sox the early lead in the same contest. As Musial before him, he played over twenty years with the same team, and he retired in 1983 with 3,419 total hits as "Yaz," a revered New England monument.

A superficial glance at Yastrzemski's career can be deceiving. Taken at face value, his lifetime statistics—.285 with 452 home runs—appear substantial but not stupendous, and one encounters a tendency to consider him a Hall of Famer more by longevity than outright excellence. As with Williams, the Red Sox's #8 also derived a certain benefit from playing in hitter-friendly Fenway Park. On the other hand, he had his best years in the midst of a pronounced pitcher's era, a fact that can distort appreciation of his real value. In 1968, when Yastrzemski won his third and final batting championship with a startlingly low mark of .301, he became a poster boy of sorts for the supposed deficiencies of modern hitters; in fact, in the context of his time, he was as imposing an offensive force that year as Al Simmons had been posting his flashier .390 in run-drunk

Carl Yastrzemski as a Red Sox rookie at a ballpark promotion. Courtesy of the Sports Museum of New England.

1931. On top of that, he gained a reputation as a deadly clutch performer, compiled an enviable record in postseason competition, and received seven Gold Gloves for defensive skill as an outfielder. All in all, Yastrzemski stands as the greatest American League player of the later sixties following the waning of Mickey Mantle.

The case of Yastrzemski likewise illustrates the progressive diminution of the role of European ethnicity within the culture of baseball. By his own account, Yaz possessed a keen sense of Polish identity. His family observed the folk customs of the old country, and his mother prayed in the ancestral tongue. As a boy, he chose favorite players because they were Poles, and when he broke into the majors, he befriended Bill Skowron for the same reason. Teammates jocularly greeted him as "Polack" inside the Red Sox clubhouse, and one of his proudest moments was a meeting with Pope John Paul II at the White House in 1979.[34] Furthermore, there was no mistaking the national origins of the Yastrzemski name, not pronounced but sneezed, according to one Boston scribe.[35] Yet, the public took no particular interest in his background, and his ethnic image was fuzzy at best. Indeed, Gene Mauch nicknamed him "Irish" as a tribute to his college pedigree from Notre Dame.[36]

Notable Slavic American players who followed Yastrzemski met a similar ethnically neutral reception. Knuckleballer Phil Niekro won 318 major league games, mostly for the Braves from 1964 to 1983, and was clearly the best pitcher of east European heritage ever to come down the pike, but he tossed his fluttery specialty for twenty-four years with barely a mention of his Polish roots. Greg "the Bull" Luzinski, a stocky, serviceable slugger for the Phillies and White Sox in the 1970s–80s, looked for all the world like a man who had escaped from the fifties via time travel, a throwback to the halcyon days when Slavic behemoths stalked the diamonds of the land.

To a great extent, the reduced profile of Slavic Americans in baseball has to do with their gradual ascent in U.S. society. Traditionally pegged as marginal, working-class groups of low status, Poles and other east European ethnics for many years almost obsessively pointed to baseball stars they had produced as proof that their boys could make it in America.[37] As a rookie in 1961, Yastrzemski would run across articles in Polish American newspapers breathlessly applauding him and other Polonia athletes as community examples and feel the pressure to uphold the honor of his people.[38] The urgency of that sentiment, so vivid not so long ago, has largely vanished. Now, with their remaining sense of ethnicity left sentimental if not vestigial, Slavic Americans are more likely to aim at business or the professions than the riskier arena of athletics. The days are gone when the Coveleskis, the Simmonses, the Musials, and the other sons of east European laborers looked to baseball as their main chance out of the mines, the smokestacks, and the drab immigrant neighborhoods; yet, while they lasted, they added a rich and colorful chapter to the lore of the summer game.

Notes

1. Stan Musial and Bob Broeg, *The Man Stan: Musial, Then and Now* (St. Louis: Bethany Press, 1977), 182.

2. This list is not exhaustive and omits a few smaller Slavic subgroups. Several Slavic nations are sometimes called by alternative names. Ukrainians are also known as "Ruthenians" or, rarely anymore, "Little Russians"; Belorussians as

"White Russians"; and Czechs as "Bohemians," although, strictly speaking, this last term is ethnically ambiguous and could refer equally to Czechs or Germans from the region of Bohemia roughly corresponding with the contemporary Czech Republic.

3. For information on Slavic immigration to the United States, see Stephan Thernstrom, ed., *Harvard Encyclopedia of American Ethnic Groups* (Cambridge, Mass.: Harvard University Press, 1980); and the classic Emily Greene Balch, *Our Slavic Fellow Citizens* (New York: Charities Publication Committee, 1910).

4. Steven A. Riess, *City Games: The Evolution of American Urban Society and the Rise of Sports* (Urbana: University of Illinois Press, 1989), 99.

5. Gary Gildner, *The Warsaw Sparks* (Iowa City: University of Iowa Press, 1990), 17; John Leo, *How the Russians Invented Baseball and Other Essays of Enlightenment* (New York: Delacorte Press, 1989), 155–56. From time to time, commentators in the Soviet Union contended that baseball in fact grew out of Russian *lapta,* to American indignation. Jonathan Fraser Light, ed., *The Cultural Encyclopedia of Baseball* (Jefferson, N.C.: McFarland, 1997), 630.

6. Balch; Roger Daniels, *Coming to America: A History of Immigration and Ethnicity in American Life* (New York: Harper Collins, 1990), both passim.

7. The Giants later claimed to have gained revenge against Harry by taunting "that big Pole" on personal grounds to the point that he could no longer pitch effectively in the National League. Christy Mathewson, *Pitching in a Pinch* (New York: Putnam, 1912), 76–82; and Fred Snodgrass interview in Lawrence S. Ritter, ed., *The Glory of Their Times* (Evanston, Ill.: Holtzman Press, 1966), 101. Brother Stan denied the story emphatically, also in Ritter, 110.

8. Ritter, 110–15.

9. Riess, *City Games,* 99, 104; Steven A. Riess, *Touching Base: Professional Baseball and American Culture in the Progressive Era* (Urbana: University of Illinois Press, 1999), 47.

10. Gerald R. Gems, "Sport and the Americanization of Ethnic Women in Chicago," in *Ethnicity and Sport in North American History and Culture,* ed. George Eisen and David K. Wiggins (Westport, Conn.: Greenwood Press, 1994), 183–84; Riess, *Touching Base,* 29; Geoffrey C. Ward and Ken Burns, *Baseball: An Illustrated History* (New York: Knopf, 1994), 124.

11. Gems, 186; Donald E. Pienkos, *One Hundred Years Young: A History of the Polish Falcons of America, 1887–1987* (Boulder, Colo.: East European Monographs, 1987), 45–46.

12. Edward (Jimmy) Adamski, "Milwaukee Poles in Sport," in *We, the Milwaukee Poles,* ed. Thaddeus Borun (Milwaukee: Nowiny Publishing, 1946), 153; George Reimann, *Sandlot Baseball in Milwaukee's South Side* (Milwaukee: Robert W. Wiesian and Associates, 1968), passim; Casimir J. B. Wronski, "Early Days of Sport among Polish Americans of Chicagoland," in *Poles of Chicago, 1837–1937* (Chicago: Polish Pageant, 1937), 145–46.

13. Riess, *Touching Base*, 29–30, 48, 186–87.

14. Riess, *Touching Base*, 191–92.

15. Ed "Dutch" Doyle, *Al Simmons, The Best: A Fan Looks at Al, the Milwaukee Pole* (Chicago: Adams Press, 1979), 6–13; Reimann, 14–20.

16. Mike Shatzkin, ed., *The Ballplayers* (New York: Arbor House, 1990), 1001.

17. Gems, 194; Wronski, 147.

18. Reimann, passim. In fact, Ripley was mistaken: the one player who did not bear a Slavic name was Polish on his mother's side.

19. Gems, 194; Wasyl Halich, *Ukrainians in the United States* (Chicago: University of Chicago Press, 1937), 130; Paul Robert Magocsi, *Our People, Carpatho-Rusyns and Their Descendants in North America* (Toronto: Multicultural History Society of Ontario, 1984), 59; Vladimir Wertsman, *The Ukrainians in America, 1608–1975* (Dobbs Ferry, N.Y.: Oceana, 1976), 14.

20. Ewa Morawska, *For Bread with Butter: The Life-Worlds of East Central Europeans in Johnstown, Pennsylvania, 1890–1940* (New York: Cambridge University Press, 1985), 110–11, 157, 170–72, 179.

21. Riess, *Touching Base*, 210–11.

22. Richard C. Crepeau, *Baseball, America's Diamond Mind, 1919–1941* (Orlando: University Presses of Florida, 1980), 165.

23. Riess, *City Games*, 106–7.

24. Musial, 5–11, 46.

25. Bill James, *The Bill James Historical Baseball Abstract* (New York: Villard, 1986), 210–11.

26. Shatzkin, 513.

27. Shatzkin, 293.

28. Ira Berkow and Jim Kaplan, eds., *The Gospel According to Casey: Casey Stengel's Inimitable, Instructional, Historical Baseball Book* (New York: St. Martin's, 1992), 140.

29. Contrary to what may be general impression, there is no historical tendency toward over-representation of first basemen and outfielders among Slavic players in the major leagues. The distribution of positions among players of east European origin has been normal, proportionate to the usual makeup of a team roster.

30. James, 210–11.

31. Pienkos, 181–82.

32. Carl Yastrzemski and Gerald Eskenazi, *Yaz: Baseball, the Wall, and Me* (New York: Doubleday, 1990); Carl Yastrzemski and Al Hirshberg, *Yaz* (New York: Viking, 1968).

33. John Thorn et al., eds., *Total Baseball*, 6th ed. (New York: Total Sports, 1999), 213.

34. Yastrzemski and Eskenazi, passim; Yastrzemski and Hirshberg, 28–30, 39.

35. Joseph McBride, *High and Inside: An A-to-Z Guide to the Language of Baseball* (Chicago: Contemporary Books, 1997), 321.

36. McBride.

37. Helena Znaniecki Lopata, *Polish Americans, Status Competition in an Ethnic Community* (Englewood Cliffs, N.J.: Prentice Hall, 1976), 75–76.

38. Yastrzemski and Eskenazi, 90–91.

★9★

The Latin Quarter in the Major Leagues: Adjustment and Achievement

SAMUEL O. REGALADO

When in November of 1998 Puerto Rican Juan Gonzalez and Dominican Sammy Sosa won the Most Valuable Player Awards for their respective leagues, it represented the highest watermark to date for Latinos in the major leagues. The dual Latin achievement capped one of baseball's most exciting seasons, which featured the fabled home run race between Mark McGwire of the St. Louis Cardinals and Sosa of the Chicago Cubs. Though both broke Roger Maris's single-season home run mark (McGwire with seventy, Sosa with sixty-six), their duel captivated the public. Sosa's fame went beyond North American borders. Indeed, Dominicans were exuberant about their native son, who had not only achieved greatness in the United States but continually expressed patriotism to his country and love to his family through a series of gestures following each home run. And this devotion, to be sure, was quite timely as the Dominican Republic was devastated by a terrific summer hurricane that rendered thousands homeless. Exhibiting great compassion, Sosa used his popularity to channel funds to his homeland. His actions, however, were not uncommon among his Latino peers and characterized the bond between them that was rooted long before he reached stardom. Like Sosa, Latins have always felt a sense of mission that had accompanied their careers as players. The advancement of their regions and communities and their self-proclaimed positions as "ambassadors" for their respective nations contributed to their campaigns to succeed. And Sosa's 1998 heroics both on and off the field simply exemplified the latest in the long and noble history of Latinos in the major leagues.

Though baseball's history is rooted in the United States, Latin Americans also adopted the game within a short time after it gained its popularity in mainstream North American culture in the mid-nineteenth century. And throughout most of baseball's past, Latins, too, have enjoyed some representation in the major leagues. But playing "America's game" as professionals in the United States did not come without a cost. North Americans had promoted baseball as an illustration of democracy and opportunity. But this promotion omitted another aspect of the United States: the "Great Colossus to the North" could also be a land of broken promise. Hence, the odyssey of Latin ballplayers in the United States included language difficulties, negative stereotypes advanced by an insensitive press, and constant bouts with Jim Crow. Though it is difficult to envision baseball today without their presence, there was a time when they were barely in existence in the majors; an era when they were baseball's real invisible men. In fact, between 1871 and 1950, only fifty-four Latins appeared on major league rosters. Still, in spite of the drawbacks, their numbers continued to increase throughout the twentieth century.

Esteban Bellán, who had originally come from Cuba to study in the United States, is credited as being the first player from Latin America to play in the big leagues. In 1871, the "Cuban Sylph" played with the Troy Haymakers of the American Association. Though he made no distinguishable mark as a player, his participation in the majors advanced the baseball enthusiasm in his homeland.

Baseball in Cuba, to be sure, was not yet ten years old by the time of Bellán's U.S. appearance. But in the next several years, the game caught fire throughout the island. The seeds of Latin baseball legend also were planted. The Habana Reds and the Almendares Blues, for instance, began operations at this time—the start of a fabled rivalry that lasted nearly a century. Between the 1870s and the end of the nineteenth century, baseball fever also expanded into the Dominican Republic, Puerto Rico, Venezuela, and the Yucatán Peninsula of Mexico. By the 1890s, there were several baseball clubs among the Yucatán elite. Hence, by 1911, a number of Latin countries already had developed a baseball past nearly as long as that of the United States. But the exposure of their players to their Norte Americanos counterparts was slim at best, and interest from the major leagues in Latin players was slimmer still. Not surprisingly, since Esteban Bellán's quiet appearance, only Venezuelan Louis Castro, in 1902, had worn a big league uniform. But after the twentieth century's first decade, this changed.

North American professionals were, by 1900, aware of Latin America's baseball environment. As early as 1890, the Cincinnati Reds, Detroit Tigers, and others had played in Cuba. In 1906, the Chicago White Sox competed in Mexico City. And as competition between Latins and North Americans increased, so too did the level of play. Cuban players, in particular, were tough. Pitcher José Méndez, for example, the island's "Black Diamond," left an indelible impression on all of the U.S. players who faced him. In 1908, Méndez threw a one-hit shutout against the Cincinnati Reds, who were then touring Cuba. Other victims included the New York Giants and Philadelphia Phillies. Giants manager John McGraw was so impressed that he placed Méndez's value at fifty thousand dollars. And the "Black Diamond" was not the only Latin star to shine against the North Americans. Cristóbal Torriente and, later, Martín Dihigo distinguished themselves against teams from the north. But, unfortunately for Torriente, Dihigo, and many others, their black skin dissuaded major league owners from signing these players onto their rosters. Consequently, only white Latinos found access to the majors. And two of them, Rafael Almeida and Armando Marsans, landed in Cincinnati.

In 1911, at the behest of manager Clark Griffith, the Reds signed the two Cubans and, in doing so, initiated a small stream of Latin players who, in the next forty years, sprinkled the majors with their presence. Of the two, Marsans made the bigger impact. The infielder from Matanzas completed seven big league seasons, including one with St. Louis of the maverick Federal League. While Marsans and Almeida toiled for Cincinnati and other clubs, in 1912, the Boston Braves signed another Cuban, a catcher named Miguel "Mike" González.

González advanced the visibility of Latin players during his seventeen-year major league career. Well respected for his baseball knowledge, in 1938 the Cuban became the first Latin to manage a team when he skippered the St. Louis Cardinals for seventeen games. A well-liked personality, he often playfully referred to himself as a "smart dummy." But baseball insiders appreciated his talents; *The Sporting News* described him as "one of the smartest hombres to ever trod a diamond."[1]

González, unfortunately, also lived in an era when stereotyping ethnic groups was quite common. At a time when racial discrimination was a way of life, ethnic stereotypes served as justification for policies and

Miguel Angel "Mike" González. *Boston Herald* photo.

attitudes about groups other than Anglos. Condescending descriptions portrayed blacks as watermelon-eating "sambos," Jews as "shylocks," and Asian groups as members of a "yellow peril." Attitudes toward Latins, too, were advanced by both folklore and even the movies of that period. Indeed, by the time of González's arrival, several Latin countries had repudiated the U.S. film industry for the negative portrayal of their people in several features.

Sportswriters, however, provided some of the most damaging descriptions. Journalists of that period were prone to chide many of the Latin players for their inability to speak clear English. Consequently, readers often saw interviews of Spanish-speaking players printed phonetically, which gave the impression of a stupid individual. These portraits were generally augmented by the long-held beliefs of Latin ignorance and laziness. As such, the negative characterizations far overshadowed any Latin achievement both in and out of baseball.

Adolfo Luque, a native of Havana, came along during this period and became the first real Latin standout in the major leagues. In a span of twenty seasons, the "Pride of Havana" earned 194 wins to 179 losses. In 1923, he led the National League with twenty-seven wins, a .771 winning percentage, twice captured the earned-run-average title, and won a game in the 1933 World Series. But the Cuban legend also won distinction in large part due to his storied temper. Though *The Sporting News* tabbed him as "Cuba's greatest gift to our national game," reporters often embellished on his propensity to throw at hitters and initiate fights against opponents. Moreover, Cuban journalists who held a disdain for Luque also fed into the stories that North American reporters favored. Indeed, a Cuban writer for Havana's *La Noche,* in a letter to the Reds, wrote that Luque was "the most illiterate man [in] captivity," and added that "outside [of] his ability to pitch [Luque] was a most perfect jackass."[2]

But though the early stereotypes dogged the incoming Latins, their presence in the majors continued to mount. By 1930, twenty Latins were listed on major league rosters; most were Cuban and most ended up on the Washington Senators. Prior to that time, the Cincinnati Reds had been the main repository for Latin players. Clark Griffith, who had managed the Reds and encouraged the signing of Rafael Almeida and Armando Marsans, was the common denominator. In 1912, Griffith joined the Washington Senators as a manager, becoming the team president in 1920. Ten years later, Griffith hired Joe Cambria, an Italian

American from New York, to his scouting staff. Though Cambria's chief finances had come by virtue of the laundry business, he at one point had owned a minor league club in Albany, New York, that was part of the International League.

Although Cambria had signed a few blue-chip players to the Senators, he faced stiff competition from seasoned scouts in the United States. Frustrated, he looked southward and unwittingly expanded baseball's horizons. Cambria's adventures in the Caribbean initiated an important step for the eventual Latin presence in the major leagues. Though Latins had appeared in the majors years earlier, they had not been actively recruited in their homelands. Before the Cambria era, Latinos had either been students already in the United States or players whose reputations had come by virtue of winter league play. What Cambria did was to set up shop in Havana. The scout, in short, became an on-site fixture of opportunity for, in this case, hungry Cuban players. From the mid-1930s until the late 1950s, Cambria, tabbed "Papa Joe" by Cuban baseball aficionados, became a magnet for Latin talent. And given the financial plight of many Cubans, recruits were in abundance—a virtual utopia for a scout often strapped for operating cash.

But while Cambria did provide opportunity for young Latino hopefuls, his "programs" also initiated another pattern—the lack of proper North American orientation for the recruits. This was not lost on insightful Cuban and North American reporters. Indeed, Bob Considine sarcastically referred to Cambria as an "ivory hunter." Players were prepared only to play baseball. Unfortunately, some North American ballplayers saw them as intruders. Furthermore, at a time when Depression-era unemployment weighed heavily on all Americans, ballplayers were not exempt, and they were often resentful toward foreign cheap labor. "The Cuban [player] has been regarded as an unsolid horse by his batwaving brethren. He is supposed to be deficient in the vicinity of the gizzard and prone to collapse in the pinches and his high-pitched Latin laughter rubs the average ex-ploughboy the wrong way," wrote the *Pittsburgh Courier*. Tales of turbulence in the Senators' locker room and the reported beating of one Latino surfaced in many articles as writers were quick to advance the stereotypes already held about Spanish-speaking people.

World War II, of course, played havoc on the major leagues. In fact, historian David Voigt has determined that by 1944, as a result of the war, the majors suffered a 60 percent personnel turnover.[3] As baseball owners sought to fill the vacuum, Joe Cambria took advantage of the opportunity and sent more Cubans than ever before northward. Twenty-seven Latinos appeared in the majors during the 1940s and of that number, twenty-two came from Cuba. Pedro "Preston" Gomez was among those whom Cambria sent to the Senators in 1944. Gomez, who played in only eight games, was destined to be the second Latino hired to manage a big league club.

Jackie Robinson's 1947 entry to the majors signaled a new period of baseball integration. The impact on American black players, of course, is well known. But the fallout from Robinson's appearance as a Brooklyn Dodger also affected the Caribbean. Black Latinos, like their North American counterparts, had been barred from the big leagues; before 1947, only those Latinos deemed to be white played in the majors. But black Latins, like Cuban Minnie Miñoso, did compete in the Negro leagues.

Saturnino Orestes Arrieta Armas "Minnie" Miñoso came to the United States from the Mantanzas Province in Cuba to play for the New York Cubans in 1946. Born in 1922 on a sugar plantation, before his

Saturnino Orestes Arrieta Armas "Minnie" Miñoso. *Boston Herald* photo.

arrival in the United States, Miñoso was already a player of prominence in his homeland, having played with Mirianao, a professional team of great distinction. He then joined the New York Cubans and starred in the 1947 Negro World Series. Signed by the Cleveland Indians that same year, Miñoso appeared briefly with the big club. But his quick appearance was noteworthy as it represented the first time a black Latin had competed in the majors. The following three seasons he bounced back and forth between the big league club and the minors until the Indians traded him off to the Chicago White Sox.

In 1951, Miñoso joined the White Sox roster and in doing so broke the major league color barrier in Chicago. His career with the White Sox also took off, and he became one of the league's most exciting players in the 1950s. In his first three White Sox seasons, he led the league in stolen bases and in triples each of those years. Moreover, his success not only debunked the old stereotype that portrayed Latins as a good fielding but nonhitting group in the majors, it also helped pave the path for a new era of Latino players.

As Miñoso's stardom grew, the number of Latin players also expanded. In fact, during the 1950s, sixty-nine players from Latin regions entered the big leagues. This number represented a huge increase. To place this in perspective, between Esteban Bellán's initial appearance in 1871 and Miñoso's debut in 1947, only fifty-two Latinos had worn major league uniforms. Clearly, the glorious event of baseball integration had widened the doors for all Latins. And not only did several more Latins come through those doors but big league scouts started to pour into all sectors of Latin America in their search for players.

C. C. Slapnicka was among those who found gold when, in 1948, he signed Mexican star Roberto Francisco "Beto" Avila. At the time of Avila's signing, he was already a prominent player both in Mexico and the Caribbean region and had been courted by the ever-present Joe Cambria. But it was the Indians who satisfied Avila's terms, and after a few seasons, he broke into the lineup in 1951. Three years later, Avila made history when he won the American League batting championship with a .341 average, thus becoming the first Latino to win a batting title.

In the wake of the achievements of Miñoso and Avila, Latinos such as Victor "Vic" Pellot Power, Edmundo "Sandy" Amorós, and others forged their way onto major league rosters. Moreover, the emergence of these players also represented baseball's expanding horizons. While Cuba continued to hold the lion's share of players in the big leagues, players from other regions started to appear in larger numbers than in the past. In fact, of the sixty-nine players who participated in the majors in the 1950s, thirty-three had come from regions other than Cuba. This was a distinct change from the previous decade, wherein only five of the twenty-seven Latin players had come from regions other than Cuba.

Though Joe Cambria was the most popular of those who had initiated on-site scouting in Latin America, in the 1950s big league scouts roamed throughout Caribbean and other Latin regions. Alex Campanis, Howie Haak, Alejandro Pompez, George Genovese, among others, like Cambria became household names among both the hopeful players and people of the region. Additionally, Robert Marin, Pedro Zorilla—men who were established coaches in the various Latin leagues both professional and amateur—became important contacts for scouts. Indeed, the difficult experiences of the scouts merit their own stories, and their importance cannot be underestimated. They became surrogate parents to the players they recruited. Parents of players entrusted their sons to these men in the hope that they might not only help guide them to the big leagues but also help orientate them to life in North America.

Pompez, in particular, was well liked. A mulatto from Key West, Florida, Pompez had been involved with the Negro leagues since the 1920s. Primarily with the New York Cubans, the bilingual Pompez was a legend by the time of the 1950s. The New York Giants, recognizing his popularity, hired him as a scout in the area; through him, the club tapped into the availability of talent there and by the 1960s, was heavily laden with Latin players on their roster. Like the Giants, the Pittsburgh Pirates, too, bore into the Latin well by virtue of the efforts of Howie Haak and George Genovese. Haak traveled extensively throughout the Caribbean, while Genovese's beat was both Cuba and Mexico. But it was Alex Campanis who found the greatest nugget of that era when he signed a Puerto Rican named Roberto Clemente.

Born in 1934 in Carolina, Clemente exhibited his skills at an open tryout hosted by the Dodgers scout. "How could I miss him? He was the greatest natural athlete that I ever saw as a free agent," remembered Campanis.[4] Following Clemente's high school graduation, the scout returned and in 1954, signed him to a contract. But following a complex set of circumstances that rendered him available to competing clubs after a year in the Dodgers farm club, the Pittsburgh Pirates signed him onto their team. Clemente's potential prompted Branch Rickey, then president of the Pirates, to order Howie Haak into the Caribbean region to seek

Roberto Clemente. From the private collection of Richard A. Johnson.

others like the young Puerto Rican slugger. "If there's anymore of those 'creatures' down there, I want 'em," bellowed Rickey.[5]

Clemente, as any baseball aficionado knows, lived up to his potential. An important element of Branch Rickey's "five-year plan," Clemente spearheaded the Pirates' attack during the 1960s. In his colorful career, Clemente captured four National League batting titles, twelve Gold Glove Awards, and the National League's Most Valuable Player Award for 1966. In 1972, he stroked his three thousandth hit and, only months after his untimely death in 1972, won enshrinement into baseball's Hall of Fame—the first Latin to enter that hallowed institution.

But Clemente's success belied the difficulties many Latinos faced upon their attempt to reach the big leagues. Cultural adjustments and encounters with racial discrimination came with the package as well. Moreover, few of the young ballplayers carried with them the bilingual capabilities to help them in their professional baseball path. Indeed, among their problems, the language barrier loomed large. "I couldn't speak English. Not to speak the language . . . that is a terrible problem. Not to speak the language meant you were different," recalled Clemente.[6] In the 1950s, major league clubs were still some twenty years away from offering cultural orientation programs designed to ease the transition from a Spanish-speaking to an English-speaking arena. Hence, players who came into the United States in the 1950s and 1960s were often left to live by their own wits. And this system created awkward and difficult circumstances for the newcomers, such as the one that Felipe Alou endured.

Following Alou's April 1956 arrival at the Giants' spring training facility in Melbourne, Florida, the club assigned him to their Class C club in Lake Charles, Louisiana, initiating what turned out to be a harrowing experience for the young Dominican. Because of the racial ordinances there, which outlawed integrated competition, Alou's time with that team lasted only five days. The Giants then sent him to their Class D team in Cocoa, Florida—a trip that advanced Alou's knowledge of Jim Crow America. Alou was appalled at the segregated policies of the South and opted to eat as little as possible on the two-and-a-half-day trip. Upon his 4:30 A.M. arrival at Cocoa, the Dominican, given few directions, slept on a park bench for the remainder of the evening. Sadly, circumstances like Alou's were not uncommon for many of his peers.

Puerto Rican Vic Power faced possible imprisonment for having purchased a soft drink at a Florida gas station, Cuban Pedro "Tony" Oliva could not stay with his white counterparts in hotels, and several southern restaurants refused to give service to Dominican Juan Marichal. Felix Mantilla of Puerto Rico, with the Braves at the outset of his career, recalled his inability and that of his fellow black Latins to attend a movie. "We had to sit on the sidewalk from seven until the bus came back at ten. Right there, a lot of the [Latins] decided to go back."[7]

As more and more Latinos reached the majors, their impact on the field increased. In fact, as opposed to earlier Latin "eras" in the majors, as the diversity of Latins expanded, so too did the extent of talent. Latins, in fact, dominated the majors in the sixties. In 1965, Cuban Zoilo

Versalles of the Minnesota Twins won the American League's Most Valuable Player Award—the first Latin to do so. One year later, Clemente did the same in the National League. Cuban Tony Oliva won the 1964 American League Rookie of the Year Award, and Clemente took four batting championships. His teammate, Dominican Mateo "Matty" Alou, won the 1966 National League batting title. And Puerto Rican Orlando Cepeda, after having won the 1958 Rookie of the Year Award, captured the 1967 Comeback Player of the Year Award and the 1968 Most Valuable Player trophy. Their legions also had success on the mound, where Dominican Juan Marichal won twenty or more games six different times. A workhorse, he also led the National League in complete games in 1964 (twenty-two) and 1968 (thirty).

But, unlike mainstream North American players, some Latins faced potentially debilitating political circumstances in their homelands. Cuban players, in particular, faced a crisis unprecedented in the major leagues. Relations between Cuba and the United States deteriorated between 1961 and 1962 to the extent that diplomatic relations came to an end. As a result, baseball players from Cuba no longer could freely shuttle between their homeland and the United States. Hence, several of them already in North America, like Tony Oliva, Orlando Peña, Atanacio "Tony" Perez, Zoilo Versalles, and others, made the difficult decision not to return to Cuba, where their loved ones lived. Some, like Luis Tiant, did not see their families for over a decade. Versalles described his emotions, and those of his Cuban teammates, following his club's 1965 American League pennant-winning victory: "I stand in front of my locker with Tony [Oliva] and Camilo [Pascual] and Sandy [Valdespino] and we don't say nothing. Tony cries. I think this is the biggest moment I ever have in my life and I can't go home and tell about it. I have nothing to do with politics. The trouble between Castro and the United States should not cause things like this." Tony Oliva recalled, "I thought about my family all the time."[8]

Cuban players also faced additional problems from the baseball hierarchy. In 1963, at the behest of the owners, then Commissioner Ford Frick issued a mandate that prevented Latin players from playing winter baseball in countries other than their own. The ruling, therefore, prevented Cuban players from playing ball in the off-season. "This ruling is not fair," pronounced an angry Pedro Ramos. "For fourteen years I play baseball. . . . It is part of my life. . . . The American boys can get jobs during the winter. They work in their hometowns. Me, I'm a stranger. I cannot get the same job an American can. My job is playing baseball in the winter."[9]

Frick's mandate also affected Dominican baseball. In January 1963, he announced that an exhibition in Santo Domingo between Cuban major leaguers and their Dominican counterparts could not take place. However, interim Dominican president Rafael Bonelli responded, "I am the president of the Dominican Republic and I say that it is alright to play." Felipe Alou, among the players in the controversy, declared, "It is unthinkable to many Dominican that someone from a foreign country would tell other Dominicans who they can play ball with and who they can't."[10]

The turbulence of the 1960s that Latins experienced, in addition to their problems in cultural adjustments, fostered calls by some that baseball should seriously address Latino concerns. Felipe Alou was among the first to trumpet his concerns publicly. "We need somebody to represent us who knows what goes on in the Latin American countries," he pronounced. Other Latinos echoed Alou's concerns. "The Latin player doesn't get the recognition he deserves. We have self-satisfaction, yes, but after the season is over nobody cares about us," stated Clemente. And in response to some of the long-held stereotypes about the Latin style of play, Tony Oliva said, "Minnie Miñoso was loved and recognized [in Cuba]. . . . They did not call him a 'hot dog.' Minnie was a hustler."[11] In 1965, Commissioner William D. Eckert appointed Bobby Maduro, former owner of the Havana Sugar Kings, to a post newly created for the purpose of tending to the needs of Latin major leaguers. However, the position was not permanent and no longer existed by the end of the decade.

Roberto Clemente's death as a result of a plane crash on New Year's Eve in December 1972 also spelled the end of an important era for Latins. Several of the players who started their careers in the 1950s completed their major league tenures in the decade of the seventies. Venezuelan Luis Aparicio retired in 1973, Felipe Alou and Orlando Cepeda in 1974, and Juan Marichal a year later. These and others like them pioneered into the North American professional baseball world in the immediate postintegrationist period. Players of their generation experienced far greater racial abuse and were more significantly tormented by cultural adjustment problems than either those who preceded them or those who came after. Moreover, many of them were victimized by the international political circumstances that rendered them virtually homeless. But it was also they whose achievements contributed directly to baseball's new expansive boundaries.

Though several Latin players such as Luis Tiant, Tony Perez, and Miguel Angel "Mike" Cuellar increased Latin visibility in the majors during the seventies, Fernando Valenzuela's rookie season in 1981 took it several important steps further. Valenzuela, a native of Sonora, Mexico, had joined the Los Angeles Dodgers in the latter part of the 1980 season. In 1981, the lefty reeled off eight consecutive wins to open that year's campaign. His success, along with his quiet but charming demeanor, also sparked a euphoria that captivated the nation. Writers playfully dubbed the excitement "Fernandomania." Though the 1981 season was scarred by a players' strike, Valenzuela tempered much of the fans' wrath toward the game. Additionally, the attention accorded to Valenzuela also increased the visibility of the Mexican community in the United States and helped to bridge gaps between them and Mexican nationals living in North America. But Valenzuela was not just a popular sideshow. That year, he won both Rookie of the Year honors and the Cy Young Award in the same season, the first major leaguer to do so. And throughout the 1980s, he established himself as one of the top pitchers of that decade.

By the end of the decade and into the 1990s, Latins also started to make their entry into baseball management. Until then, only two Latinos, Mike González, who managed the St. Louis Cardinals for all of seventeen games in 1938 and six in 1940, and Preston Gomez, who, beginning in 1969, held a similar post for seven years with the San Diego Padres, Houston Astros, and Chicago Cubs, had skippered a club in the big leagues. In 1988, another Cuban, Octavio "Cookie" Rojas, took over the California Angels. But his position was only an interim one and lasted but half the season. Not until 1992 did another Latino win the opportunity to manage in the majors.

Felipe Alou, who had toiled in the Montreal Expos' minor league system since 1975, took over the parent club while it floundered in fourth place in May of 1992. His impact was immediate, and he led the club to a second-place finish that year. Two years and many more wins later, Alou won the National League Manager of the Year Award.

By the time of Alou's success and the achievement of both Sammy Sosa and Juan Gonzalez four years later, the Latin impact throughout the history of the majors was clear. They simply had changed the face of professional baseball in the United States. Seen as virtual novelties prior to integration, the major leagues expanded their operations to recruit them in the period thereafter. Moreover, as their presence contributed to the success of the game, organizations began to hire Spanish-speaking personnel, establish orientation academies and, as a throwback to an earlier era, send major league clubs to play in Latin America. But the Latin impact on the field also transcended the foul lines. The press corps, which had once chided Latino players for their inability to speak English, had, by the 1980s, incorporated bilingual employees to conduct interviews. The Spanish-language media, too, expanded. As a result of the "Fernandomania" experience, clubs other than the Dodgers began to use Spanish-language radio broadcasts. And cable television also started to send games into the Latin regions. Lastly, advertisers, many of whom had ignored Spanish-speaking players in the past, started to hire players for endorsements both in English and in Spanish. Not coincidentally, the rising impact of the Latin player in the major leagues enhanced the rising presence of Latino culture in the United States. The Latin players and the fame they achieved contributed greatly to advancing a positive image of Latins in the United States and establishing a vital legacy to the history of major league baseball.

Notes

1. *The Sporting News,* undated clipping in González's biographical file, National Baseball Library, Cooperstown.

2. Letter dated 21 January 1923, in Luque's biographical file, National Baseball Library, Cooperstown.

3. David Q. Voigt, *American Baseball: From the Commissioners to Continental Expansion* (University Park: Pennsylvania State University Press, 1983), 264.

4. Samuel O. Regalado, *Viva Baseball! Latin Major Leaguers and Their Special Hunger* (Urbana: University of Illinois Press, 1998), 118–19.

5. Regalado, 57.

6. Regalado, 91.

7. Regalado, 78.

8. Regalado, 142.

9. Regalado, 143.

10. Regalado, 143, 144.

11. Regalado, 124, 125, 144.

★10★

Baseball and Racism's Traveling Eye: The Asian Pacific American Experience

JOEL S. FRANKS

Baseball has long played an ambiguous role in the construction of racial and ethnic relations in the United States. It has furnished a sense of commonality among diverse racial and ethnic groups and even equalized, in specific contexts, otherwise hierarchical power relations among these groups. Still, while baseball can mediate profound social and cultural differences, it can also exaggerate differences and help transform them into useful arguments for discrimination, exploitation, and marginalization.

Asian Pacific Americans have, accordingly, encountered baseball as a contradictory force in the United States. Asian Pacific American baseball merits attention from historians concerned with popular culture and sports. In the first place, only a few scholars have examined this topic. Second, aside from the work of Harold Seymour, most baseball historians ignore the multiethnic, multicultural experiences of Asian Pacific Americans, who might possess Chinese, Japanese, Korean, Filipino, Asian Indian, Southeast Asian, or mixed ancestry. Instead, when such scholars look toward Asian Pacific Americans, they generally focus on Japanese Americans. Third, historians who explore Asian Pacific American baseball more closely will escape the East Coast bias of much of baseball history. This East Coast bias is admittedly understandable, but it tends to reduce race and ethnicity to white/black terms rather than consider seriously the experiences of Native Americans, Latinos, and Pacific Islanders, in

addition to Asian Pacific Americans. Fourth, Asian Pacific American baseball history offers researchers a chance to examine sport from a less elitist
perspective. Baseball history embraces more than the achievements of the
game's great players, managers, or owners. An inclusive baseball history
would also consider the contributions of people who will never see their
likenesses on a baseball card, let alone a plaque in the National Baseball
Hall of Fame. Finally, some fine studies have focused on the baseball and
sporting experiences of African American and other ethnic groups such
as Jewish Americans yet, as Ronald Takaki writes, "one pursuit of our
multicultural past has been the study of history of a specific group, fo-
cusing on its separate memory." While necessary, these works, Takaki
adds, "fragmentize the study of society and thus deny the opportunities for different groups to learn about one another." The Asian Pacific
American legacy, despite various attempts to homogenize it, has been
culturally diverse and multiethnic. And, most assuredly, we should not
isolate that legacy from the histories of non-Asian Pacific groups.[1]

Baseball and Cultural Theory

Baseball has offered a shared code for Asian Pacific American and
other racial and ethnic groups—a shared code that has helped culturally
diverse Americans cross cultural boundaries as they were often crossing
geographic boundaries. A growing legion of academic and nonacademic
scholars and writers have used relevant spatial metaphors such as "middle
grounds" and "borderlands" to describe the sites of dynamic, yet often
conflictive, cultural interactions crossing over racial, ethnic, class, gender,
and geographic borders. These cultural analysts lead us away from static
notions of culture and cultural interactions among social groups: away
from simplistic arguments for essentialism, on the one hand, or assimilation, on the other.[2]

The point is that cultural change is multidirectional, a product of
interactions, sometimes engaged in voluntarily and sometimes involun-
tarily. It can emerge from racial, ethnic, gender, class, religious, regional,
and national crosscurrents. Cultural change seemingly disdains homoge-
neity, but while it inspires differences among social groups, it also sup-
ports often hard-won commonalities. Still, as we try to understand the
cultural interactions helping to shape the lives of Asian Pacific Americans,
we should try to recognize that the interplays among social groups are

significantly, to quote Robin D. G. Kelley, "constellations of power relations," "constellations" of inequitable and overlapping racial, ethnic, gender, and class relations.[3]

In this essay, I will focus on how baseball as a site of cultural interactions among diverse racial and ethnic groups connects to those "constellations of power relations." I will, more specifically, attempt to show how baseball has been used to aid "racializing" and "deracializing" processes. In other words, I accept the scholarship that asserts that race is as much (if not more) a social construct as it is a biologically viable category. Accordingly, a cultural practice such as baseball can both erect and cross racial and other boundaries socially and often invidiously established to separate Asian Pacific American ethnic groups from non-Asian Pacific American groups.[4]

I will analyze four areas of Asian Pacific American baseball. First, I will explore some of the limited amount of information available regarding Asians and baseball in nineteenth-century America. Second, I will discuss the experiences and perceptions of baseball players of Asian Pacific ancestry who crossed the Pacific from Japan and Hawaii during the early decades of the twentieth century to play on the American mainland. The relationship between baseball and Asian Pacific American community development and support will be the essay's third focus. Finally, I will explore the problem of Asian Pacific American baseball and cultural boundary crossings. I hope to show that the baseball experiences of culturally diverse people of Asian Pacific ancestry discredits prepackaged formulations of racial and ethnic identities. Asian Pacific American baseball wriggles free of essentialism and veers away from assimilationist models. It also discloses the importance of migration and cultural interactions, on the one hand, and, to quote Elaine Kim, racism's powerful "traveling eye," on the other.[5]

Asian Pacific Americans and Racism's "Traveling Eye"

People of Asian Pacific ancestry have historically struggled against racism in the United States. The first naturalization law enacted by the U.S. government in 1790 declared that only free, white immigrants were qualified for citizenship. This law helped make it possible to deny citizenship rights to Asian Pacific immigrants until World War II. And it helped to create conditions for subsequent national, state, and local laws targeting people of Asian Pacific ancestry after the California gold rush of the late 1840s and early 1850s lured Chinese immigrants in significant numbers to the United States. Meanwhile, immigrants from European countries, however frequently despised by many native-born Americans, were defined as white and therefore eligible to acquire the fruits of American citizenship.

In the United States, Asian Pacific immigrants generally faced a racial ideology that characterized them, like other people of color, as dependent, childish, and servile. Asian Pacific immigrants were stereotyped as "toiling machines" unthinkingly driven to take jobs away from hard-working white people. Disproportionately male, these Asian Pacific immigrants were decried as unmanly. They were unfit for citizenship and, considering they were generally poor and seemingly quite culturally different from European Americans, many whites argued that Asian Pacific immigrants were unassimilable and therefore unfit to live in the United States.

Consequently, a popular anti-Asian Pacific movement emerged in the second half of the nineteenth century and won several political victories from the 1850s through World War II. Among these victories was the Chinese Exclusion Act, passed in 1882. In 1907, the United States negotiated with Japan an agreement denying Japanese laborers entrance into the United States. Ten years later, the United States barred immigrants from India. And in 1934, the Tydings-McDuffie Act closed off entry to Filipinos previously allowed into America because they were categorized as U.S. nationals.

The responses by people of Asian Pacific ancestry to these and other examples of institutionalized racism varied. To a significant extent, where Asian Pacific Americans lived made a difference. Unlike European immigrants and their progeny, Asian Pacific Americans inhabiting the continental United States could not easily empower themselves by substantial involvement in politics or popular culture or by rendering themselves economically indispensable. This does not mean that Asian Pacific Americans on the mainland were passive victims. It does mean that for decades, Asian Pacific Americans on the mainland were very likely too few in number outside of the Pacific Coast and too well marginalized by institutionalized racism to effectively struggle against discrimination and exclusion.

The experiences of Asian Pacific people in Hawaii differ dramatically from their mainland counterparts. Brought to the islands to perform contract labor on Hawaiian sugar plantations, Asian Pacific Hawaiians encountered racism and class oppression. But they did not encounter systematic efforts on the part of a white majority to bar them from the islands or Hawaii's economic mainstream. Indeed, European Americans constituted a generally elite minority on the islands—an elite minority who enthusiastically populated the Hawaiian working class with Asians and native Hawaiians and strove mightily to limit that working class to nonwhites. Thus, unlike California in 1900, the vast majority of people living in Hawaii were people of color, divided by ethnicity but often sharing similar class experiences.

Asian Pacific Hawaiians developed and maintained fewer of what scholars describe as isolated ethnic communities or enclaves than did Asian Pacific American mainlanders, who reasonably perceived themselves as creating ethnic islands in a sea of European American hostility. To be sure, Asian migrants to Hawaii transplanted their cultures to the islands and nurtured their cultures as best they could in the new environment. This task was made a bit easier for them than on the mainland because Asian Pacific Hawaiians were more likely to live with spouses and family members. It was less costly for plebeian Chinese, Japanese, or Korean people to travel to Hawaii than to the mainland. At the same time, Hawaiian plantation owners tended to believe that workers who brought their families would compose a more stable, quiescent labor force, and they were similarly aware that the toil of women and children could supplement that of the male plantation workers quite nicely and inexpensively.[6]

Nevertheless, the subsequent emergence of a second generation, relatively stronger in presence than on the mainland, helped to break down ethnic isolation as these young men and women worked, went to school, and socialized with people of other Asian nationalities as well as Pacific Islanders and European Americans. According to scholar William Carlson Smith, writing in the 1930s, second-generation Hawaiian Chinese and Japanese seemed more at ease both with dominant European American culture and their own cultural heritages than were their mainland counterparts. Still, as Ronald Takaki points out, people like Chinese Hawaiians did not need their children to overcome ethnic barriers. Takaki writes, "by about 1900, about 1,500 Chinese men married or lived with Hawaiian women, and their children represented the first Chinese-Hawai'ian generation."[7]

The Nineteenth Century

During the second half of the nineteenth century, baseball became America's national pastime. In the process, too many Americans regarded it as the white man's particular pastime. People of color and women tried to challenge this assumption, but it remained an integral aspect of America's sporting canon for decades and, arguably, remains so today. People of Asian Pacific ancestry also tried to dispel stereotypes of them as physically, intellectually, and emotionally inadequate to compete in baseball. During the late nineteenth century, their efforts seem to have been largely ignored.

Patrician Chinese students living in Hartford, Connecticut, took up baseball in Gilded Age America. Members of the Chinese Educational Mission formed a nine called the Orientals and, according to observers such as William Phelps, played the game well. As the United States headed toward passing the Chinese Exclusion Act, the Chinese government ordered the mission to return home. While waiting in San Francisco for a China-bound steamer in 1881, the mission team was challenged by an Oakland baseball club. Wen Bing Chung, a mission student, remembered that "the Oakland men imagined that they were going to have a walk-over with the Chinese. Who had seen Celestials playing baseball?" However, the Chinese nine won, surprising their opponents and the spectators who witnessed a "strange phenomenon—Chinese playing their national ball game and showing the Yankees some of the thrills of the game."[8]

Despite the Chinese Exclusion Act, the Chinese presence in the United States continued to pose a dilemma for American nativism and racism. In 1884, *Sporting Life* reported that a "California man is trying to teach a lot of Chinamen how to play baseball with a view to organizing a Chinese base ball team." However, *Sporting Life* assured readers that "he has met with little success thus far and will meet with less in the future."[9] In 1885, the *San Francisco Chronicle* reported on a multiracial, multiethnic baseball game played by "Spaniards, Dutch, Americans, and Chinese."[10]

The majority of Chinese immigrants living in the United States lacked the patrician background of those young men involved in the Chinese Educational Mission. Most were laborers who in increasing numbers by the 1880s inhabited overcrowded "ethnic enclaves" such as the one existing in San Francisco. There, according to one *San Francisco Chronicle* reporter, interesting games of baseball were played in 1887. *Chronicle* readers were told that on "any Sunday afternoon on Stockton Street one may see a team of rising Mongolians wrestling with the technicalities of the Great American game, while different pawnbrokers, pork butchers, and influential high binders and their wives beam down approvingly from the rickety balconies."[11]

While some Chinese Americans showed a passion for playing nineteenth-century baseball, in Kansas City, a Chinese American laundry operator got involved in the entrepreneurial end of the national pastime of the 1890s. Quong Fong, indeed, did more than that, as he crossed racial and ethnic boundaries to organize an African American nine called Wall's Laundry Grays.[12]

However, as baseball could serve as a cross-cultural bridge builder, it could also clearly reinforce barriers between Chinese and non-Chinese Americans. The anti-Chinese movement remained active after the Chinese Exclusion Act. In 1886, anti-Chinese Californians began a statewide boycott of Chinese-owned businesses and non-Chinese-owned businesses hiring Chinese or dealing commercially with Chinese Americans. To publicize the boycott, a group of young men living in Sacramento formed a nine called the Boycotters.[13]

Pacific Crossings

In 1905, a baseball team representing Japan's Waseda University arrived in the United States. Commentators on baseball history as varied as Albert G. Spalding and Harold Seymour noted the event as a milestone in the internationalization of America's national pastime. At least as important is how the recognition of Japanese by the American press and authorities such as Spalding sustained the racialization of Japanese people and, by extension, Americans of Japanese ancestry.

The timing of the Japanese ballplayers coming to the United States was significant. The anti-Asian movement had turned its attention from the Chinese to the Japanese, as more first-generation Japanese immigrants took up residence in Hawaii and the American mainland. Moreover, the fact that Japan had emerged as a major rival to U.S. interests in Asia and the South Pacific reinforced American distrust of the Japanese and Japanese immigrants.

Nevertheless, baseball seemed to furnish A. G. Spalding an excuse to praise the Japanese while depicting them as exotic cultural others.

Noting the Japanese enthusiasm for baseball in his book, *America's National Game* (originally published in 1911), Spalding maintained that "the fact is quite in keeping with what we know of the little brown men of the Orient." Baseball, according to Spalding, was a combative game, embraced by aggressive, competitive, and progressive people. The Japanese, argued Spalding, shared these attributes, at least, with white Americans.[14]

Yet, the reference to "the little brown men of the Orient" declared that the Japanese were, after all, not like white Americans. Press stories on the Waseda nine supported Spalding's ambiguous reflections on Japanese baseball. The *Sporting Life*'s R. S. Ransom complimented the Waseda nine's fine ballplaying skills. Yet, Ransom stressed their physical and cultural exoticism. For Ransom, as well, the Japanese ballplayers were "little brown men." Only these "little brown men" hailed from the mysterious Orient, "from the realm of the Mikado."[15] The *Los Angeles Times* also expressed admiration for the Waseda ballplayers' talents. Still, when the Waseda nine visited the Los Angeles area, the *Times* reported on the "wiry Japs" and the "little short-legged black haired [Waseda] base runners."[16]

Press coverage of the Waseda team, moreover, commented ambivalently on the responses of San Francisco's, Los Angeles's, and Seattle's Japanese immigrant communities to the university players. When Waseda played Stanford in San Francisco, the *San Francisco Chronicle* reported that of the two thousand people in attendance, two-thirds possessed Japanese ancestry. The grandstand took on the appearance of a "holiday in Nagasaki."[17] In southern California, Los Angeles's Japanese community supported the Waseda team. The *Los Angeles Times* observed that many of the eight hundred who showed up to watch Waseda beat Los Angeles High School were Japanese with "bright colored pennants." The *Times* added, "it was the firm conviction of the Japs that the 'white boys' could not play with the men from Tokio [sic]."[18] The *Seattle Times* maintained that during a game between Waseda and the University of Washington, "the sympathy of the crowd was all with the Japs and there was an oriental tinge to the grand stand, given by a few hundred Seattle Japs, who smoked cigarettes, cracked peanuts, and rooted for the Waseda bunch."[19] To the American press, it was not a matter of insulting the people of Japanese ancestry who rooted for the Waseda nine. Rather, the press declared what many European Americans took for granted; that, in the words of Ronald Takaki, Japanese immigrants and their progeny were "strangers from a different shore."[20]

A somewhat similar reaction was elicited by the mainland appearance of the top-notch Chinese Hawaiian club in the 1910s. But the point should be made that unlike the Waseda ballplayers, these particular young men were from a U.S. territory and they were therefore U.S. citizens and American athletes, however they were perceived and however they might have perceived themselves.

Baseball had been played in Hawaii for decades before the Chinese Hawaiian club's arrival. Apparently, Chinese Hawaiian workers in the late 1800s were taught America's national pastime. Indeed, Sun Yat-sen, Chinese statesman, reportedly played baseball in Hawaii. When Japanese workers were recruited in the 1890s and 1900s to work on Hawaiian sugar plantations, many of them and other Japanese immigrants brought their love of baseball with them. Labor unrest in the early decades of the twentieth century, according to Ronald Takaki, prompted planters to encourage the organization of worker nines and leagues as a way to divert their labor forces from organizing unions and strikes. Accordingly, Hawaiian nines were often multiethnic, while all-Japanese and all-Chinese clubs also formed.[21]

Beginning as early as 1910, a team ostensibly representing the University of Hawaii in Honolulu made annual treks to the mainland for several years. The teams they played included college, semiprofessional, Pacific Coast League, and African American clubs. And despite their so-called "exotic" characteristics, they did well. Harold Seymour reported that on their 1910 trip, the Chinese Hawaiians won 66, lost 44, and tied 4 games. In 1913, they won 105 games, while losing 38 and tying 1.[22]

In March 1914, the Chinese Hawaiians traveled down to southern California after beating respectable Stanford and Santa Clara University nines in the San Francisco Bay Area. The *Los Angeles Times* dispatched mixed signals regarding the Chinese Hawaiian ballplayers. In publicizing an upcoming game between Occidental College and the Chinese Hawaiians, the *Times* published cartoons depicting stereotypical images of "exotic" Chinese trying to play the white man's game. One cartoon showed European American players stepping on queues of Chinese Hawaiian base runners. The caption reads: "A practical way to stop a base stealer." Conversely, the text included praise for the Chinese Hawaiian "sensational base running and perfect fielding."[23]

After the game, a *Times* headline declared that "nine little China-men" beat the Occidental team. An accompanying cartoon used stereo-typical images to portray the Chinese Hawaiian ballplayers. But the actual text of the story reporting on the game reveals Chinese Hawaiians tran-scending racial stereotypes. The victorious nine not only won the game but also seemed to have a darn good time in the process. Hardly queued "exotics," the Chinese Hawaiians were expert bench jockeys as they rode the umpire and the opposition persistently. When the Occidental catcher tried the hidden ball trick, En Sue, described by the *Times* as "the Ty Cobb of the South Seas," yelled, "I thought we were going to learn something about baseball by coming across the Pacific Ocean. I didn't expect to see anyone try such a bush league trick at least a century old."[24] Los Angeles's Chinese community also supported the Chinese Hawaiian nine. The *Times* estimated that about 150 spectators at the Occidental game were Chinese. After the game, the community feted the team to an impressive banquet.[25]

As they toured the mainland, the Chinese Hawaiian team represented what some important contemporary cultural theorists describe as cultural border crossings. Who they were, what they did, and how they were per-ceived disclose shifting cultural identities and exchanges. For example, several of the players possessed no fixed Chinese or Chinese American identity. In 1914, the *Los Angeles Times* called pitcher Foster Hueng a "big half caste."[26] Two years later, Bill Inman, identified simply as a Ha-waiian when he wore a Pacific Coast League uniform in 1915, pitched and played outfield for the Chinese Hawaiians. Very likely, Inman, like growing numbers of Hawaiians, possessed Chinese ancestry along with other racial and ethnic forebears.[27]

If anything, moreover, the Chinese Hawaiian ball team represented the early-twentieth-century development of a "local" culture in Hawaii, a culture that intermingled native Hawaiian, Asian, and "haole" material. For example, a Chinese Hawaiian choir would accompany the ballplayers on their treks to the U.S. mainland. Indeed, some of the ballplayers doubled as choir members. The Chinese Hawaiians were heard to sing both Hawaiian songs and popular U.S. tunes. The touring Chinese Ha-waiians were often feted by Chinese American communities on the main-land, but they also mastered the art of bench jockeying and the slang prevalent in U.S. popular culture in the early twentieth century. Thus, like Hawaii itself, the Chinese Hawaiian team stood out as a cultural crossroads.[28]

As mentioned earlier, the Chinese University of Hawaii's ball club crossed racial and ethnic borderlands to play formidable African American nines such as the Taylor ABCs of Indianapolis. The African American newspaper the *Chicago Defender* reported that with Inman pitching, the Chinese Hawaiians barely lost (4-3) to the ABCs in 1916. The *Defender,* like European American newspapers, seemed prone to express an ethnocentric amazement that the Chinese Hawaiians could play baseball so well. It claimed that "some of the Chinese act like real ballplayers and there is no doubt that they like the game. They were caught on the bases several times by snappy throws, but appeared to know many of the American tricks."[29] That the Hawaiians were, indeed, not simply Chinese but U.S. Americans and Hawaiian "locals" apparently escaped the *Defender* reporter and other non-Asian Pacific people who watched them play.

Community

Baseball reflected and reinforced diverse Asian Pacific American communities. Community nines seemed to surface in the first decades of the twentieth century as second-generation Chinese Americans grew in number and first-generation Japanese Americans or Issei familiar with baseball occupied places like Los Angeles's "Little Tokyo." In February 1915, a Sacramento team of Japanese Americans barely lost to the Victory College nine, 8-7. Two years later, the *San Jose Mercury* declared that "a Jap team from Los Angeles" had lost to a local nine, 21-0.[30] In San Francisco's Chinatown, an organization called the Chinese Athletic Club formed a baseball team by 1918.[31]

The late 1910s through the 1930s witnessed a proliferation of Asian Pacific American community nines in urban and rural areas. These baseball clubs were organized in part as expressions of community pride and rootedness in the United States. In San Jose, however, Japanese American community leaders saw a need understood by other American early-twentieth-century reformers, regardless of race and ethnicity: that young people required diversions from certain "unwholesome," criminal, and even dangerous activities. Mas Akizuki, one of these leaders, wanted to steer young men away from gambling, which apparently pervaded San Jose's Japanese American community. With the help of a few European American acquaintances, Akizuki organized the Asahi Baseball Club in 1920. At first, the community was cool to the new organization, but after a couple of years, Asahi baseball became popular among Japanese San Joseans.[32]

The Asahi club was just one of several Japanese American nines formed on the U.S. mainland's Pacific Coast. While the U.S. Congress explored ways to restrict Japanese immigration to the United States, the Asahi club forged links to European Americans living in and around San Jose. According to a *San Jose Mercury* sportswriter, "the Japanese boys" who played for the Asahis "have proved to be thorough sports and are highly spoken of among the other teams playing in the winter league."[33]

California's Central Valley became a hotbed of Japanese American baseball during the 1920s. Marysville's Japanese American community petitioned the city council for help in constructing a second ball park, claiming that one park would not fit the needs of European American and Japanese American young people alike. The petitioners, however, assured the council that white youngsters could use the proposed park as well.[34]

The Japanese American Yamato Colony was represented by a ball club, which faced Central Valley opponents such as the semiprofessional Lodi nine in 1926: a game that the Yamato team lost, 1-0. In Sacramento, a team called the Nippon Cubs played in the city's Municipal Baseball League in 1927. During the Great Depression, the Church Division of Sacramento's Twilight League had clubs called the Japanese Baptists and the Japanese Presbyterians, who played nines representing the First Evangelicals and the Church of Latter Day Saints.[35]

Oakland's Chinese American community was well represented in the 1930s by a tough semiprofessional nine called the Wah Sungs. One-time Pacific Coast Leaguer Al Bowen, whose real name was Lee Gum Hong, coached them, and many of the Wah Sungs were considered professional material. Oakland was also a Chinese American softball center. Among the most notable softball teams in the 1930s was the Dragonettes, a powerful female contingent, led by pitching star Gwen Wong. According to *Chinese Digest* sportswriter Herbert Eng, Wong was "a left-handed Amazon."[36]

Baseball also found a following among the Filipinos living in the United States during the 1920s and 1930s. Soon after the United States occupied the Philippines, American colonizers used baseball as a way to pacify a population that at least to some extent preferred independence over the Philippines becoming an American protectorate. In Harold Seymour's *Baseball: The People's Game*, we find this passage: "'You see that

Filipino?' asked a Catholic priest of his visitor at a summer camp in 1908. 'He is looked upon as a good American because he plays a first class game of baseball.'"[37]

In the United States, Filipino American writer and labor activist Carlos Bulosan recounted the importance of baseball played by Filipino cannery workers on an Alaskan island during the early 1930s: "It was only at night that we felt free, although the sun seemed never to disappear from the sky. It stayed on in the western horizon and its magnificence inflamed the snows on the island, giving us a world of soft, continuous light, until the moon rose at about ten o'clock to take its place. Then trembling shadows began to form on the rise of the brilliant snow in our yard, and we would come out with baseball bats, gloves, and balls, and the Indian girls who worked in the cannery would join us, shouting huskily like men."[38]

In California, Filipino baseball clubs and leagues were organized in the San Francisco Bay Area as well as in Los Angeles during the 1920s and 1930s. In 1927, the Filipino All Star club competed in San Francisco's semiprofessional mid-winter league. In Depression-ridden Los Angeles, Filipinos organized the Indoor Baseball League, with one hundred participants representing the Ilocos Sur Association of America, the Filipino Patriotic Association, Pangasian Youth, La Union Association, the Catholic Filipino Club, Filipino Youth, and the Sons of Cebu.[39]

During and after World War II, Asian Pacific American nines persisted. Of course, matters changed substantially for West Coast Japanese Americans in the months after the attack on Pearl Harbor. Nevertheless, Japanese Americans continued to employ baseball to sustain a sense of community among them while first placed in assembly centers and then interned in concentration camps. At the Gila, Arizona, camp, thirty-two nines were organized, according to Jay Feldman. Tule Lake internees removed canvas covers from government-issued mattresses and sewed them together to make uniforms. However, the *Manzanar Free Press,* an internee-produced newspaper, reported that at one time in 1944, female softball teams attracted more participation than male baseball teams.[40]

World War II and the cold war years witnessed some significant easing of legalized patterns of discrimination against Asian Pacific Americans. For example, during the war, Chinese immigrants could acquire citizenship, and in 1946, Korean, Asian Indian, and Filipino immigrants became eligible for naturalization. Japanese immigrants were compelled to wait until 1952. At the same time, community nines endured in the late

1940s and 1950s. In 1946, the *San Francisco Chronicle* let readers know that every Sunday, two Chinese American nines called the Bears and the Cobras played each other in Golden Gate Park. In one game, the "Bears got but 2 hits, while their opponents got five, and the youngsters were playing good ball all the way."[41] Five years later, clubs such as the Nisei Clippers and the Chinese Merchants played on Bay Area sandlots. In Santa Clara County, one of the top semiprofessional nines was the San Jose Zebras, a team consisting of second-generation Japanese Americans, or Nisei.[42]

Crossing Foul Lines, Crossing Cultural Boundaries

Regardless of skill level, Asian Pacific Americans, individually and collectively, crossed cultural boundaries many times when they stepped on baseball diamonds such as San Jose's Asahi Field. Sometimes, it seems that they allow us to see baseball as transcending racial and ethnic barriers. Sometimes, however, baseball remains quite capable of reinforcing such barriers despite the best efforts of Asian Pacific American ballplayers.

For many decades of the twentieth century, baseball transmitted contradictory messages to highly accomplished players of Asian Pacific ancestry. We know that the legendary All Nations club, playing out of Kansas City, fielded players of Asian Pacific descent. A box score of one game reported on by the *Chicago Defender* in 1916 reveals that the All Nations pitcher was a fellow named Hong Long. A Filipino Hawaiian named Frank Blukoi, moreover, played with the All Nations nine before joining the Kansas City Monarchs in 1920.[43]

Organized European American baseball expressed some interest in individual Asian Pacific American ballplayers during the 1910s. Walter McCreadie, owner of the Pacific Coast League's Portland Beavers, signed Lang Akana, a Chinese Hawaiian player, to a contract for the 1915 season. The *San Francisco Chronicle* described Akana as "a left-handed hitter with a burst of speed."[44] However, McCreadie felt compelled to let Akana go before spring training. The Beavers' owner complained that Akana's skin was insufficiently light to please PCL players, who were planning a boycott. Referring to the heated racial atmosphere then enveloping American sport and society, McCreadie lamented that some players griped that Akana was as dark-skinned as controversial African American boxer, Jack Johnson.[45]

More fortunate in a manner of speaking were two Asian Pacific American pitchers who appeared in Pacific Coast League uniforms during the early 1930s. In 1932, the Great Depression could have grievously hurt the attendance and profit margins of PCL teams if their owners had not turned to creative marketing strategies such as night ball games. Toward the end of the season, the Sacramento Solons came up with an interesting marketing strategy to stimulate attendance figures. The team hired Kenso Nushida, a Japanese American pitcher of Hawaiian background who pitched for local Japanese American community nines. While marketed and perceived as something of a novelty, Nushida pitched adequately. Later, however, the Oakland Oaks signed Lee Gum Hong, who, as previously mentioned, pitched for the Wah Sungs. It was not likely a coincidence that Hong was put in an Oaks uniform just in time to take the box against Nushida and the Solons.[46]

The Nushida-Hong duel occurred while Japan and China engaged in a violent struggle over Manchuria, a war that Americans of Japanese and Chinese ancestry could not easily ignore and over which they frequently expressed bitter partisanship. Despite the bloodshed resulting from the Chinese and Japanese warfare, Nushida's and Hong's PCL employers seemed willing to transform tragedy into profits. To be fair, however, Nushida and Hong, as well as some of the people with whom they shared their ethnic experiences, were willing to allow this transformation to take place. Thus, Yoichi Nagata quotes Hong before he took the mound against Nushida: "This is a battle of nations. I represent China. Nushida represents Japan. And China shall win."[47]

Like the Waseda nine nearly thirty years earlier, Nushida attracted Japanese American support. When the Solons played the Los Angeles Angels at Wrigley Field, *Los Angeles Times* reporter Harry Williams declared that "there was a distinct saffron sheen reflected by the crowds and the lights, perhaps a third of the crowd of 7,000 being Japanese out to see their countryman do his stuff." Three large bouquets of chrysanthemums were presented to Nushida "by a pretty little Japanese sheba dolled up in a gay kimono."[48] With no obviously bad intention, European American journalists such as Williams represented Nushida and other Japanese Americans as racialized aliens.

Other Asian Pacific Americans played in the North American minor leagues and higher in subsequent years. Wally Yonamine, a Hawaiian of Japanese Okinawan descent, comes to mind. In many ways, Yonamine's career illustrates how baseball can encourage cultural border crossings.

Yonamine has been likened to Jackie Robinson, and the comparison makes at least some sense. Like Robinson, Yonamine was a great all-around athlete. A son of agricultural workers, he played both professional football and baseball while traversing substantial racial, ethnic, class, and national barriers in the process. After World War II, Yonamine could be found playing in interethnic, interracial baseball leagues in Hawaii as well as in the All American Football Conference for the San Francisco 49ers. In 1950, Yonamine played for the Pioneer League's Salt Lake City franchise. Yonamine hit .335 for Salt Lake City, prompting one Brooklyn Dodger pitcher to claim that the best hitter he ever saw was "Y-A-N-A-M-I-N-I-, maybe. He's a Jap."[49] In subsequent years, Yonamine crossed another cultural barrier by playing in the Japanese major leagues. He wracked up several fine years and despite being American-born, became a well-respected coach and manager in the Japanese "Show." Yonamine, indeed, was ultimately selected to Japan's Baseball Hall of Fame.[50]

Other players of Asian Pacific ancestry defied the stereotype of Asian Pacific people as deficient in sports such as baseball. Filipino American Bobby Balcena knocked around the minor leagues for several years after World War II. Nevertheless, in 1957, he played briefly for the Cincinnati Reds.[51] Chinese Hawaiian Mike Lum played solid ball for several years in the 1960s and 1970s. Japanese Hawaiian Lenn Sakata was a durable utility infielder for Earl Weaver's Baltimore Orioles club. "Hapa" Atlee Hammaker pitched well for the San Francisco Giants before an arm injury derailed his career. Speaking of the Giants, Wendell Kim carved out a fine career as a player and manager in the Giants' organization before serving as a third-base coach for the parent club. Most recently, Kim coached third base for the Boston Red Sox. The one-time hurler for the New York Mets and the Oakland Athletics, Ron Darling, possesses some Chinese ancestry. Benny

Mike Lum. Courtesy of the Atlanta Braves.

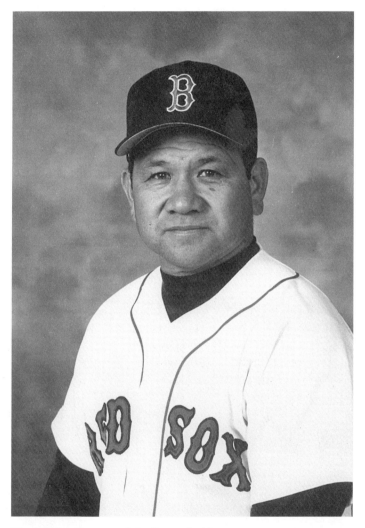

Wendell Kim. Courtesy of the Boston Red Sox.

Agbayani, who had solid seasons for the New York Mets in 1999 and 2000, is a Hawaiian of Filipino and Samoan ancestry, while a Hawaiian of Japanese ancestry, Onan Masaoka, pitched adequately as a reliever for the Los Angeles Dodgers.

Yet, what truly matters is not how many representatives of any racial and ethnic group have made it into or near the big leagues. The larger issue is whether baseball has offered Asian Pacific Americans, regardless of age and command of the game, opportunities to assert their stereotype-defying humanity and have some fun in the process. Here, as elsewhere, baseball has provided indeterminate service. One could argue, as Peter Levine does for Jewish Americans, that baseball has denoted something of a "middle ground" for Asian Pacific Americans. The baseball diamond, therefore, can stand as a relatively neutral terrain for interchange among Asian Pacific and non-Asian Pacific groups. Undoubtedly, many Asian Pacific Americans on the mainland and Hawaii found joy and respect in baseball. However, what seems to make the fit between the metaphor of a "middle ground" and Asian Pacific American experiences less than useful is "racism's traveling eye." Baseball could remind Asian Pacific people of their racialized "otherness" in the United States: what Ronald Takaki refers to as the Asian Pacific American's "racial uniform," which has for decades permitted non-Asian Pacific Americans to perceive them as "strangers from a different shore."[52] Perhaps, the more active metaphor of boundary crossings works best. Boundaries express the politicization of nationality, race, and ethnicity—social categories that have often been created by people for unjust purposes but that can be transcended at times by people, even baseball playing and watching people, for very just, grand, and humble purposes. At the same time, the notion of boundary crossings captures the dynamic character of people at play, shifting in and out of socially constructed identities such as race as they race for home or to field a Texas leaguer.

Notes

1. Ronald Takaki, "Teaching American History Through a Different Mirror," *Perspectives: American Historical Association Newsletter* (October 1994): 1, 9–12.

2. Renato Rosaldo, *Culture and Truth: The Remaking of Social Analysis* (Boston: Beacon Press, 1989); Gloria Anzaldua, *Borderlands/La Frontera: The New Mestiza* (San Francisco: Spinsters/Aunt Lute, 1987); Richard J. White, *The Middle Ground: Indians, Empires, and Republics in the Great Lakes Region, 1650–1815* (New York: Cambridge University Press, 1991); Peter Levine, *Ellis Island to Ebbets Field: Sport and the American Jewish Experience* (New York: Oxford University Press, 1991); Paul Gilroy, *The Black Atlantic: Modernity and Double Consciousness* (Cambridge, Mass.: Harvard University Press, 1993).

3. Robin D. G. Kelly, "Notes on Deconstructing 'The Folk,'" *American Historical Review* 97 (December 1992): 1,408.

4. Michael Omi and Howard Winant, *Racial Formation in the United States from the 1960s to the 1990s,* 2d ed. (New York: Routledge, 1994).

5. Elaine Kim, preface to *Charlie Chan Is Dead: An Anthology of Contemporary Asian American Fiction,* ed. Jessica Hagedorn (New York: Penguin Books, 1993).

6. Ronald Takaki, *Strangers from a Different Shore: A History of Asian Americans* (Boston: Little, Brown, 1989), ch. 4.

7. Takaki, *Strangers,* 169; William Carlson Smith, *Americans in Process* (1937; reprint, New York: Arno Press, 1970), ch. 2.

8. Cited in Ruthanne Lum McCunn, *Chinese American Portraits: Personal Memories, 1828–1988.* (San Francisco: *San Francisco Chronicle* Books, 1988), 22–23.

9. *Sporting Life,* 10 June 1884, 7.

10. *San Francisco Chronicle,* 19 May 1885, 4.

11. *San Francisco Chronicle,* 25 November 1887, 6.

12. Harold Seymour, *Baseball: The People's Game* (New York: Oxford University Press, 1990), 566.

13. *Sacramento Bee,* 15 April 1886, 3.

14. Albert G. Spalding, *America's National Pastime* (1911; reprint, Lincoln: University of Nebraska Press, 1992), 395.

15. Cited in Spalding, 396.

16. *Los Angeles Times,* 18 May 1905, 8; 21 May 1905, part 3, p. 1.

17. *San Francisco Chronicle,* 3 May 1905, 8.

18. *Los Angeles Times,* 18 May 1905, 8.

19. Cited in Seymour, *People's Game,* 169.

20. Ronald Takaki, *Strangers,* ch. 1.

21. Ronald Takaki, *Pau Hana: Plantation Life and Labor in Hawai'i, 1835–1920* (Honolulu: University of Hawaii Press, 1983); Seymour, *People's Game,* 179.

22. Seymour, *People's Game,* 173.

23. *Los Angeles Times,* 10 March 1914, part 3, p. 2.

24. *Los Angeles Times,* 15 March 1914, part 7, p. 7.

25. *Los Angeles Times,* 15 March 1914, part 7, p. 7.

26. *Los Angeles Times,* 15 March 1914, part 7, p. 7.

27. *Chicago Defender,* 19 May 1916, 4.

28. Joel S. Franks, *Crossing Sidelines, Crossing Cultures: Sport and Asian Pacific American Sporting Experiences* (Lanham, Md.: University Press of America, 2000).

29. *Chicago Defender,* 20 May 1916.

30. *Sacramento Bee,* 1 March 1915, 10; *San Jose Mercury,* 6 August 1917, 8.

31. *San Francisco Chronicle,* 16 February 1918, 24.

32. Jay Feldman, "Baseball Behind Barbed Wire," *National Pastime: A Review of Baseball History,* no. 12 (summer 1992): 37; Valerie Matsumoto, *Farming the Homeplace: A Japanese American Community in California, 1919–1982* (Ithaca, N.Y.: Cornell University Press, 1993), 79–82; Steven Misawa et al., *Beginnings: Japanese Americans in San Jose* (San Jose: Japanese American Community Senior Services, 1981), 14.

33. *San Jose Mercury,* 3 February 1923, 12.

34. *Sacramento Bee,* 2 June 1925, 18.

35. *Sacramento Bee,* 5 March 1927, 2 and 2 July 1933, sports section, p. 2; *San Francisco Chronicle,* 5 October 1926, 2H.

36. *Chinese Digest* (June 1937): 17 and (March 1938): 18.

37. Seymour, *People's Game,* 96.

38. Carlos Bulosan, *America Is in the Heart* (Seattle: University of Washington Press, 1979), 102.

39. *San Francisco Chronicle,* 1 March 1927, 2H; Bencio Catupusan, *The Filipino Occupation and Recreational Activities in Los Angeles,* (Saratoga, Calif.: R & E Research Associates, 1975), 34.

40. Feldman, "Barbed Wire," 38–39; Samuel Regalado, "Sport and Community in California's Japanese American 'Yamato Colony,' 1930–1945," *Journal of Sport History* 19 (summer 1992): 130–44; *Manzanar Free Press,* 8 July 1944, 4.

41. *San Francisco Chronicle,* 1 April 1946, 3H.

42. *San Francisco Chronicle,* 19 August 1951, 2H; *San Jose Mercury,* 9 May 1954, 45.

43. Janet Bruce, *The Kansas City Monarchs: Champions of Black Baseball* (Lawrence: University of Kansas Press, 1985), 15; *Chicago Defender* (1916).

44. Steven Riess, *Touching Base: Professional Baseball and American Culture in the Progressive Era* (Westport, Conn.: Greenwood Press, 1980), 193–94; *San Francisco Chronicle,* 10 December 1914, 9.

45. *Chicago Defender,* 16 January 1915, 4.

46. Yoichi Nagata, "The First All-Asian Pitching Duel in Organized Baseball: Japan vs. China in the PCL," *Baseball Research Journal,* no. 21 (1992): 14.

47. Nagata; *San Francisco Examiner,* 21 September 1932, 17, 28 September 1932, 10, and 29 September 1932, 20.

48. *Los Angeles Times,* 16 September 1932, 9.

49. *Honolulu Star-Advertiser,* 1 July 1948, 10; *The Sporting News,* 8 April 1953, 7.

50. Robert Whiting, *You Gotta Have Wa* (New York: Vintage Books, 1989), 143–44.

51. Franks, ch. 3.

52. Levine; Takaki, *Strangers.*

Contributors

Index

Contributors

The grandson of Italian immigrants, **Lawrence Baldassaro** grew up in Chicopee, Massachusetts, where he played high school, American Legion, and semipro baseball. He is a professor of Italian and comparative literature and the director of the University Honors Program at the University of Wisconsin–Milwaukee. He has edited *The Ted Williams Reader* (1991) and has published articles on baseball in numerous journals. He is also a regular contributor to *Lead Off*, the Milwaukee Brewers' magazine, and, for a few weeks in 1992, pitched batting practice for the Brewers.

Joel S. Franks teaches Asian American and ethnic studies at San Jose State University and De Anza College in Cupertino, California. He is the author of *Crossing Sidelines, Crossing Cultures: Sport and Asian Pacific American Cultural Citizenship* (2000) and *Whose Baseball?: The National Pastime and Cultural Diversity in California, 1859–1941* (2001).

Larry R. Gerlach, a professor of American sports history at the University of Utah and past president of the Society for American Baseball Research, grew up in a Volga Deutsch neighborhood in Lincoln, Nebraska, where he learned more about ethnicity and baseball than he realized at the time. He became a Yankee fan at age eight after seeing his first movie, *The Pride of the Yankees,* which poignantly brought together his love for baseball and his German heritage. He is the author of *The Men in Blue: Conversations with Umpires* (1980; rev. ed., 1994).

Frederick Ivor-Campbell edited *Baseball's First Stars* (1996) and has contributed to numerous encyclopedias and journals, including *Total Baseball, Biographical Dictionary of American Sports, The National Pastime,* and *American National Biography.* He was twice elected vice president of the Society for American Baseball Research.

Richard A. Johnson, who has served as the curator of the Sports Museum of New England since 1982, is the author or coauthor of seven books, including *DiMaggio: An Illustrated Life* (1995), *Ted Williams: A Portrait in Words and Pictures* (1991), *Red Sox Century* (2000) and, most recently, *Boston Braves* (2001).

Neal Pease is an associate professor of history at the University of Wisconsin–Milwaukee, with specialties in modern Poland, central Europe, and church history. He also teaches a course on baseball in American history and is a member of the Society for American Baseball Research. His attempt to introduce baseball to Polish university students in the 1970s while on an academic exchange never made it past batting practice—when an apt pupil broke the window of the dean's office.

Richard F. Peterson is the editor of the Southern Illinois University Press Writing Baseball series and the author of *Extra Innings: Writing on Baseball* (2001). His baseball essays have appeared in the *Chicago Tribune, Creative Nonfiction, Pittsburgh Sports, Elysian Fields Quarterly, Sport Literate, Aethlon,* and *NINE.*

Samuel O. Regalado is a professor of history at California State University–Stanislaus. A 1994 Smithsonian Faculty Fellow and specialist in ethnic and immigration history, he has published numerous articles on the topic of Latins in American professional baseball and Japanese Americans in community baseball. He is the author of *Viva Baseball! Latin Major Leaguers and Their Special Hunger* (1998).

Steven A. Riess is a professor of history at Northeastern Illinois University. The former editor of the *Journal of Sport History,* he has written and edited several books on American sport history, including *Touching Base: Professional Baseball and American Culture in the Progressive Era* (1980; rev ed., 1999), *City Games: The Evolution of American Society and the Rise of Sports* (1989), and *Sports and the American Jew* (1998).

Jules Tygiel is a professor of history at San Francisco State University. He is the author of *Baseball's Great Experiment: Jackie Robinson and His Legacy* (1983; rev. ed., 1997) and *Past Time: Baseball as History* (2000).

Index

Marsans, Armando, 164, 166
Martin, Billy, 112
Martin Park (Memphis), 73
Masaoka, Onan, 193
Mathewson, Christy, 113n. 2
Mathis, Verdell, 71, 75
Mauch, Gene, 158
Mayer, Erskine, 122
Mayer, Sam, 122
Mays, Willie, 71–72
Mazeroski, Bill, 153
McCaffrey, Lawrence, 57
McCarthy, Tom, 58
McCormick, Barry, 122
McCreadie, Walter, 190
McDuffie, Terris, 87
McGill, Willie, 58
McGraw, John: at Gleason's funeral, 63; as a manager, 68, 95, 102, 119, 125, 164; as a player, 55, 61–62; as a racetrack owner, 123; on Wagner, 33
McGuire, James Deacon, 63–64
McGwire, Mark, 2, 162
McLean, Billy, 62
Meine, Heinie, 38–39
Meister, George, 29
melting pot, xiii–xiv, 3, 4, 45, 56
Melvin, Bob, 133, 140n. 51
Memphis Blues, 71, 74–75
Memphis Red Sox, 78
Menderson, Nathan, 118
Méndez, José, 164
Mendoza, Ramiro, 2
Merkle, Fred, 33, 104
Messersmith, Andy, 48
Mexico, xiv, 163, 175
Meyerle, Levi, 30, 40
Meyers, Lon, 136n. 3
Michaels, Cass, 143, 150
Miller, Joseph, 29
Miller, Marvin, 134
Mills Brothers, 73
Milwaukee, Wisconsin, 147, 148, 149
Miñoso, Saturnino Orestes Arrieta Armas "Minnie," 168–69, 174
Mirianao, 169
Monroe, Marilyn, 112
morality. *See* alcohol; cheating; gambling; Sunday games

Moriarty, George, 127
Morris, William, 42
Morse, Jacob C., 134
"Mrs. Robinson" (Simon), 112
Muchnick, Isadore, 130
Muehlebach Stadium (Kansas City), 79
Mullin, Willard, 109
Murnane, Tim, 64
Musial, Stan, 142, 150–52, 154, 156
Myer, Buddy, 126, 127

Nagata, Yoichi, 191
Naismith, James, 7
names: of Babe Ruth, 53n. 51, 98; derogatory (*see* prejudice); ethnicization of, 111; of German Americans, 37–39, 41–42, 47–48, 52n. 32; of Irish Americans, 62–63; of Italian Americans, 93, 96, 99–100; of Jews, 122, 125; of Slavic Americans, 143, 148, 157–58
Nashville Elite Giants, 78
"National Agreement," 19
National Association for the Advancement of Colored People (NAACP), 71, 85
National Association of Base Ball Players, 13, 18, 29
National Association of Colored Professional Clubs of the United States and Cuba, 81
National Association of Professional Base Ball Players, 117
National Commission, 36, 41
National Game, The (Spink), 63–64
National League: ethnicity of players in, 29; formation of, 13, 16–17, 18, 26n. 26, 65; Jewish owners in, 119; officers in, 36; other leagues and, 20–21, 30, 37; policies of, 17, 19, 20, 22, 30
Native Americans, 177
nativism. *See* prejudice
Natural, The (Malamud), 56, 135
Negro American League, 84
Negro National League: attendance at, 75–76; booking agents in, 80–84; community-based nature of, 69, 71–74; demise of, 85–88; Eastern Colored League and, 75, 81–83; formation of, 68–70; owners in, 70–71, 80–85; play-